The Gift of Black Folk

The Gift of Black Folk

W. E. B. DU BOIS

New Introduction by
Herbert Aptheker

KRAUS-THOMSON ORGANIZATION LIMITED, MILLWOOD, N.Y.

Introduction copyright, 1975 by Herbert Aptheker
All Rights Reserved
First Printing 1975

Library of Congress Cataloging in Publication Data

Du Bois, William Edward Burghardt, 1868-1963.
    The gift of Black folk.

    Reprint of the 1924 ed. published by the Stratford
Co., Boston, in series: Knights of Columbus racial
contribution series.
    1. Negroes—History.   2. United States—Race
question. I. Title. II. Series: Knights of Columbus
racial contribution series.
E185.D83   1975   973'.004'96   75-1447
ISBN 0-527-25310-3

Printed in the United States of America

INTRODUCTION

In his "Opinion" department that opened *The Crisis* for August, 1922, under the heading, "Americanization," Du Bois delineated the roots of his eighth book. He warned that "the same dry rot of aristocracy is entering New England and Harvard that has ruined in other days the aristocracies of the world."

Everyone, then, was talking of "Americanization"; for Du Bois: "What we think we mean by Americanization is the making of this country one great homogeneous whole working for the same ideals, defending its integrity, preserving its hard found liberty." But the so-called "Americanization" that was then being used as a facade for a campaign of bigotry, racism and repression, was, he wrote, ". . . but a renewal of the Anglo-Saxon cult; the worship of the Nordic totem, the disfranchisement of Negro, Jew, Irishman, Italian, Hungarian, Asiatic and South Sea islander—the world rule of Nordic white through brute force." But, he pointed out, "the majority of people in the United States are not of English descent." He concluded:

> The same forces south and east that are fighting democracy in the United States are fighting black men and fighting Jews. The great alliance then between the darker people the world over, between disadvantaged groups like the Irish and the Jew and between the working classes everywhere is the one alliance that is going to keep down privilege as represented by New England and old England. (24:154)

Dramatic illustrations of the condition against which Du Bois was polemizing included the rabid anti-Semitic campaigns financed and led by Henry Ford and his *Dearborn Independent,* and the extraordinary growth of the Ku Klux Klan, which had some five million members by 1924 and exerted profound political influences not only throughout the South but also in such states as Indiana, Oregon, Colorado and Ohio. Its most grisly forms were the lynching phenomenon which claimed hundreds of victims in the years from 1918 to 1924 and the so-called race riots—or, rather, pogroms—in which scores of Black men, women and children from Tulsa, Oklahoma to Chicago, Illinois, to Elaine, Arkansas were murdered.

The so-called eugenics movement, associated with racist fanatics such as H.H. Laughlin, C.B. Davenport, Lothrop Stoddard, Madison Grant, John B. Trevor and Lee Roy Henry, had great influence in these same years—with millions of dollars provided by Mrs. E.H. Harriman, wife of the railroad tycoon. A result was the passage in 1921 and, more importantly, 1924, of restrictions on immigration explicitly based on anti-Semitic, anti-colored, anti-Catholic, and so-called Nordic prejudices.

In 1921, Vice President Coolidge, in *Good Housekeeping* magazine (February; 72:14), had asserted that "Nordics" deteriorate when mixed with other peoples, and in his first Annual Message as President, in December, 1923, he had urged that America be kept American—by which he meant the same thing. In 1924 he signed the very restrictive and racist immigration law.[1]

It was not only people like the leaders of the KKK, or savants like Madison Grant and Lothrop Stoddard, or politicians like Calvin Coolidge who were making explicit the most blatant kind of racism. One of Du Bois' two history professors at Harvard—Edward Channing—was publishing in 1925, in the sixth volume of his *History of the United States,* sentences like these:

> . . . it appears that it is about as hard for the Ethiop to change his institutional and racial conceptions as it is for him to alter the color of his skin. Both his institutions and his skin are matters of heredity. They have come down from a very remote past and are, even today, being handed on unchanged to future generations. In his pure condition undiluted by white or yellow blood, the Negro is essentially a communist and a fatalist.

While, as Professor Higham has pointed out in the already cited book, *Strangers in the Land,* liberal organs like *The Nation* and *The New Republic* were flabby in opposing this poisonous ideology and activity, Black organizations, certain Jewish and Catholic groups, the Left, and significant segments of more rational opinion in the South offered resistance. As to the latter, Du Bois again was especially alert. Typical was his reportage entitled "Inter-Racial Activities in the South"—*The Crisis,* April, 1921 (21:249-50)—where generous quotations were offered from proceedings of inter-racial committees in Louisiana and Kentucky and a Woman's Inter-Racial Conference in Memphis.

Indeed, in the course of his making known this aspect of white Southern thought and effort, Du Bois quoted a paragraph from the public statement made by one such meeting that is very nearly a pros-

---

[1] See, for example, John Higham, *Strangers in the Land* (New Brunswick, 1955), chapter 11; K. M. Ludmerer, *Genetics and American Society* (Baltimore, 1972); G. E. Mowry, *The Urban Nation, 1920-1960* (N.Y., 1965), pp. 31-34; F. Haller, *Eugenics: Hereditarian Attitudes in American Thought* (New Brunswick, 1963).

pectus for *The Gift of Black Folk*. In January, 1922, impelled by the appalling situation, certain Southern white professors in the universities of Alabama, Arkansas, Florida, Georgia, Mississippi, North Carolina, South Carolina, Tennessee, Texas and Virginia made a plea for "cooperation" among Black and white in resolving "such vital community problems as better schools, good roads, more healthful living, and more satisfactory business relations." Somewhat more pointed and less traditional was the final paragraph of their statement, which Du Bois published in *The Crisis* (August, 1922; 24:155):

> No fact is more clearly established than that Hatred and Force only complicate race relations. The alternative to this is counsel and co-operation among men of character and good-will, and, above all, of intelligent and comprehensive knowledge of the racial problem. The number of those who possess specific knowledge upon which to base intelligent thinking, and, ultimately, wise action is still too small. There is great need, therefore, that facts now available concerning the advancement of the Negro race in education, in professional accomplishment, in economic independence and in character, be studied by thoughtful students in our colleges. Such facts as are definitely established could well be made, as has already been done in some institutions, the basis of instruction in race conditions and relations as a part of a regular course in social science. This body of information would undoubtedly allay race antagonism and would serve as a foundation for tolerant attitude and intelligent action in every direction of inter-racial co-operation.

At the same time and for similar considerations, a leading Catholic organization was reaching substantially identical conclusions. Thus, Dr. Edward McSweeney (1864-1928), who was chairman of the Historical Commission of the Knights of Columbus and had been assistant U.S. Commissioner of Immigration at Ellis Island (1893-1902), in an address before the Supreme Council of the Knights in San Francisco in August, 1921, excoriated what he felt was English-inspired propaganda about the superiority of the Anglo-Saxon. Such ideas were vicious nonsense, said Dr. McSweeney; the population of the United States was made up of diverse peoples, all with their own values and features, none inferior to any other. This, he said, was the essence of the history of the United States and of the American idea, while concepts of co-called "mongrelization" were wrong and hurtful. In the spirit of this address, the Knights launched that year a history program, complete with contests for children, to convey this position.[2]

---

[2] This speech is in *Bulletin No. One,* Knights of Columbus History Commission, 1921, in the N.Y. Public Library. The Knights also issued (in 1923) a pamphlet by McSweeney, *The Racial Contribution to the United States,* which is almost identical with the essay in *The Gift of Black Folk,* constituting its first 29 pages.

Another part of the Knights' history program was a projected series of volumes which would convey positive features of the history of different nationalities and peoples within the general context of the history of the United States. Dr. McSweeney was in overall charge of this effort and a Boston publishing house, The Stratford Company, was to produce the volumes. As it turned out, three such books were issued, all in 1924; it is as part of this series that *The Gift of Black Folk* was published.[3] That the Knights would seek the services of Du Bois was altogether natural; he was at that time, without any question, the best known Black person in the United States. He possessed an international reputation as a scholar, was a leader of the outstanding civil rights organization in the nation, the N.A.A.C.P., and was editor of *The Crisis,* which in 1919 had achieved a circulation of 100,000 copies and in the early 1920s still was bought by some 60,000 people and read by perhaps a quarter of a million. He contributed at that time to leading journals, such as *New Republic, Foreign Affairs,* the *Atlantic;* his efforts on behalf of the Pan-African movement were widely known and in 1923 he was named by President Coolidge to represent him, as Ambassador, at the inauguration of the Liberian President in January, 1924.

It is likely that sometime in 1922, Dr. McSweeney and Dr. Du Bois reached agreement on his contribution to the series; probably early in 1923 the first draft of Du Bois' book reached McSweeney. Certainly a letter from McSweeney—dated Boston, July 30, 1923—exists in which Dr. Du Bois is told: "I am anticipating receipt of your revised manuscript and hoping that as soon as it comes we may proceed to get the matter in shape for ultimate publication."

The revised manuscript must have been received shortly thereafter since Dr. Du Bois left New York City on October 28, 1923 for attendance, in Lisbon, beginning in December at the Third Pan-African Conference. The precise date of the publication of *The Gift of Black Folk* is not known; it must have appeared, however, in the summer of 1924 for the first advertisement of the book was in the September, 1924 issue of *The Crisis.*

On June 16, 1923 Dr. McSweeney wrote to Dr. Du Bois enclosing a copy of the introduction to—as he put it—"the series of studies on the racial contributions to the United States." He asked for Dr. Du Bois' advice as "to the best method of distribution." On July 13, 1923 Du

---

[3]The two other books were: F. F. Schrader, *The Germans in the Making of America* and George Cohen, *The Jews in the Making of America.* Each contains the same introduction by McSweeney. The Schrader book was reprinted by Haskell House (N.Y.) in 1972. See John B. Kennedy, "The Knights of Columbus History Movement," in *Current History,* December, 1921 (15:441-443). This contains a photograph of McSweeney.

Bois replied, directing McSweeney to Monroe Work's *Negro Year Book* and citing the pages within that book which listed names and addresses of leaders of significant organizations and institutions among the Afro-American people; in addition, Du Bois enclosed what he called a "Proposed Statement to go to the Colored Leaders" to accompany a copy of McSweeney's introduction. That reads as follows:

> The Knights of Columbus Historical Commission has undertaken the exceedingly important work of letting Americans know how many diverse elements have contributed to American civilization. Many people think of America as simply the work of English Colonists; they forget large numbers of Irish, Germans, Jews, Poles and others who, from the very beginning, have helped to make America. Especially are people apt to assume that America was founded and made entirely by white people. The contribution which Negroes have made to American civilization not only as passive slaves and workers but as active doers and thinkers, is one which must not be forgotten.
>
> One of the volumes to be published by the Knights of Columbus Historical Commission is written by Dr. W.E.B. Du Bois, Editor of *The Crisis* magazine, and is entitled: "The Gift of Black Folk." It will deal with contributions that Negroes have made as laborers, explorers, soldiers and artists.[4]

Among the Du Bois Papers there is a four-page typed "MEMORANDUM ON THE CONTRIBUTIONS OF THE NEGRO TO AMERICAN LIFE." Above this, in pencil, in Du Bois' hand, is the notation "Knights of Columbus." The memorandum is not dated but it clearly was prepared as a kind of outline for the volume to be written; it is likely that it was seen by Dr. McSweeney. It may, then, be considered as prepared sometime in 1922, probably early that year. It is certainly fundamental to the history of this particular Du Bois volume and is therefore given below in full:

> After the heading as given above, appears this:
> (Set down approximately in the order of their importance.)
> 1. Labor
> The American Negro through his labor has been the chief cause of the commercial importance of four great modern crops, sugar, rice, tobacco and cotton. These crops have revolutionized modern commerce and modern life. In addition to this the Negro has been the back-bone of farming industry in the South and still forms one fifth of the farm operators in a country where he is only one tenth of the population and nearly one third of the farmers and farm laborers in the whole land. His employment as common laborer and servant throughout the history of the land has released for other employment

---

[4] Quotations from the Du Bois correspondence come from the papers left by him in the Editor's custody; in 1973 these were acquired by the University of Massachusetts and are now in the library of that University.

millions of white persons and thus enabled America to develop economically and spiritually at a rate unparalleled elsewhere in modern history. In addition to common labor the American Negro has through invention added to American industry some of the basic inventions on the telephone by Granville Woods; practically the whole system of locomotive lubrication by Elijah McCoy; the machine for making a complete shoe by mechanical contrivance by Matzeliger, and in all some five hundred patented inventions.

Particularly in the case of women, American Negroes have been pioneers voluntary and involuntary in the appearance of the economically independent woman. More than any other group in the United States colored women are self supporting. Nearly 39% of colored women being gainfully employed as compared with 18½% of white women. The colored woman as a nurse both for children and in sickness has an unforgettable record.

During the World War Negroes carried off the riveting and pile-driving records and the late Booker T. Washington did more than any single man to popularize industrial education for all children in the United States.

2. Art

Perhaps even greater than his contribution to America as a laborer has been the Negro's contribution to American art. The only real American music is Negro music. The Negro folk song which arose in the days of slavery has been developed into modern syncopated music and in other lines by colored composers like Harry Burleigh, Coleridge-Taylor, Rosamond Johnson, R. Nathaniel Dett, Will Marion Cook and others. Negro music has also more or less directly influenced white composers like Stephen Foster and other modern writers. The peculiarly African gift of rhythm has been developed by American Negroes and others both in song and markedly in dancing throughout the modern world.

Other forms of art where the American Negro has made a notable contribution are in painting in the case of Bannister, Tanner and Scott, and in sculpture in the case of Edmonia Lewis, Warrick and Jackson. On the stage we have had Ira Aldridge who was decorated by nearly every crowned head in Europe, Bert Williams, George Walker and Charles Gilpin. We have given the world a peculiar and characteristic kind of stage humor and comedy.

Many wonderful voices have been possessed by colored singers as that of the Black Swan in 1851, the Fisk Singers in 1870, Flora Batson in 1887, and Roland W. Hayes in our day.

3. Literature

The gift of the Negro to American literature may be divided into two parts; *first,* his tragic history has been the inspiration of perhaps a larger part of American literature than any other single series of facts in American life. In this connection we have only to think of Sewall, Emerson, Whittier, Holmes, Lowell, Harriet Beecher Stowe, Julia Ward Howe, Walt Whitman,

Thomas Nelson Page and George W. Cable. Several of the great masterpieces of American literature like "Uncle Tom's Cabin" are based on the Negro. On the other hand there has arisen an important American literature by Negroes, in which we may notice Phillis Wheatley, Paul Laurence Dunbar, Charles W. Chesnutt and George W. Williams. The Uncle Remus tales are pure Negro folk lore written down by a white man. Especially notable are biographies like those of Frederick Douglass and Booker T. Washington and the work of William Stanley Braithwaite as a critic of poetry.

4. Social Uplift

Directly and indirectly the Negro has contributed to the social advancement in the United States. He was not merely the passive beneficiary of emancipation but his work as fugitive slave, orator, agitator and organizer was decisive by making the abolition of slavery possible in the United States. Notable in this leadership was Paul Cuffee, Elijah Johnson, Harriet Tubman, Sojourner Truth, Denmark Vesey, Nat Turner and Frederick Douglass.

In religion the Negro has not simply been a devotee of the more emotional type but has furnished the country real religious leaders like George Lisle, one of the first American missionaries, Lott Carey, Richard Allen, founder of the African Methodist Episcopal Church, Lemuel Haynes, pastor of a white New England church, John Chavis and Lunsford Lane of Virginia and Carolina.[5]

It was the Negro as a legislator that established the free public school system in the south and from the beginning of American history down to the present time the Negro has in a peculiar way and by his own action and aspiration been the test and measure of American democracy. If democracy finally triumphs in the world it will be because in America the Negro was found capable of participating in democratic government and has been accepted by the nation as a fellow citizen.

5. Exploration and Defense

It is of interest to remember that the only living human being who has stood at the North Pole is an American Negro and that a Negro, Estevanico, was the first person of the eastern hemisphere to discover Arizona, New Mexico and the southwest and with all the early explorers there were Negro leaders and laborers. Negroes were with Balboa, Cortez and Pizarro.

If it had not been for Touissaint L'Ouverture and the Haitian revolt there is every reason to believe that the Mississippi could never have been acquired by America and certainly not for the nominal sum which Jefferson paid for it. It was the Haitian revolt that drove France out of the Mississippi valley. On the other hand the Negro not only helped to find the land but to defend it and colored soldiers have been decided factors in the Revolutionary War, when Crispus Attucks was the first to fall; the War of 1812, on Lake Erie and at New Orleans; in the Civil War, where the 200,000 Negro soldiers were ac-

[5] This was a slip; both Chavis and Lane were from North Carolina.

cording to Lincoln indispensable to victory; the Spanish American War, where
they saved Roosevelt at El Caney and the World War.

In the World War 77.6% of the Negroes were fit for service as against
67.7% of the whites. The Negro's record in exploration and defense as well as
in labor has been dependent upon his physical fitness. While poverty and
crime have made inroads upon the physique of the children of slaves, nevertheless their record in athletics has been notable. In pugilism we have had as
world champions Jack Johnson, Joe Walcott, Joe Gans and George Dixon. In
football we have had three men named on all-American teams and in track
and field athletics we have had Sol Butler, the army champion, Desmond,
Drew, Jackson and others.

Among the Du Bois Papers, in connection with his work on *The Gift,*
are scattered work sheets serving perhaps as outlines or as drafts of
thoughts to be developed. Two, on onion skin paper, are numbered
pages 9 and 10, and are fragmentary. Certain thoughts here are note-
worthy. Thus, one finds: "There will be those who think that the role
of the Negro as laborer is his fateful one in America and others who
think that his work, active and passive, in emancipation is the most important thing; but it is quite possible that posterity will find that the
great contribution of the Negro to America and the world is a contribution to art, an appreciation for beauty and a conception of beauty new
and peculiar and gripping." Further, we find this:

> Above and beyond all we have mentioned and perhaps least tangible but
> just as true is the peculiar spiritual quality which the Negro has injected into
> American life and civilization. Sometimes this is loosely called his spirit of
> happiness and jollity but it is far more subtle than this: it is an unfailing
> faith in the world, an unfaltering hope for betterment and a wide and patient
> tolerance for opposition and hatred. It is this which is at the basis of Negro
> religion and with all the loose organization of the Negro church the individual
> religious characteristics [here the manuscript breaks off]

Du Bois often worked graphically—with charts and drawings that apparently he found useful to sharpen or highlight some aspect of his effort. This was true as he prepared *The Gift* and among his papers is a
chart in the form of a pyramid which conveys much of what he had in
mind in this book. It is reproduced below; one peculiarity in Du Bois'
writing may cause difficulty: he made his written z very much like his r.
Thus to the left of the pyramid, adjacent to "Defense," are the words
"Shaw frieze" by which he was referring to the words, reprinted in this
volume on pages 125-126, that appear on the Boston monument to
Robert Gould Shaw, an officer commanding Black troops in the Civil

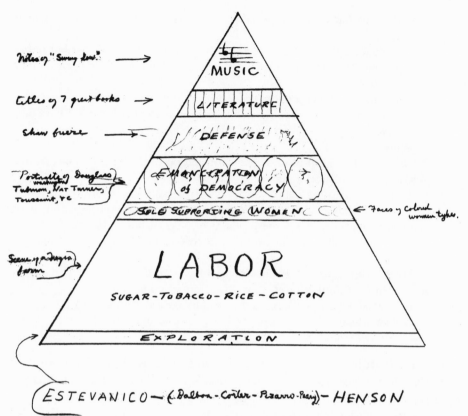

Notes of "Swing low." ⟶

Titles of 7 great books ⟶

Shaw statue ⟶

Portraits of Douglass washington Tubman, Nat Turner, Toussaint, &c

Scenes of a negro farm

MUSIC
LITERATURE
DEFENSE
EMANCIPATION of DEMOCRACY
SELF SUPPORTING WOMEN ⟵ Faces of Colored women types.
LABOR
SUGAR - TOBACCO - RICE - COTTON
EXPLORATION

ESTEVANICO — (Balboa - Cortez - Pizarro - Peary) — HENSON

War. Similarly, the names of explorers written beneath the pyramid include Cortez and Pizarro.

Finally, among the Du Bois Papers there is a typed "Memorandum on Criticisms of 'The Gift of Black Folk'." It is a carbon copy of an original no doubt sent to Dr. McSweeney; it is not dated but must have been prepared either rather late in 1922 or early in 1923. Unfortunately the criticisms to which Dr. Du Bois refers have not survived; still, their general tenor can be adduced from his reply. Certainly, the latter is of great interest:

1. This monograph is based mainly upon secondary works. It is not an attempt at new research but rather an interpretation of well known facts.
2. The conclusions are in many cases contrary to the accepted historical opinion and in those cases I have followed the advice of the critic and inserted detailed references. I think footnotes in a monograph of this character are out of place but I have furnished them.
3. I have tried to rearrange the paper in better proportions to avoid repetition

and to cut out details. Especially in the chapter on Negro soldiers have I done this.

4. This monograph is not an attempt to present lights and shadows but rather achievements so that in this respect I have not followed the suggestion of the critic.

5. I have made no change in the tone. If it is bitter it must remain so.

6. I have mentioned Dr. Booker T. Washington in his proper place. I have not, however, exaggerated the work which some white people suppose that he did.[6]

7. I have tried to keep in mind the contribution of the Negro to the country as a whole and [not] to be merely laudatory.[7]

Turning now to the detailed reports I have made the following changes: I have shown that Negro labor even in the north was important because northern commerce depended upon the products of Negro labor. I do not think that the anti-Negro riots of the thirties and forties were simply economic and not racial.

My whole chapter on Reconstruction has been changed. I have rewritten it three times. I think it meets most of the criticisms passed on it.

In general I have not hesitated to emphasize an attitude with relation to the Negro which to most people will seem untrue and fantastic but nevertheless is to my mind absolutely true.

Certain features of this volume deserve emphasis. As already pointed out, this book was one in a series which was to show the contributions of different peoples to the making of the United States. The other volumes were entitled "Germans in the Making of America" and "The Jews in the Making of America." But with Du Bois, this form was a sub-title; his title was *The Gift of Black Folk*. The difference points to something deep in Du Bois' thinking and occurs in his 1890 address at the Harvard commencement. Here, in treating the theme of "Jefferson Davis as a Representative American," Du Bois emphasized that while Davis' aggressiveness and assertiveness reflected basic currents in the American experience and psyche, the African contribution was important—all the more important—and it was one of compassion, mercy, and above all of *service*.

This runs as a theme through the present book and is at the heart of its title. The gift of Black folk was not only the obvious things—labor and productivity; but also, and perhaps above all, spiritual, artistic and somehow intangible qualities coming out of their special backgrounds and experiences. All this may be summed up, perhaps, in the meaning

[6]Booker T. Washington is mentioned four times in *The Gift*, once substantively (p. 258) and then more favorably than was usual for Du Bois.

[7]The bracketed word is inserted by the Editor; the context clearly suggests the addition.

of "soul"; its evocation and exposition constitute a basic element in Du Bois' thought from his youth to his death and is expressed with particular force in his *The Souls of Black Folk* (1903) and his *The Gift of Black Folk.* Indeed, Du Bois' making *gift* singular rather than plural helps underline the point here being made.

In his writings on labor, Du Bois emphasizes that among Black people this was not only labor of brawn but also of brain and that skilled work and scientific and inventive contributions mark that labor. Thus, "It must not be assumed, however, that the labor of the Negro has been simply the muscle-straining unintelligent work of the lowest grade. On the contrary he has appeared as both personal servant, skilled laborer and inventor . . . Negroes did most of the mechanical work in the South before the Civil War." And as for the slave system itself, Du Bois noted of the master class: "They provided punishment by physical torture, death or sale, but they always left some minimum of incentive by which the slave could have the beginnings of private possession."[8] (See pp. 61, 64-65, 66, 69)

Another theme in Du Bois' writing is made explicit in this book, namely: "Dramatically the Negro is the central thread of American history" (p. 135). Also present and relatively new in the early 1920s was Du Bois' insistence upon the active and decisive role of Black people in U.S. history in general and in the advancement of his own status. Further, the organic relationship between the democratic advancement of society in general in the United States and the enhancement in the condition of Black people was a persistent theme in Du Bois' thought and is in this book.

The ever-contemporaneous quality of Du Bois is present in this work; thus, one might think he was describing the Double V concept that dominated the Black people's response to World War II in this passage:

> His problem as a soldier was always peculiar: no matter for what America fought and no matter for what her enemies fought, the American Negro always fought for his own freedom and for the self-respect of his race. Whatever the cause of the war, therefore, his cause was peculiarly just. He appears, therefore, in American wars always with double motive,—the desire to oppose the so-called enemy of his country along with his fellow white citizens, and

---

[8]These features of slave and pre-Civil War Black history are well-known, of course, to experts in the field; attention is called to their reiteration in Du Bois' work of 1924 because they seem to have been "discovered"—in caricatured form—and are being hailed as break-throughs in historiography in the work published in 1974 entitled *Time on the Cross,* by R. W. Fogel and S. L. Engerman (Boston: Little, Brown).

before that, the motive of deserving well of those citizens and securing justice
for his folk. (p. 82)

Du Bois' contributions to political philosophical thought are major;
in no area is this greater than in that of democracy and its meaning. In
this respect, the fourth chapter of this book will repay most careful
study; note, for example, these two sentences:

> The democracy established in America in the eighteenth century was not,
> and was not designed to be, a democracy of the masses of men and it was
> thus singularly easy for people to fail to see the incongruity of democracy
> and slavery. It was the Negro himself who forced the consideration of this
> incongruity, who made emancipation inevitable and made the modern world
> at least consider if not wholly accept the idea of a democracy including men
> of all races and colors. (p. 139)

The active and dynamic role of Black people themselves was new in
published writings in the early 1920s and still is not reflected in the
main body of dominant United States writing. It was basic to Du Bois'
thinking from his high school days in the early 1880s, and is stated
clearly in this book. Thus, referring to the Abolitionist movement and
commending the work of those white people who participated in it, he
states that it is a mistake to then consider the struggle against slavery as
a kind of white man's benevolent enterprise. For, he emphasizes, one
must keep in mind "the inescapable fact that the attitude, thought and
action of the Negro himself was in largest measure back of this [white]
heart searching, discomfort and warning; and first of all was the physical
force which the Negro again and again and practically without ceasing
from the first days of the slave trade down to the war of emancipation,
used to effect his freedom." (p. 146)

Very few men in the history of the United States were as aware of
and as opposed to male supremacy as was Dr. Du Bois. This also is a
feature of his writing, beginning with his days as an editor of the college paper at Fisk University in the late 1880s. It is prominent in *Gift*
and forms the content of perhaps the book's most original chapter, "The
Freedom of Womanhood," pp. 259-273. The last lines in this book's
text are meant to summarize the gift of Black Folk; simultaneously it
summarizes the life of W.E.B. Du Bois: ". . . a thing of questing for
eternal youth, of fruitful labor, of joy and music, of the free spirit and
of the ministering hand, of wide and poignant sympathy with men in
their struggle to live and love which is, after all, the end of being."

And Du Bois' confidence in the triumph of reason among all people,
a triumph long in the coming but certain nonetheless, forms the "post-

script" in this book written for the Knights of Columbus and geared largely for a white readership: ". . . listen to the Souls that wing and thrill and weep and scream and sob and sing above it all. What shall these things mean, O God the Reader? You know. You know."

* * *

Of *The Gift*, Du Bois wrote some fifteen years after its appearance, that it was "basically sound . . . but too hurriedly done, with several unpardonable errors."[9] As indicated earlier, it is likely that Du Bois did not put in more than twelve months on the production of this book; and they were not twelve months devoted only to the writing of the book! Haste, then, certainly marked the book's creation. It marked also its production and many of the errors—whether unpardonable or not will depend on the reader—no doubt resulted from the fact that it is unlikely that Dr. Du Bois read the galleys or the pages of this book prior to its publication. As we have seen, late in July, 1923, Dr. McSweeney was writing to ask for the return of the revised manuscript and presumably this reached him either in August or September. But, as we also have noted, by the end of October, 1923 Du Bois was on the high seas beginning a journey that was to see him in Europe and Africa, not to return to the United States until March 19, 1924. And almost at once he was off on his annual lecture tour, for in May and June, 1924 Du Bois visited and spoke publicly in Virginia, South Carolina, Georgia, Ohio, Tennessee and Kentucky—and the book appeared that summer.

Leaving proof-reading entirely to others is dangerous indeed for the author of any book; but to leave this vital task in the hands of the Knights of Columbus back in the early 1920s was a grievous mistake. Surely this at least helps explain the very large and often quite serious slips, typographical errors and mistakes which do blemish *The Gift*. The errors will be listed below in tabular form; we begin with the text and conclude with the footnotes:

page	line	error	should be
55, in the table under 1910, the percentage of Negro population in the South is given as 2.61; this should be 26.1.			
86	13	1779	1770
123	9	asking	asked
125	16	M.H. Delaney	M.R. Delany
161	20	Pittsburg	Pittsburgh
233	20	committe	committee

[9] In his *Dusk of Dawn* (N.Y.: Harcourt, Brace, 1940), p. 269.

page	line	error	should be
257	23	American	America
272	1	1858	1859
293	12	George U. Cable	George W. Cable
293	13	Thomas Dixson	Thomas Dixon
297	4	Virgina	Virginia
300	19	Delaney	Delany
300	25	Samuel Northrop	Solomon Northup
302	22	Frank	Francis
303	27	Mitchell	Williams
304	2	H.F.M.	F.H.M.
304	11	Lawrence	Laurence
304	17	Claud	Claude
308	8	Claud	Claude
332	10	Hayes	Haynes
333	20	Virgina	Virginia

Footnotes

page	line	error	should be
36	2	Thurston	Thruston
36	2	De Charnay	D. Charnay
36	3	publicati . . . quorto	pubblicati . . . quarto
38	7	Essalante Fontanedo	Escalante Fontaneda
153	18	Coppin	Coffin
154	20	Talmadge	Talmage
158	25	I. W. Cromwell	J. W. Cromwell
220	24	7	5
249	39	p. 871	p. 781
268	5	p. 326ff.	Vol. II, p. 326ff.
304	7	Schomberg	Schomburg
308	8	Claud	Claude
332	5	J.E. Bassett	J. S. Bassett

Note: Naturally many of the errors in the text are carried over into the index. In addition, errors appear in the index that are not in the text; for example, Lydia Marcia Child instead of Lydia Maria Child, Charles W. Chestnutt instead of Charles W. Chesnutt and Freemont instead of Fremont, etc.

Figures on the sales of *The Gift* seem no longer available; one might guess that the original printing was about three thousand. Certainly by the end of December, 1928 it was out of print, for on December 15 of that year the accounting department of its publisher, The Stratford Company, wrote *The Crisis* that it was unable to fill an order for six copies because the title was sold out. On April 29, 1930, Du Bois wrote the Company stating: "We have had a proposition from a publisher for a cheap edition of this book," and asking if plates were extant and could they be purchased. No reply from the Company seems to have survived, if one was forthcoming. There was a paperback reprint, with an introduction by Truman Nelson, issued in 1970 by the Washington Square Press in New York City. This edition omitted not only the essay by Dr. McSweeney but also the foreword by Dr. Du Bois. In 1972 the AMS press in New York City issued a photographic reproduction, in cloth, of the 1924 book.

* * *

The reviews of *The Gift* were fairly numerous and usually quite favorable and perceptive. A brief notice appeared in the *American Review of Reviews,* October, 1924 (70:448), making the point that "most readers of the white race" would be surprised at the data brought forward by Du Bois; especially was this true, thought the reviewer, of the material on Black people as explorers. The comment in *The Bookman,* November, 1924 (60:357) was fuller and deeper. Du Bois, said the reviewer, "has the gift of style and polemic" and he called attention to Du Bois' material on women, literature, music and science in particular, noting also the "special emphasis upon the spiritual gifts of his group with their perpetual challenge to American democracy." A commentary in the Chicago *Daily News* (March 11, 1925) came from Willis A. Ellis, who felt that "no one in America is better fitted by knowledge and education than Mr. Du Bois to present the record of the Negroes." Mr. Ellis added: "A tendency toward bitterness and even belligerency which he has occasionally shown is entirely absent from this book and the presentation which he makes of the gift of his people is in truth an impressive one." Dr. Du Bois may well have smiled to find that this reviewer discovered an absence of "bitterness" while the critic for the publisher had lamented its presence!

A review that can only be called disgusting came from Virginia Moore[10] and was published in the N.Y. *Evening Sun,* July 18, 1925. Du Bois' book was "grossly biased"; it "stubbornly refuses" to see contrary evidence; much in it is either "questionable" or "flagrantly fal-

---

[10] Virginia Moore was born in Virginia in 1903; she published poetry, fiction and biographies—her biographies of Emily Bronte (1936) and of William Butler Yeats (1954) remain in print. For a time she was married to Louis Untermeyer. Her book, *Virginia as a State of Mind* (N.Y. Dutton, 1942), is of gone-with-the wind vintage.

lacious" and "any honest person who has lived in the thick of a largely negro population" would recognize the "shameless garbling" marking Dr. Du Bois' book.

Black reviewers rejoiced that the book was published and hailed it as a contribution in the struggle against racism. J. A. Rogers (1880-1966), the prolific columnist and historian, found *Gift* to be "a less impassioned book" than Du Bois' *Soul,* but thought this was logical since the later book was meant to be a straight-forward accounting of data. In this effort, wrote Rogers, the book succeeded despite the occurrence of factual slips—"mere trivialities"—and so might well have a positive effect "on the minds of those for whom such works are primarily intended—the oppressors." (N.Y. *Amsterdam News,* October 1, 1924)

Walter White, in the Sunday N.Y. *Herald Tribune* (September 21, 1924), also gave the book a very positive review; the points he made were substantially those made by Rogers. White also called attention to the "careless proof reading," doing so in no carping spirit but rather seeing them as blemishes in a book of great value for the time and place of publication.

Benjamin G. Brawley[11] provided an illuminating estimate of the book for *Opportunity,* the organ of the National Urban League (December, 1924; 2:377-378). As did White and Rogers, he commented on the poor proofing of the book and then added that it seemed to have been written under pressure of time. Still, the book was extremely valuable, dealing as it did with "vital subjects" and doing so with the grace and verve characteristic of the author. Brawley was especially pleased by "its optimistic temper, its constructive spirit, and its catholicity of interest" and by the generosity with which it treated personalities and groups engaged in the effort to eliminate racism.

.George S. Schuyler hailed the book in a magazine not overly friendly to Du Bois—*The Messenger,* December, 1924 (12:384-385). Schuyler wrote that a feeling of inferiority pervaded the minds of many Black people—of all classes—and that this restrained the forward movement of the people. Du Bois' new book, he felt, could do much to overcome this for it showed convincingly and in moving prose the actual accomplishments of Afro-American people. He concluded by remarking that every

---

[11] Dr. Brawley (1882-1939) was born in South Carolina. He was educated at Morehouse, Chicago and Harvard Universities and served as a professor of English and a dean at Morehouse, Howard and Shaw. His studies of drama and of literature were published by Harcourt, Brace and by Knopf and his books on the history of Black people by Macmillan, beginning in 1913. Several of his works remain in print.

cloud did indeed have a silver lining; here, as a result of the attacks upon Catholics and Jews, were the Knights of Columbus sponsoring a series which allowed our foremost author to state our case. "Probably," concluded Schuyler, "the Klan has some value."

* * *

In *The Gift of Black Folk,* the reader has before him a summing up of the views and hopes of the foremost Black thinker in the midst of what contemporaries referred to as the period of the Harlem Renaissance.

May, 1974   Herbert Aptheker

THE
GIFT *of* BLACK FOLK

The Negroes in the
Making of America

by

W. E. Burghardt DuBois
PH. D. (HARV.)

Author of "The Souls of Black Folk," "Darkwater," etc.
Editor of *The Crisis*

Introduction by
EDWARD F. McSWEENEY, LL. D.

1924

THE STRATFORD CO., *Publishers*
BOSTON, MASSACHUSETTS

CONTENTS

Chapter   Page

       Foreword i

       Prescript 33

   I   The Black Explorers 35

  II   Black Labor 52

 III   Black Soldiers 80

  IV   The Emancipation of Democracy . 135

   V   The Reconstruction of Freedom . . 184

  VI   The Freedom of Womanhood . . 259

 VII   The American Folk Song 274

VIII   Negro Art and Literature 287

  IX   The Gift of the Spirit 320

FOREWORD

It is not uncommon for casual thinkers to assume that the United States of America is practically a continuation of English nationality. Our speech is English and the English played so large a part in our beginnings that it is easy to fall more or less consciously into the thought that the history of this nation has been but a continuation and development of these beginnings. A little reflection, however, quickly convinces us that at least there was present French influence in the Mississippi Valley and Spanish influence in the southeast and southwest. Everything else however that has been added to the American nationality is often looked upon as a sort of dilution of more or less doubtful value: peoples that had to be assimilated as far as possible and made over to the original and basic type. Thus we continually speak of Germans and Scandinavians, of Irish and Jews, Poles, Austrians and Hungarians; and, with few exceptions, we regard the coming of the Negroes as an unmitigated error and a national liability.

It is high time that this course of our thinking should be changed. America is conglomerate.

i

This is at once her problem and her glory—perhaps indeed her sole and greatest reason for being. Her physical foundation is not English and while it is primarily it is not entirely European. It represents peculiarly a coming together of the peoples of the world. American institutions have been borrowed from England and France in the main, but with contributions from many and widely scattered groups. American history has no prototype and has been developed from the various racial elements. Despite the fact that our mother tongue is called English we have developed an American speech with its idiosyncrasies and idioms, a speech whose purity is not to be measured by its conformity to the speech of the British Isles. And finally the American spirit is a new and interesting result of divers threads of thought and feeling coming not only from America but from Europe and Asia and indeed from Africa.

This essay is an attempt to set forth more clearly than has hitherto been done the effect which the Negro has had upon American life. Its thesis is that despite slavery, war and caste, and despite our present Negro problem, the American Negro is and has been a distinct asset to this country and has brought a contribution without which America could not have been; and that perhaps the essence of our so-called Negro problem is the failure to recognize this fact and to continue to act as though the Negro was what we once imagined and wanted to imagine him — a representative of a subhuman species fitted only for subordination.

A moment's thought will easily convince open minded persons that the contribution of the Negro to American nationality as slave, freedman and citizen was far from negligible. No element in American life has so subtly and yet clearly woven itself into the warp and woof of our thinking and acting as the American Negro. He came with the first explorers and helped in exploration. His labor was from the first the foundation of the American prosperity and the cause of the rapid growth of the new world in economic and social importance. Modern democracy rests not simply on the striving white men in Europe and America but also on the persistent struggle of the black men in America for two centuries. The military defense of this land has depended upon Negro soldiers from the time of the Colonial wars down to the struggle of the World War. Not only does the Negro appear, reappear and persist in American literature but a Negro American literature has arisen of deep significance, and Negro folk lore and music are among the choicest heritages of this land.

Finally the Negro had played a peculiar spiritual rôle in America as a sort of living, breathing test of our ideals and an example of the faith, hope and tolerance of our religion.

THE RACIAL CONTRIBUTIONS
TO THE UNITED STATES

By Edw. F. McSweeney, LL. D.

In a general way, the Racial Contribution Series in the Knights of Columbus historical program is intended as a much needed and important contribution to national solidarity. The various studies are treated by able writers, citizens of the United States, each being in full sympathy with the achievements in this country of the racial group of whom he treats. The standard of the writers is the only one that will justify historical writing; — the truth. No censorship has been exercised.

No subject now actively before the people of the United States has been more written on, and less understood, than alien immigration. Until 1819, there were no official statistics of immigration of any sort; the so-called census of 1790 was simply a report of the several states of their male white population under and over 16 years of age, all white females, slaves, and others. Statements as to the country of origin of the inhabitants of this country were, in the main, guesswork, with the result that, while the great bulk of such estimates was honestly and patriotically done, some of the most quoted during the present day were inspired, obviously to prove a predetermined case, rather than to recite the ascertained fact.

1

From the beginning the dominant groups in control in the United States have regarded each group of newer arrivals as more or less the "enemy" to be feared, and, if possible, controlled. A study of various cross-sections of the country will show dominant alien groups who formerly had to fight for their very existence. With increased numerical strength and prosperity they frequently attempted to do to the later aliens, frequently even of their own group, what had formerly been done to them: — decry and stifle their achievements, and deny them opportunity, — the one thing that may justly be demanded in a Democracy, — by putting them in a position of inferiority.

To attempt, in this country, to set up a "caste" control, based on the accident of birth, wealth, or privilege, is a travesty of Democracy. When Washington and his compatriots, a group comprising the most efficiently prepared men in the history of the world, who had set themselves definitely to form a democratic civilization, dreamed of and even planned by Plato, but held back by slavery and paganism, they found their sure foundations in the precepts of Christianity, and gave them expression in the Declaration of Independence. The liberty they sought, based on obedience to the law of God as well as of man, was actually established, but from the beginning it has met a constant effort to substitute some form of absolutism tending to break down or replace democratic institutions.

What may be called, for want of a better term, the colonial spirit, which is the essence of hyphenism, has persisted in this country to hamper national progress and national unity. Wherever this colonial spirit shows itself it is a menace to be fought, whether the secret or acknowledged attachment binds to England, Ireland, France, Germany, Italy, Greece or any other nation.

Jefferson pointed out that we have on this soil evolved a new race of men who may inexactly be called "Americans". This term, as a monopoly of the United States, is properly objected to by our neighbors, North and South — yet it has a definite meaning for the world.

During the Great War one aspect of war duty was to direct the labor activities growing out of the war, to divert labor from "non-essential" to "essential" industry and to arbitrate and mediate on wage matters. It was found necessary to study and to analyze the greatly feared, but infrequently discovered "enemy alien"; and as a preparation for this duty, with the assistance of several hundred local agents, the population of Massachusetts was separated into naturally allied groups based on birth, racial descent, religious, social and industrial affiliations. The astonishing result was that, counting as "native Americans" only the actual descendants of all those living in Massachusetts in 1840, of whatever racial stock prior to that time, only two-sevenths, even with the most liberal classification, came within the group of colonial descent, while the remaining five-sevenths were found in the various racial groups coming later than 1840. More than this: While the "Colonial" group had increased in numbers for three decades after 1840, in 1918 they were found actually to be fewer in number than in 1840, a diminution due to excess of deaths over births, proceeding in increasing ratio.

Membership in the Society of Mayflower descendants is eagerly sought as the hallmark of American ancestry. In anticipation of the tercentenary of the Mayflower-coming in 1620, about a dozen years ago a questionnaire was sent to every known eligible for Mayflower ancestry, and the replies were submitted to the experts in one of the national universities for review and report. When this report was presented later, it contained the statement that, considering the prevailing number of marriages in this group, and children per family, — when the six-hundredth celebration of the Pilgrims' Landing is held in 2220, three hundred years hence, a ship the size of the original Mayflower will be sufficient to carry back to Europe all the then living Mayflower descendants.

The future of America is in the keeping of the 80 per cent. of the population, separate in blood and race from the colonial descent group. Love of native land is one of the strongest and noblest passions of which a man is capable. Family life, religion, the soil which holds the dust of our fathers, sentiment for ancestral property, and many other bonds, make the ties of home so strong and enduring, and unite a man's life so closely with its native environment, that grave and powerful reasons must exist before a change of residence is contemplated. Escape from religious persecution and political tyranny were unquestionably the chief reasons which induced the early comers to America to brave the dangers of an unknown world. Yet that very intolerance against which this was a protest soon began to be exercised against all those unwilling to accept in their new homes the religious leadership of those in control.

It is not necessary to go into the persecutions due to religious bigotry of the colonial period. While the spirit of liberty was in the free air of the colonies and would finally have secured national independence, it is not possible to underestimate the support brought to the revolting colonials because of the attitude of Great Britain in allowing religious freedom to Canada after it had been taken from the French. After the victory of New Orleans, a spirit of national consciousness on a democratic basis was built up and the narrow spirit of colonialism and of religious intolerance was to a great degree repudiated by the people, when they had become inspired with the American spirit, — only to be revived later on.

The continued manifestation of intolerance has been the most persistent effort in our national life. It has done incalculable harm. It is apparently deep-rooted, an active force in almost every generation. Present in the 30's, 40's and 50's, stopped temporarily for two decades by the Civil War, it has recurred subsequently again and again; revived since the Armistice, it is unfortunately shown to-day in as great a virulence and power of destructiveness as at any time during the last hundred years.

After the 70's, as the aliens became numerically powerful and began to demand political representation, movements based on religious prejudice were started from time to time, some of which came to temporary prominence, later to die an inglorious death; but all these movements which attempted to deprive aliens of their right of freedom to worship were calculated to bring economic discontent and to add to the measure of national disunion and unhappiness.

Sixty years ago[1] the bigoted slogan was *"No Irish need apply."* During the World War, the principal attack was on the German-American citizens of this country, whose fathers had come here seeking a new land as a protest against tyranny. To-day the current attempt is

---

[1] In the fifties it was customary for the merchants, etc., to have posted at their door a list of help wanted. Many of these help wanted signs were accompanied by another which read "No Irish need apply." During the Civil War there was an Anti-Draft song with a refrain to the effect that when it came to drafting they did not practice "No Irish need apply."

to deprive the Jews[2] of the right to educational equality. In short, while there have been spasmodic manifestations of movements based on intolerance in many countries, the United States has the unenviable record for continuous effort to keep alive a bogey based on an increasing fear of something which never existed, and cannot ever exist in this country.

For a hundred years the potent cause which has poured millions of human beings into the United States has been its marvellous opportunities, and unprecedented economic urge.   Ever since 1830 a graphic chart of the variations in immigration from year to year will reflect the industrial situation in the United States for the same period.   In 1837, the total immigration was 79,430.[3]   After the panic of that year it decreased in 1838 to 38,914.[4]   In 1842, it increased to 104,565,[5] but a business depression in 1844 caused it to shrink to 78,615.[6]   Thus the influx of aliens increased or decreased according to the industrial conditions prevalent here.   The business prosperity of the United States was not only the urge to entice immigrants hither, but it made their coming possible as they were helped by the savings of relatives and friends already here.

The English were not immigrants, but colonists, merely going from one part of national territory to another.   With few exceptions, the majority of the early colonists came from England.   The first English settlement was made in Virginia under the London Company

---

[2] "Americans only" in a real estate advertisement to-day usually means "No Jews need apply."   It sometimes means Irish (i. e., Catholic) also.

[3] Wm. J. Bromwell, *History of Immigration to United States*, p. 96.

[4] *Ibid.*, p. 100.

[5] *Ibid.*, p. 116.

[6] *Ibid.*, p. 124.

in 1607. It took twelve years of hard struggling to establish this colony on a permanent basis.

The New England region was settled by a different class of colonists. Plymouth was the first settlement, in 1620, followed in 1630 by the Massachusetts Bay Colony, which later absorbed the Plymouth settlement. Population, after the first ten years, increased rapidly by natural growth, and soon colonies in Rhode Island, New Hampshire and Connecticut resulted from the overflow in the original settlements.

While this English settlement was going on North and South, the Dutch, under the Dutch West India Company, took possession of the region between, and founded New Netherlands and New Amsterdam, later New York City. Intervening, as it did, between their Northern and Southern colonies, New Netherlands, which the English considered a menace, was seized by the English during a war with Holland, and became New York and New Jersey.

Early in the seventeenth century there was a substantial French immigration to the Dutch colonies. There was a constant stream of French immigration to the English colonies in New England and in Virginia by many of the Huguenots who had originally emigrated to the West Indies.

In 1681, Penn settled Pennsylvania under a royal charter and thus the whole Atlantic coast from Canada to Florida became subject to England. During the colonial period, England contributed to the population of the colonies. But, by the middle of the seventeenth century, the coming of the English to New England was practically over. From 1628 to 1641 about 20,000 came from England to New England, but for the next century and a half more persons went back to Old England than came

from there to New England.[7]   Due to the relaxing of
religious persecution of dissenting Protestants in England,
the great formerly impelling force to seek a new home
across the ocean in America had ceased.

In 1653 an Irish immigration to New England, much
larger in numbers than the original Plymouth Colony, was
proposed.   Bristol merchants, who realized the necessity
of populating the colonies to make them prosperous,
treated with the government for men, women and girls
to be sent to the West Indies and to New England.[8]   At
the very fountain head of American life we find, therefore,
men and women of pure Celtic blood from the South of
Ireland, infused into the primal stock of America.   But
these apparently were only a drop in this early tide of
Irish immigration.[9]

[7] *Commercial Relations of the United States,* 1885-1886, Appendix
III, p. 1967.

[8] "The Commissioners for Ireland gave them orders upon the governors of garrisons, to deliver to them prisoners of war; upon the keep-
ers of gaols, for offenders in custody; upon masters of workhouses, for
the destitute in their care 'who were of an age to labor, or if women
were marriageable and not past breeding'; and gave directions to all in
authority to seize those who had no visible means of livelihood, and
deliver them to these agents of the Bristol sugar merchants, in execution
of which latter direction Ireland must have exhibited scenes in every
part like the slave hunts in Africa.   How many girls of gentle birth
have been caught and hurried to the private prisons of these man-
catchers none can tell.   Messrs. Sellick and Leader, Mr. Robert
Yeomans, Mr. Joseph Lawrence, and others, all of Bristol, were active
agents.   As one instance out of many: Captain John Vernon was employed by the Commissioners for Ireland into England, and contracted in
their behalf with Mr. David Sellick and Mr. Leader under his hand,
bearing date the 14th September, 1653, to supply them with two hundred
and fifty women of the Irish nation above twelve years, and under the
age of forty-five, also three hundred men above twelve years of age, and
under fifty, to be found in the country within twenty miles of Cork,
Youghal, and Kinsale, Waterford and Wexford, to transport them into
New England."   J. P. Prendergast, *The Cromwellian Settlement of
Ireland,* London, 1865.   2d. ed., pp. 89-90.

[9] "It is calculated that in four years (1653-1657) English firms of
slave-dealers shipped 6,400 Irish men and women, boys and maidens, to
the British colonies of North America."   A. J. Theband, *The Irish Race
in the Past and Present,* N. Y., 1893, p. 385.

No complete memorial has been transmitted of the emigrations that took place from Europe to America, but (from the few illustrative facts actually preserved) they seem to have been amazingly copious. In the years 1771-72, the number of emigrants to America from the North of Ireland alone amounted to 17,350. Almost all of these emigrated at their own charge; a great majority of them were persons employed in the linen manufacture, or farmers possessed of some property which they converted into money and carried with them. Within the first fortnight of August, 1773, there arrived at Philadelphia 3,500 emigrants from Ireland, and from the same document which has recorded this circumstance it appears that vessels were arriving every month freighted with emigrants from Holland, Germany, and especially from Ireland and the Highlands of Scotland.[10]

That many Irish settled in Maryland is shown by the fact that in 1699 and again a few years later an act was passed to prevent too great a number of Irish Papists being imported into the province.[11] Shipmasters were required to pay two shillings per poll for such. "Shipping records of the colonial period show that boatload after boatload left the southern and eastern shores of Ireland for the New World. Undoubtedly thousands of their passengers were Irish of the native stock."[12] So besides the so-called Scotch-Irish from the North of Ireland, the distinction always being Protestantism, not race, it is indisputable that thousands, Celtic in race and Catholic in religion, came to the colonies. These newcomers made

[10] Rev. T. A. Spencer, *History of the United States,* Vol. 1, p. 305.
[11] Henry Pratt Fairchild, *Immigration: A world movement, and its American significance,* N. Y., 1913, p. 47. See also *Archives of Maryland,* Vol. 22, p. 497.
[12] Charles A. and Mary R. Beard, *History of the United States,* N. Y., 1921, p. 11.

their homes principally in Pennsylvania, Virginia, Maryland, the Carolinas and the frontiers of the New England colonies. Later they pushed on westward and founded Ohio, Kentucky and Tennessee. An interesting essay by the well-known writer, Irvin S. Cobb, on *The Lost Irish Tribes in the South* is an important contribution to this subject.

The Germans were the next most important element of the early population of America. A number of the artisans and carpenters in the first Jamestown colony were of German descent. In 1710, a body of 3,000 Germans came to New York — the largest number of immigrants supposed to have arrived at one time during the colonial period.[13] Most of the early German immigrants settled in New Jersey, the Carolinas, and Pennsylvania. It has been estimated that at the end of the colonial period the number of Germans was fully two hundred thousand.

Though the Irish and the Germans contributed most largely to colonial immigration, as distinguished from the English, who are classed as the Colonials, there were other races who came even thus early to our shores. The Huguenots came from France to escape religious persecution. The Jews, then as ever, engaged in their age-old struggle for religious and economic toleration, came from England, France, Spain and Portugal. The Dutch Government of New Amsterdam, fearing their commercial competition, ordered a group of Portuguese Jews to leave the colony, but this decision was appealed to the home Government at Holland and reversed, so that they were allowed to remain. On the whole, their freedom to live and to trade in the colonies was so much greater than in their former homes that there were soon flourishing

[13] Fairchild, p. 35.

colonies of Jewish merchants in Newport, Philadelphia and Charleston.

In 1626 a company of Swedish merchants organized, under the patronage of the Great King Gustavus Adolphus, to promote immigration to America. The King contributed four hundred thousand dollars to the capital raised, but did not live to see the fruition of his plans. In 1637, the first company of Swedes and Finns left Stockholm for America. They reached Delaware Bay and called the country New Sweden. The Dutch claimed, by right of priority, this same territory and in 1655 the flag of Holland replaced that of Sweden. The small Swedish colony in Delaware came under Penn's rule and became, like Pennsylvania, cosmopolitan in character.

The Dutch in New York preserved their racial characteristics for more than a hundred years after the English conquest of 1664. At the end of the colonial period, over one-half of the 170,000 inhabitants of New York were descendants of the original Dutch.

Many of the immigrants who came here in the early days paid their own passage. However, the actual number of such is only a matter of conjecture. From the shipping records of the period we do know positively that thousands came who were unable to pay. Shipowners and others who had the means furnished the passage money to those too poor to pay for themselves, and in return received from these persons a promise or bond. This bond provided that the person named in it should work for a certain number of years to repay the money advanced. Such persons were called "indentured servants" and they were found throughout the colonies, working in the fields, the shops and the homes of the colonists. The term of service was from five to seven years. Many found it

impossible to meet their obligations and their servitude
dragged on for years. Others, on the contrary, became
free and prosperous. In Pennsylvania often there were
as many as fifty bond servants on estates. The condition
of indentured servants in Virginia "was little better than
that of slaves. Loose indentures and harsh laws put them
at the mercy of their masters."[14] This seems to have been
their fate in all the colonies, as their treatment depended
upon the character of their masters.

Besides these indentured servants who came here voluntarily, a large number of early settlers were forced to
come here. The Irish before mentioned are one example.
In order to secure settlers, men, women and children were
kidnapped from the cities and towns and "spirited away"
to America by the companies and proprietors who had
colonies here. In 1680 it was officially computed that
10,000 were sent thus to American shores. In 1627,
about 1,500 children were shipped to Virginia, probably
orphans and dependents whom their relatives were unwilling to support.[15] Another class sent here were convicts, the scourings of English centers like Bristol and
Liverpool. The colonists protested vehemently against this
practise, but it was continued up to the very end of the
colonial period, when this convict tide was diverted to
"Botany Bay."

In 1619, another race was brought here against their
will and sold into slavery. This was the Negro, forced to
leave his home near the African equator that he might
contribute to the material wealth of shipmasters and
planters. Slowly but surely chattel slavery took firm root
in the South and at last became the leading source of the

[14] Henry Cabot Lodge, *A Short History of the English Colonies in
America*, N. Y., 1881, p. 70.
[15] Beard, p. 15.

labor supply. The slave traders found it very easy to seize Negroes in Africa and make great profits by selling them in Southern ports. The English Royal African Company sent to America annually between 1713 and 1743 from 5,000 to 10,000 slaves.[16] After a time, when the Negroes were so numerous that whole sections were overrun, the Southern colonies tried ineffectually to curb the trade. Virginia in 1710 placed a duty of five pounds on each slave but the Royal Governor vetoed the bill. Bills of like import were passed in other colonies from time to time, but the English crown disapproved in every instance and the trade, so lucrative to British shipowners, went on. At the time of the Revolution, there were almost half a million slaves in the colonies.[17] The exact proportions of the slave trade to America can be but approximately determined. From 1680 to 1688 the African Company sent 249 ships to Africa, shipped there 60,783 Negro slaves, and after losing 14,387 on the middle passage, delivered 46,396 in America. The trade increased early in the eighteenth century, 104 ships clearing for Africa in 1701; it then dwindled until the signing of the Assiento, standing at 74 clearances in 1724. The final dissolution of the monopoly in 1750 led — excepting in the years 1754-57, when the closing of Spanish marts sensibly affected the trade — to an extraordinary development, 192 clearances being made in 1771. The Revolutionary War nearly stopped the traffic, but by 1786 the clearances had risen again to 146.

To these figures must be added the unregistered trade of Americans and foreigners. It is probable that about 25,000 slaves were brought to America each year between

[16] Beard, p. 16.
[17] W. S. Burghardt DuBois, *Suppression of the Slave Trade,* Harvard Historical Studies, No. 1, p. 5.

1698 and 1707. The importation then dwindled but after the Assiento rose to perhaps 30,000. The proportion of these slaves carried to the continent now began to increase. Of about 20,000 whom the English annually imported from 1733 to 1766, South Carolina alone received some 3,000. Before the Revolution the total exportation to America is variously estimated as between 40,000 and 100,000 each year. Bancroft places the total slave population of the continental colonies at 59,000 in 1714; 78,000 in 1727; and 293,000 in 1754. The census of 1790 showed 697,897 slaves in the United States. Not all the Negroes who came to America were slaves and not all remained slaves. There were the following free Negroes in the decades between 1790 and 1860:

1790	59,557
1800	108,435
1810	186,446
1820	233,634
1830	319,599
1840	386,293
1850	434,495
1860	488,070

Immigration of Negroes is still taking place, especially from the West Indies. It has been estimated that there are the following foreign-born Negroes in the United States:

1890	19,979
1900	20,336
1910	40,339
1920	75,000

In 1790, Negroes were one-fifth of the total population; in 1860 they were one-seventh; in 1900 one-ninth;[18] to-day they are approximately one-tenth.

With the beginning of the national era — 1783 — all peoples subsequently coming to the United States must be classed as immigrants. During the first years of our national life, no accurate statistics of immigration were kept. The Federal Government took no control of the matter and the State records are incomplete and unreliable. A pamphlet published by the Bureau of Statistics in 1903, *Immigration into the United States,* says, "The best estimates of the total immigration into the United States prior to the official count puts the total number of arrivals at not to exceed 250,000 in the entire period between 1776 and 1820."

From 1806 to 1816, the unfriendly relations which existed between the United States and England and France precluded any extensive immigration to this country. England maintained and for a time successfully enforced the doctrine that "a man once a subject was always a subject." The American Merchant Service, because of the pay and good treatment given, was very attractive to English sailors and a very great enticement to them to come to America and enter the American service. However, the fear of impressment deterred many from so doing. The Blockade Decrees of England against France in 1806 and the retaliation decrees of France against England in that same year were other influences which retarded immigration. These decrees were succeeded by the British Orders in Council, the Milan Decree of Napoleon, and the United States law of 1809 prohibiting intercourse with both Great Britain and France.

[18] John R. Commons, *Races and Immigrants in America,* N. Y., 1907, p. 53.

In 1810, the French decrees were annulled and American commerce began again with France, only to have the vessels fall into the hands of the British. Then came the War of 1812. The German immigration suffered greatly from this condition of affairs, as the Germans sailed principally from the ports of Liverpool and Havre. At these points ships were more numerous and expenses less heavy. In December, 1814, a few days before the Battle of New Orleans, a treaty of peace was concluded between the United States and England and after a few months immigration was resumed once more.

In 1817, about 22,240 persons arrived at ports of the United States from foreign countries. This number included American citizens returning from abroad. In no previous year had so many immigrants come to our shores.

In 1819 a law was passed by Congress and approved by the President "regulating passenger ships and vessels." In 1820, the official history of immigration began. The Port Collectors then began to keep records which included numbers, sexes, ages, and occupations of all incoming persons. However, up to 1856, no distinction was made between travellers and immigrants.

Immigration increased from 8,358 in 1820 — of which 6,024 came from Great Britain and Ireland — to 22,633 in 1831.[19] The decade of the twenties was a time of great industrial activity in the United States. The Erie Canal was built, other canals were projected, the railroads were started, business increased by leaps and bounds. As a consequence, the demand for labor was imperative and Europe responded. During the entire period of our

[19] Adam Seybert, *Statistical Annals of the United States,* Phila., 1818, p. 29.

early national life, the United States encouraged the coming of foreign artisans and laborers as the necessity for strength, skill and courage in the upbuilding of our country began to be realized.

From 1831 the number of immigrants steadily increased until from September 30, 1849, to September 30, 1850, they totaled 315,334[20]   The largest increases during those years were from 1845 to 1848, when the famine in Ireland and the revolution in Germany drove thousands to the shores of free America.   These causes continued to increase the number of arrivals until in 1854 the crest was attained with 460,474[21] — a figure not again reached for nearly twenty years.

From September 30, 1819, when the official count of immigrants began to be taken, to December 31, 1855, a total of 4,212,624 persons of foreign birth arrived in the United States.[22]   Of these Bromwell, who wrote in 1856 a work compiled entirely from official data, estimates that 1,747,930 were Irish.[23]   Next comes Germany,[24] with 1,206,087; England third with 207,492; France fourth with 188,725.

The exodus of the Irish during those famine years furnishes one of the many examples recorded in history of a subject race driven from its home by the economic injustice of a dominant race.   Later, we see the same thing true in Austria-Hungary where the Slavs were tyrannized by the Magyars; again we find it in Russia where the Jew sought freedom from the Slav; and once again in Armenia and Syria where the native people fled from the Turk.

[20] Young, *Special Report on Immigration*, Phila., 1871, p. 5.
[21] Bromwell, p. 145.
[22] *Ibid.*, p. 16.
[23] *Ibid.*, p. 18.
[24] *Ibid.*, pp. 16-17.

After 1855, the tide of immigration began to decrease steadily. During the first two years of the Civil War, it was less than 100,000.[25] In 1863, an increase was noticeable again and 395,922[26] immigrants are recorded in 1869.

During all these years up to 1870, the great part of the immigration was from Northern Europe. The largest racial groups were composed of Irish, Germans, Scandinavians and French. About the middle of the nineteenth century French-speaking Canadians were attracted by the opportunities for employment in the mills and factories of New England.

The number of Irish coming here steadily decreased after 1880 until it has fallen far below that of other European peoples. Altogether, the total Irish immigration from 1820 to 1906 is placed at something over 4,000,000, thus giving the Irish second place as contributors to the foreign-born population of the United States. The Revolution of 1848 was the contributing cause of a large influx of Germans, many of whom were professional men and artisans. From 1873 to 1879 there was great industrial depression in Germany and consequently another large immigration to America took place. Since 1882, there has also been a noticeable decline in German immigrants. From 1820 to 1903, a total of over 5,000,-000 Germans was recorded as coming to the United States.[27]

In the period from 1880 to 1910 immigration from Italy totaled 4,018,404. It will be remembered that the law requiring the registration of outgoing aliens was not passed until 1908, and it may, therefore, be estimated that

[25] Young, p. 6.
[26] Ibid., p. 6.
[27] Special Consular Reports, Vol. 30, p. 8.

3,000,000 represents the total number of arrivals from Italy, who remained here permanently.

After 1903, up to the outbreak of the Great War, the number of alien arrivals steadily increased. In 1905, it was more than 1,000,000; in 1906, it passed the 1,100,000 mark and in 1907 the 1,200,000 mark; in 1913 and 1914, the total number for each year exceeded 1,400,000.[28]

During the ten years from 1905 to 1915, nearly 12,-000,000 aliens landed in the United States, a yearly average of 1,200,000 arrivals. These alone form more than 37 per cent. of all recorded immigration since 1820 and make up about 88 out of every 100 of our present total foreign-born population.[29]. Until interrupted by the European War, the immigration to the United States was the greatest movement of the largest number of peoples that the world has ever known. Of course, there have been economic upheavals from time to time which have noticeably affected this movement. The Civil War, as before noted, and financial panics and industrial depressions in our country interrupted the incoming tide repeatedly. The Great War with its social and economic upheaval had a tremendous effect on our immigration. The twelve months following the declaration of war shows the smallest number of alien arrivals since 1899. The number was slightly over 325,000. The statistics compiled by the Federal Bureau of Immigration show that by far the greater part of the immigrants who come to the United States are from Europe. Of the 1,403,000 alien immigrants who came here in 1914, about 1,114,000 were from Europe; about 35,000 came from Asia; the remainder, about 254,000, came from all other countries

[28] *Immigration and Emigration,* Bureau of Labor Statistics, Washington, 1915, p. 1099.
[29] *Ibid.*

combined, principally Canada, the West Indies, and Mexico. Eighty out of every 100, therefore, came from Europe. As many as sixty of that eighty came from the three countries of Italy, Austria-Hungary and Russia. Italy sent 294,689; Austria-Hungary was second with 286,059; Russian contributed 262,409. From all of England, Ireland, Scotland and Wales came only 88,000 or about 6 out of every 100; and from Norway, Sweden and Denmark came about 31,000 or 2 out of every 100.

Greece, France, Portugal, Bulgaria, Montenegro, Spain, Turkey, the Netherlands, Belgium, Switzerland, and Roumania contributed virtually all the remainder of our 1914 immigrants from Europe, given in the order of importance.

However, we should bear in mind always that the country of origin or nationality or jurisdiction (as determined by political boundaries) is not always identical with race. Immigration statistics have followed national or political boundaries. Take the immigrants from Russia. The statistics say that 262,000 arrived from that country in 1914. But of this number, less than 5 out of every 100 are Russians; the rest or 95 out of every 100, are Hebrews, Poles, Lithuanians, Finns and Germans.

Austria-Hungary was another country made of a medley of races. The Germanic Austrians who ruled Austria and the Hungarian Magyars who ruled Hungary were less than one-half of the total population of the one time Austria-Hungary.

The record of alien arrivals from Poland is not accurate because it is divided into three national statistical divisions — Russia, Germany and Austria-Hungary. The best estimate is that the total Polish arrivals to the United States since 1820 approximates 2,500,000.

The Slav, the Magyar, the German, the Latin, and the Jew were all in Austria-Hungary and moreover, these were all numerously subdivided. The most numerous of the Slavs are the Czechs and Slovaks. These gave the United States in 1914 a combined immigration of 37,000. Poles, Ruthenians and Roumanians also came here from northern Austria, and from the vicinity of the Black Sea came Roumanians more Latin than Slavic. Besides these, the one time dual kingdom sent Jews, Greeks and Turks.

Although the most important Slavic country of Europe is Russia, yet it was from Austria-Hungary that we received most of our Slavic immigrants. In 1914, as many as 23 out of every 100 of our total immigration were Slavic, and the larger part of this racial group which reached 319,000 that year, came from Austria-Hungary.

That mere recording of country or origin does not give accurate racial information is illustrated in the case of the many Greeks under Turkish rule, and the large number of Armenians found in almost all large Turkish towns. The Armenians are probably the most numerous of the immigrants from Asia. In 1914, the total immigration from Turkey was about 20,000, but the actual Turkish immigration was only 3,000. The remaining 27,000 were Greeks, Bulgarians, Serbians, Montenegrins, Syrians, Armenians and Hebrews.[30]

The "country of origin" tells us almost nothing about the large Hebrew immigration which comes to the United States. The Jew comes from many countries. The greater part of all our recent Jewish immigration comes from Russia, from what is called the "Jewish Pale of Settlement" in the western part of that country. Other Jews come from Austria, Roumania, Germany and Tur-

[30] *Reports of Department of Labor*, Washington, 1915.

key.   In 1914, the Jews were the fourth largest in numbers among our immigrants, nearly 143,000.[31]

We must also bear in mind that all of these millions
who came to America do not remain with us.   There is a
constant emigration going on, a departure of aliens back
to their native land either for a time, or for all time.   Up
to 1908, the Bureau of Immigration kept no record of the
"ebb of the tide" but since that time vessels taking aliens
out of the United States, are obliged by law to make a list
containing name, age, sex, nationality, residence in the
United States, occupation, and time of last arrival of each
alien passenger, which must be filed with the Federal
Collector of Customs.

The first year of this record, 1908, followed the financial panic of October, 1907, and due to the economic
conditions prevalent in the United States a very large
emigration to Europe was disclosed.

The records show also that the volume of emigration,
like that of immigration, varies from year to year.   Just
as prosperity here increases immigration, "bad" times increase emigration from our shores.

There was a time when emigration was so slight that it
was of little importance, but since the early nineties it
has assumed large proportions.   After the panic of 1907,
for months a larger number left the country than came
into it, and thousands and thousands swarmed the ports
of departure awaiting a chance to return home.   In the
earlier years, the immigrant sometimes spent months making the journey here.   Besides the difficulty of the trip,
ocean transportation was more expensive.   Therefore, the
earlier immigrants came to remain, to make homes here
for themselves and their children.   The Irish, the Ger-

[31] *Ibid.*

mans, the early Bohemians, the Scandinavians, and in fact all the early comers brought their families and their "household goods", ready to settle down for all time and to become citizens of their adopted country.

A large number of the alien arrivals of recent years come here initially with only a vague intention of remaining permanently, and these make up the large emigration streaming constantly from our ports. However, it is only fair to say that eventually many of these people come back to America and become permanent residents. Anyone who has had experience at our ports of entry can substantiate the statement that during a period of years the same faces are seen incoming again and again.

Although immigrants have come by millions into the United States, and have been the main contributing cause of its wonderful national expansion, yet opposition to their coming has manifested itself strongly at different times.

In the colonial period the people objected, and rightly, to the maternal solicitude which England evidenced by making the colonies the dumping ground for criminals and undesirables. However, these objections were disregarded and convicts and criminals continued to come while the colonies remained under British rule.

After the national era, immigration was practically unrestricted down to 1875. At different periods there were manifestations of a strong desire to restrict immigration, but Congress never responded with exclusion laws. The alien and sedition laws of 1798 had for their object the removal of foreigners already residents in the United States. The naturalization laws passed that same year, lengthening the time of residence necessary for citizenship to fourteen years, were another severe measure against

resident aliens. The native American and the Know-
nothing uprisings were still other indications of that same
spirit of antagonism to the alien based on religious
grounds. This religious antagonism in many of the States
took the form of opposition to immigration itself and a
demand for restrictions. But this all proved futile, for
the National Government recognized the necessity of
settling the limitless West. Then, too, another subject
loomed large and threatening at this time, and engrossed
the attention of the people away from the dire evils which
the Irish and the Catholics would precipitate upon "our
free and happy people". This was the State Rights and
Slavery question; and soon the country forgot immigration in the throes of the Civil War.

By an act of March 3, 1875, the National Government
made its first attempt to restrict immigration; this act
prohibited the bringing in of alien convicts and of women
for immoral purposes. On May 6, 1882, Congress passed
and the President approved another act "to regulate
immigration", by which the coming of Chinese laborers
was forbidden for ten years. The story which led up to
this Act of Congress is a long one, and the details cannot
be given here. Briefly, conditions in California following
the Burlingame treaty of 1868, owning to the influx of
Chinese labor, resulted in the organization of a workingman's party headed by Dennis Kearney, and forced the
Chinese question as one of the dominant issues of State
politics. Resolutions embodying the feelings of the people
on Chinese immigration were presented to the Constitutional Convention of 1879. The State Legislature enacted laws against this immigration. Subsequently pressure was brought to bear on the National Government, a
new treaty with China was negotiated, and finally the law

of 1882 was passed by Congress, restricting for ten years the admission of Chinese laborers, both skilled and unskilled, and of mine workers also.

Ever since the passage of this law, the Federal Government has pursued a more restrictive and exclusive immigration policy. The next law was passed in August, 1882, prohibiting the immigration of "any convict, lunatic, idiot, or any person unable to take care of himself or herself without becoming a public charge." Then, in 1885, came another act known as the "Alien Contract Labor Law", forbidding the importation and immigration of foreigners and aliens under contract or agreement to perform labor in the United States. In 1891 came the law called the "Geary Act" which amended "the various acts relative to immigration and the importation of aliens under contract or agreement to perform labor". This act extended Chinese exclusion for another ten years, and required the Chinese in the country to register and submit to the Bertillon test as a means of identification. In 1893 two acts were passed; one which gave the quarantine service greater powers and placed additional duties upon the Public Health Service, and another which properly enforced the existing immigration and contract labor laws. In 1902 the law of exclusion was made permanent against Chinese laborers. So, since 1875, the United States has passed laws excluding Chinese entirely and virtually excluding the Japanese, and both these races are ineligible to citizenship. In 1907, an act was passed "to regulate the immigration of Aliens into the United States", which excluded imbeciles, epileptics, those so defective either physically or mentally that they might become public charges; children under sixteen not with a parent, etc.

A far more restrictive measure known as the "literacy"

or "educational" test has been before Congress at different times and has, on three different occasions, falied to become a law. President Cleveland vetoed it in 1897, Taft in 1913, and Wilson in 1915. All three Presidents objected to this bill principally on the ground that it was such "a radical departure" from all previous national policy in regard to immigration. President Wilson's veto of 1917 was overcome and the bill became a law by a two-thirds majority vote of both houses. This law requires that entering aliens must be able to read the English language or some other language or dialect. The one thing which the literacy test was designed to accomplish — to decrease the volume of immigration — was brought about suddenly and unexpectedly by the European War. From the opening of the war, the number of immigrants steadily decreased until, for the year ending June 30, 1916, it was only 298,826[32] and for the year ending June 30, 1917, only 110,618.[33] Then it began again to increase steadily until for the year ending June 30, 1920, it reached a total of 430,001.[34]

On June 3, 1921, an emergency measure known as the three per cent. law was passed. This act provided that the number of aliens of any nationality who could be admitted to the United States in any one year should be limited to three per cent. of the number of foreign-born persons of such nationality resident in the United States as determined by the census of 1910. Certain ones were not counted, such as foreign government officials and their families and employees, aliens in transit through the United States, tourists, aliens from countries having immigration treaties with the United States, aliens who

[32] *Reports of Department of Labor,* Washington, 1918, p. 208.
[33] *Reports of Department of Labor,* Washington, 1920, p. 400.
[34] *Reports of Department of Labor,* Washington, 1921, p. 365.

have lived for one year previous to their admission in Canada, Newfoundland, Mexico, Central America, or South America, and aliens under eighteen who have parents who are American citizens. More than twenty per cent. of a country's full quota could not be admitted in one month except in the case of actors, artists, lecturers, singers, nurses, clergymen, professors, members of the learned professions or domestic servants who could always come in even though the month's or the year's quota had been used.

A well organized effort is under way in the Congress which began its session in December 1923, to reduce the quota to two per cent. of the immigrants recorded as coming to the United States in 1890. This bill, which will probably be passed, is being opposed vigorously, by the Jews and Italians who are immediately the particular racial groups to be affected, but since neither the Jews nor Italians, separately or collectively, have political strength to be a voting factor to be considered, except in a half dozen of the industrial states, the passage of the bill seems to be inevitable.

The recent immigration restriction laws make a decided break with past national history and tradition. There is little doubt that these laws are in part the fruit of an organized movement which, especially since the war, is attempting to classify all aliens, except those of one special group, as "hyphenates" and "mongrels". These laws are haphazard, unscientific, based on unworthy prejudice and likely, ultimately, to be disastrous in their economic consequences. The present three per cent. immigration law is not based on any fundamental standard of fitness. Once the percentage of maximum admissions is reached, in any given month, the next alien applying for entrance may be a potential Washington, Lincoln or Edison to whom the unyielding process of the law must deny admission. Such laws, worked out under the hysteria of "after war psychology", seem to be one of the instances, so frequent in history, where Democracy must take time to work out its own mistakes.

Under the circumstances, there is all the more reason that the priceless heritage of racial achievement by the descendants of various racial groups in the United States be told.

The United States has departed a long way from the policy which was recorded in 1795 by the series of coins known as the "Liberty and Security" coins, on which appeared the words "A Refuge for the Oppressed of all Nations".

ARRIVALS OF ALIEN PASSENGERS AND IMMIGRANTS IN THE UNITED STATES FROM 1820 TO 1892

Prepared by the Bureau of Statistics and published in 1893 by the Government Printing Office.

Countries Whence Arrived	1821 to 1830	1831 to 1840	1841 to 1850	1851 to Dec. 31, 1860	Jan. 1 1861 to June 30, 1870	Fiscal Years 1871 to 1880	Fiscal Years 1881 to 1890	Fiscal Years 1891 and 1892	Total
Austria-Hungary		22			7,800	72,969	353,719	151,178	585,665
Belgium	27	1,063	5,074	4,738	6,734	7,221	20,177	7,340	51,333
Denmark	169	539	539	3,749	17,094	31,771	88,132	21,252	163,769
France	8,497	45,575	77,262	76,358	35,984	72,206	50,464	13,291	379,637
Germany	6,761	152,454	434,626	951,667	787,468	718,182	1,452,970	244,312	4,748,440
Italy	408	2,253	1,870	9,231	11,728	55,759	307,309	138,191	526,749
Netherlands	1,078	1,412	8,251	10,789	9,102	16,541	53,701	12,466	113,340
Norway and Sweden	91	1,201	13,903	20,931	109,298	211,245	568,362	107,157	1,032,188
Russia and Poland	91	646	656	1,621	4,536	52,254	265,088	192,615	517,507
Spain and Portugal	2,622	2,954	2,759	10,353	8,493	9,893	6,535	5,657	49,266
Switzerland	3,226	4,821	4,644	25,011	23,286	28,293	81,988	14,219	185,488
United Kingdom									
England (a)	22,167	73,143	263,332	385,643	568,128	460,479	657,488	104,575	2,534,955
Scotland	2,912	2,667	3,712	38,331	38,768	87,564	149,869	24,077	347,900
Ireland	50,724	207,381	780,719	914,119	435,778	436,871	655,482	111,173	3,592,247
Total United Kingdom	75,803	283,191	1,047,763	1,338,093	1,042,674	984,914	1,462,839	239,825	6,475,102
All other countries of Europe	43	96	155	116	210	656	10,318	4,954	16,548
Total Europe	98,816	495,688	1,597,502	2,452,657	2,064,407	2,261,904	4,721,602	b1,152,457	14,845,033
British North American Possessions	2,277	13,624	41,723	59,309	153,871	383,269	392,802	(c)	1,046,875
Mexico	4,817	6,599	3,271	3,078	2,191	5,362	1,913	(c)	27,231
Central America	105	44	368	449	96	210	462	576	2,310
South America	531	856	3,579	1,224	1,396	928	2,304	1,344	12,162
West Indies	3,834	12,301	13,528	10,660	9,043	13,957	29,042	5,673	98,038
Total America	11,564	33,424	62,469	74,720	166,597	403,726	426,523	7,593	1,186,616

Alien Passengers from October 1, 1820, to December 31, 1867, and Immigrants from January 1, 1868, to June 30, 1892.

(a) Includes Wales and Great Britain not specified. According to William J. Bromwell's *History of Emigration to the United States*, published in 1856 by Redfield of New York, 1,000,000 of this number were from Ireland, which is probably accurate. During and after the Irish famine large numbers of Irish who could not find money for the passage to the United States did find it possible to go to England to work in coal mines, factories, and in seasonal agricultural employment; the money secured from which enabled them to embark for the United States from various English ports, which explains Bromwell's estimate.

(b) Includes 777 from Azores and 5 from Greenland.

(c) Immigrants from British North American Possessions and Mexico are not included since July 1, 1885.

Author's Note: Official statistics of immigration to the United States began in 1819, so that statements as to the number of aliens arriving prior to that time are largely guesswork.

The "panic" of 1893 had the effect to turn the alien tide the other way—back to Europe. Official statistics as to aliens returning from the United States were not required by law until 1908.

The quarter of a century which has passed since the character of alien arrivals to the United States beginning in the forties, changed so markedly in the decade of 1880 to 1890, is not long enough for accurate analysis of the economic, political and social influence on the United States of the coming of these newer races, so that the statistical records here given do not extend beyond 1892.

THE GIFT OF BLACK FOLK

PRESCRIPT

Who made America? Who made this land that swings its empire from the Atlantic to the Sea of Peace and from Snow to Fire — this realm of New Freedom, with Opportunity and Ideal unlimited?

Now that its foundations are laid, deep but bare, there are those as always who would forget the humble builders, toiling wan mornings and blazing noons, and picture America as the last reasoned blossom of mighty ancestors; of those great and glorious world builders and rulers who know and see and do all things forever and ever, amen! How singular and blind! For the glory of the world is the possibilities of the commonplace and America is America even because it shows, as never before, the power of the common, ordinary, unlovely man. This is real democracy and not that vain and eternal striving to regard the world as the abiding place of exceptional genius with great black wastes of hereditary idiots.

We who know may not forget but must forever spread the splendid sordid truth that out of the most lowly and persecuted of men, Man made America. And that what Man has here begun with all its want and imperfection, with all its magnificent promise and grotesque failure will some day blossom in the souls of the Lowly.

CHAPTER I

THE BLACK EXPLORERS

How the Negro helped in the discovery of America and gave his ancient customs to the land.

Garcia de Montalvo published in 1510 a Spanish romance which said: "Know ye that on the right hand of the Indies there is an island called California very near the Terrestrial Paradise which is peopled with black women without any men among them, because they were accustomed to live after the fashion of the Amazons. They were of strong and hardy bodies, of ardent courage and of great force."[1]

The legend that the Negro race had touched America even before the day of Columbus rests upon a certain basis of fact: First, the Negro countenance, clear and unmistakable, occurs repeatedly in Indian carvings, among the relics of

---

[1] From a Spanish Romance called *La Sergas de Espladian,* by Garcia de Montalvo, published in 1510; translated in Beasley's *The Negro Trail Blazers of California,* p. 18.

the Mound Builders and in Mexican temples.[2]
Secondly, there are evidences of Negro customs
among the Indians in their religious worship; in
their methods of building defenses such as the
mounds probably were; and particularly in customs of trade.   Columbus said that he had been
told of a land southwest of the Cape Verde
Islands where the black folk had been trading and
had used in their trade the well known African
alloy of gold called guanin.[3]

"There can be no question whatever as to the
reality of the statement in regard to the presence
in America of the African pombeiros[4] previous to
Columbus because the guani is a Mandingo
word and the very alloy is of African origin.   In
1501 a law was passed forbidding persons to sell
guanin to the Indians of Hispaniola."[5]

Wiener thinks "The presence of Negroes with
their trading masters in America before Columbus
is proved by the representation of Negroes in

[2] Cf. Wiener, *Africa and the Discovery of America,* Vol. 1, pp. 169-
70, 172, 174-5; Vol. 3, p. 322; Thurston, *Antiquities of Tennessee,* etc.,
1890, p. 105; De Charnay, *Ancient Cities of the New World* (trans. by
Gonino and Conant, 1887), pp. 132ff.; Kabell, *America för Columbus,*
1892, p. 235.

[3] J. B. Thacher, *Christopher Columbus,* 1903, Vol. 2, pp. 379-80;
*Raccolta di documenti e studi publicati dalla R. Commissione Colombiana
pel quorto centenario dalla scoperta dell' America,* parte I, Rome, 1892,
Vol. 1, p. 96.

[4] i. e., Negro Traders.

[5] Thacher, Vol. 2, pp. 379, 380; Wiener, Vol. 2, pp. 116-17.

American sculpture and design, by the occurrence
of a black nation at Darien early in the 16th century, but more specifically by Columbus' emphatic
reference to Negro traders from Guinea, who
trafficked in a gold alloy, guanin, of precisely the
same composition and bearing the same name, as
frequently referred to by early writers in Africa."[6]

And thirdly, many of the productions of America
which have hitherto been considered as indigenous
and brought into use especially by the Indians, may
easily have been African in origin, as for instance,
tobacco, cotton, sweet potatoes and peanuts. It
is quite possible that many if not all of these came
through the African Negro, being in some cases
indigenous to Negro Africa and in other cases
transmitted from the Arabs by the Negroes. Tobacco particularly was known in Africa and is mentioned in early America continually in connection
with the Negroes. All of these things were spread
in America along the same routes starting with
the mingling of Negroes and Indians in the West
Indies and coming up through Florida and on to
Canada. The Arawak Indians, who especially
show the effects of contact with Negroes, and
fugitive Negroes, together with Negroid Caribs,
migrated northward and it was they who led

[6] Wiener, Vol. 3, p. 365.

Ponce de Leon to search for the Fountain Bimini where old men became young.[7]

Oviedo says that the sweet potato "came with that evil lot of Negroes and it has taken very well and it is profitable and good sustenance for the Negroes of whom there is a greater number than is necessary on account of their rebellions."[8] In the same way maize and sugar cane may have been imported from Africa.

Further than this the raising of bread roots, manioc, yam and sweet potatoes may have come to America from Guinea by way of Brazil. From Brazil the culture of these crops spread and many of the words referring to them are of undoubted African origin.

Negroes probably reached the eastern part of South America from the West Indies while others from the same source went north along the roads marked by the Mound Builders as far as Canada.

"The chief cultural influence of the Negro in America was exerted by a Negro colony in Mexico, most likely from Teotihuacan and Tuxtla, who may have been instrumental in establishing the city of Mexico. From here their influence pervaded

[7] *Memoir of Hernando de Essalante Fontanedo, respecting Florida,* translated from the Spanish by Buckingham Smith, Washington, 1854.
[8] Oviedo y Valdes, *Historia general,* etc., Vol. 1, p. 286.

the neighboring tribes and ultimately, directly or indirectly, reached Peru."[9]

The mounds of the "Mound Builders" were probably replicas of Negro forts in Africa. "That this tendency to build forts and stockades proceeded from the Antilles, whence the Arawaks had come in the beginning of the sixteenth century, is proved by the presence of similar works in Cuba. These are found in the most abandoned and least-explored part of the island and there can be little doubt that they were locations of fugitive Negro and Indian stockades, precisely such as were in use in Africa. It is not possible to prove the direct participation of the Negroes in the fortifications of the North American Indians, but as the civilizing influence on the Indians to a great extent proceeded from Cuba over Florida towards the Huron Country in the north, the solution of the question of the Mound Builders is to be looked for in the perpetuation of Arawak or Carib methods, acquired from the Negroes, as well attested by Ovando's complaint in 1503 that the Negroes spoiled the manners of the Indians; and transferred to the white traders, who not only adopted the methods of the Indians, but frequently lived among the Indians as part of them, especially in

[9] Wiener, Vol. 3, p. 365.

Brazil where we have ample documentary evidence of the fact."[10]

All this is prehistoric and in part conjectural and yet it seems reasonable to suppose that much in custom, trade and religion which has been regarded as characteristic of the American Indian arose from strong Negro influences of the pre-Columbian period.

After the discovery of America by Columbus many Negroes came with the early explorers. Many of these early black men were civilized Christians and sprung from the large numbers of Negroes imported into Spain and Portugal during the fifteenth century, where they replaced as laborers the expelled Moors. Afterward came the mass of slaves brought by the direct African slave trade.

From the beginning of the fifteenth century mention of the Negro in America becomes frequent. In 1501 they were permitted to enter the colonies; in 1503 the Governor of Hispaniola sought to prohibit their transportation to America because they fled to the Indians and taught them bad manners. By 1506 they were coming again because the work of one Negro was worth more than that of four Indians. In 1518 the new sugar culture in Spain and the Canary Islands began

[10] Wiener, Vol. I, p. 190.

to be transferred to the West Indies and Negroes were required as laborers. In 1521 Negroes were not to be used on errands because they incited Indians to rebellion and the following year they rose in rebellion on Diego Columbus' mill. In 1540, in Quivera, Mexico, there was a Negro priest and in 1542 there were at Guamango, Mexico, three Brotherhoods of the True Cross of Spaniards, one of which was of Negroes and one of Indians.

Thus the Negro is seen not only entering as a laborer but becoming a part of the civilization of the New World. Helps says: "Very early in the history of the American Continent there are circumstances to show that Negroes were gradually entering into that part of the New World. They constantly appear at remarkable points in the narrative. When the Marquis Pizarro had been slain by the conspirators, his body was dragged to the Cathedral by two Negroes. The murdered Factor, Illan Suarez, was buried by Negroes and Indians. After the battle of Anaquito, the head of the unfortunate Viceroy, Blasco Nunez Vela, was cut off by a Negro. On the outbreak of the great earthquake at Guatemala, the most remarkable figure in that night's terrors was a gigantic Negro, who was seen in many parts of the city, and who assisted no one, however much he was

implored.   In the narrative of the return of Las
Casas to his diocese, it has been seen that he was
attended by a Negro.   And many other instances
might be adduced, showing that, in the decade
from 1535 to 1545, Negroes had come to form
part of the household of the wealthier colonists.
At the same time, in the West Indian Islands
which had borne the first shock of the conquest,
and where the Indians had been more swiftly destroyed, the Negroes were beginning to form the
bulk of the population; and the licenses for importation were steadily increasing in number."[11]

Continually they appear with the explorers.
Nuflo de Olana, a Negro, was with Balboa when
he discovered the Pacific Ocean,[12] and afterward
thirty Negroes helped Balboa direct the work of
over 500 Indians in transporting the material for
his ships across the mountains to the South Sea.[13]

Cortes carried Negroes and Indians with him
from Cuba to Mexico and one of these Negroes
was the first to sow and reap grain in Mexico.
There were two Negroes with Velas in 1520 and
200 black slaves with Alvarado on his desperate
expedition to Quito.   Almagro and Valdivia in
1525 were saved from death by Negroes.[14]

[11] Helps, *Spanish Conquest in America,* Vol. 4, p. 401.
[12] J. F. Rippy in *Journal of Negro History,* Vol. 6, p. 183.
[13] Helps, Vol. 1, p. 421.
[14] Rippy, *loc. cit.*

As early as 1528 there were about 10,000 Negroes in the New World. We hear of one sent as an agent of the Spanish to burn a native village in Honduras. In 1539 they accompanied De Soto and one of them stayed among the Indians in Alabama and became the first settler from the old world. In 1555 in Santiago de Chile a free Negro owns land in the town. Menendez had a company of trained Negro artisans and agriculturalists when he founded St. Augustine in 1565 and in 1570 Negroes founded the town of Santiago del Principe.

In most of these cases probably leadership and initiative on the part of the early Negro pioneers in America was only spasmodic or a matter of accident. But this was not always true and there is one well-known case which, despite the propaganda of 400 years, survives as a clear and important instance of Negro leadership in exploration. This is the romantic story of Stephen Dorantes or as he is usually called, Estevanico, who sailed from Spain in 1527 with the expedition of Panfilo de Narvaez.[15] This fleet of five

[15] The following narrative is based on: H. O. Flipper, *Did a Negro discover Arizona and New Mexico* (contains a translation of parts of the narrative of Pedro de Castaneda de Majera) ; Pedro de Castaneda, "Account of the Expedition to Cibola which took place in the year 1540. . . . . ." translated in *Spanish Explorers in the Southern United States* (J. F. Jameson Ed.) ; Beasley, *Trail Blazers of California,* Chapter 2; Rippy, in *Journal of Negro History,* Vol. 6, pp. 183ff.; *American Anthropologist,* Vol. 4.

vessels and 600 colonists and soldiers started from Cuba and landed in Tampa Bay in 1582. But disaster followed disaster until at last there were but four survivors of whom one was Estevanico "an Arab Negro from Azamor on the Atlantic coast of Morocco"; he is elsewhere described as "black" and a "person of intelligence." Besides him there was his master Dorantes and two other Spaniards, de Vaca and Maldonado.[16] For six years these men maintained themselves by practicing medicine among the Indians, and were the first to reach Mexico from Florida by the overland route.

Estevanico and de Vaca went forward to meet the outposts of the Spaniards established in Mexico. Estevanico returned with an escort and brought on the other two men. The four then went west to the present Mexican cities, Chihuahua and Sonora and reached Culiacan, the capital of the state of Sinaloa, in April, 1536.

Coronado was governor of Sinaloa and on hearing the story of the wanderers, he immediately hastened with them to the viceroy, Mendoza, in the city of Mexico. They told the viceroy not only of their own adventures but what they had heard of the rich lands toward the North and of

[16] A fifth survivor, a Spaniard, stayed with the Indians and was afterward found by DeSoto.

the cities with houses four and five stories high
which were really the Pueblos of New Mexican
Indians. Mendoza was eager to explore these
lands. He had already heard something about
them and he and Cortes had planned to make the
exploration together but could not agree upon
terms. Cortes therefore hurried to fit out a small
fleet in 1537. He took 400 Spaniards and 300
Negroes, sailed up the Gulf of California and
called the country "California". He then returned
to Spain for the last time.

Meantime, de Vaca and Maldonado after several unsuccessful attempts also went to Spain
leaving Dorantes and Estevanico. Dorantes refused to take part in the proposed expedition to the
North but sold his slave Estevanico to Mendoza.
Certain Franciscan Monks joined the expedition
and Fray Marcos de Niza became the leader,
having already had some experience in exploration
in Peru. Estevanico, because of his knowledge of
the Indian language and especially of the sign language, was the guide, and the party started North
for what the viceroy dreamed were the Seven
Cities of Cibola. They left March 7th, 1539,
and arrived at Vacapa in central Sinaloa on the 21st.
Fray Marcos, probably from timidity, sent Estevanico on ahead with an escort of Indians whom

he could send back as messengers.[17]   The Negro
marked his journey by large wooden crosses and in
this way with Estevanico far ahead they traveled
for two weeks until suddenly Fray Marcos was
met by a fleeing band of badly frightened Indians
who told him that Estevanico had reached Cibola
and had been killed.   Fray Marcos named the
country "El Nueva Reyno de San Francisco" but
being himself scared, distributed among the Indians everything which his party had in their
packs, except the vestments for saying Mass, and
traveling by double marches, returned to Mexico.

Meantime let us follow the adventure of Estevanico: Knowing how much depended upon
appearance in that unknown and savage land,
Estevanico traveled in magnificence, decorated
with bells and feathers and carrying a symbolic
gourd which was recognized among the Indian
tribes thereabouts as a symbol of authority. When
he reached the Pueblos, the Indian chiefs were in a
quandary.   First of all they recognized in Estevanico's retinue, numbers of their ancient Indian
enemies.   Secondly, they were frightened because
Estevanico informed them "that two white men
were coming behind him who had been sent by a
great Lord and knew about the things in the sky

[17] Another story is that Estevanico and the Monks did not get on
well together.

and that they were coming to instruct them in divine matters." They had good reason to fear that this meant the onslaught of some powerful enemy. And, moreover, they were puzzled because this black man came as a representative of white men: "The Lord of Cibola, inquiring of him whether he had other brethren, he answered that he had an infinite number and that they had a great store of weapons with them and that they were not very far thence. When they heard this, many of the chief men consulted together and resolved to kill him that he might not give news unto these brethren where they dwelt[18] and that for this cause they slew him and cut him into many pieces, which were divided among all the chief Lords that they might know assuredly that he was dead. . . ."

This climax is still told in a legend current among the Zuni Indians today: "It is to be believed that a long time ago, when roofs lay over the walls of Kya-ki-me, when smoke hung over the housetops, and the ladder rounds were still unbroken in Kya-ki-me, then the black Mexicans came from their abodes in Everlasting Summerland. One day, unexpectedly, out of Hemlock Canon they came, and descended to Kya-ki-me.

[18] The story that Estevanico was killed because of his greed is evidently apocryphal.

But when they said they would enter the covered way, it seems that our ancients looked not gently at them; for with these black Mexicans came many Indians of So-no-li, as they call it now, . . . who were enemies of our ancients. Therefore, these our ancients, being always bad-tempered, and quick to anger, made fools of themselves after their fashion, rushing into their town and out of their town, shouting, skipping and shooting with their sling-stones and arrows and tossing their war-clubs. Then the Indians of So-no-li set up a great howl, and thus they and our ancients did much ill to one another. Then and thus was killed by our ancients, right where the stone stands down by the arroyo of Kya-ki-me, one of the black Mexicans, a large man with chilli lips [i. e., lips swollen from eating chilli peppers] and some of the Indians they killed, catching others. Then the rest ran away, chased by our grandfathers, and went back toward their country in the Land of Everlasting Summer. . . .[19]

The village reached by Estevanico was Hawi-kih as it was called by the Indians and Grenada as the Spaniards named it. It is fifteen miles southwest of the present village of Zuni and is thus within New Mexico and east of the boundary

[19] Legends of the Zuni Pueblos of New Mexico quoted in Lowery *Spanish Settlements in the United States,* 1513-1561, pp. 281-82.

between New Mexico and Arizona. Thus Estevanico was the first European to discover Arizona
and New Mexico. Fray Marcos returned with
Coronado and came as far as the village in 1540
while Mendoza sent others to pursue explorations
that same year within the present confines of
Arizona and they brought back various stories of
the death of Estevanico.

After that for 40 years explorations rested
until 1582 when again the Spaniards entered the
territory. With all the Spanish explorers in
Florida, Texas, Arizona, New Mexico and Kansas, there were Negro slaves and helpers but none
with the initiative, perseverance and success of
Estevanico.

In the after pioneering that took place in later
days in the great western wilderness, the Negro
was often present. There was a black man with
Lewis and Clark in 1804; Jacob Dodson, a free
Negro of Washington, volunteered to accompany
Fremont in his California expedition of 1843.
He was among the 25 persons selected by Fremont
to accompany him in the discovery of Clamath
Lake and also in his ride from Los Angeles to
Monterey. Among the early settlers of Cali-
fornia coming up from Mexico were many Ne-
groes and mulattoes.[20]

[20] Cf. Beasley, Chapter 10.

William Alexander Leidsdroff was the most distinguished Negro pioneer of California and at one time lived in the largest house in San Francisco. He owned the first steamship sailing in San Francisco Bay, and was a prominent business man, a member of the City Council and treasurer and member of the school committee. H. H. Bancroft says: "William Alexander Leidsdroff, a native of Danish West Indies, son of a Dane by a mulattress, who came to the United States as a boy and became a master of vessels sailing between New York and New Orleans, came to California as manager of the 'Julia Ann,' on which he made later trips to the Islands, down to 1845." His correspondence from 1845, when he became United States Vice-Consul is a valuable source of historical information. Many Negroes came in the rush of the "forty-niners" as pioneers and miners as well as slaves.

The Negro's work as a pioneer extends down until our day. The late Commodore Peary who discovered the North Pole said: "Matthew A. Henson, my Negro assistant, has been with me in one capacity or another since my second trip to Nicaragua in 1887. I have taken him on each and all of my expeditions, except the first, and also without exception on each of my farthest sledge trips. This position I have given him primarily because of his adaptability and fitness for the work, and secondly on account of his loyalty. He is a better dog driver and can handle a sledge better than any man living, except some of the best Esquimo hunters themselves." This leaves Henson today as the only living human being who has stood at the North Pole.

CHAPTER II

BLACK LABOR

How the Negro gave his brawn and brain to fell the forests, till the soil and make America a rich and prosperous land.

The primary reason for the presence of the black man in America was, of course, his labor and much has been written of the influence of slavery as established by the Portuguese, Spanish, Dutch and English. Most writers have written of slavery as a moral and economic evil or of the worker, white and black, as a victim of this system. In this chapter, however, let us think of the slave as a laborer, as one who furnished the original great labor force of the new world and differed from modern labor only in the wages received, the political and civil rights enjoyed, and the cultural surroundings from which he was taken.

Negro labor has played a peculiar and important part in the history of the modern world. The black man was the pioneer in the hard physical work which began the reduction of the Ameri-

can wilderness and which not only hastened the
economic development of America directly but
indirectly released for other employment, thousands of white men and thus enabled America to
grow economically and spiritually at a rate pre-
viously unparalleled anywhere in history. It was
black labor that established the modern world
commerce which began first as a commerce in the
bodies of the slaves themselves and was the primary cause of the prosperity of the first great
commercial cities of our day. Then black labor
was thrown into the production of four great
crops — tobacco, sugar, rice and cotton. These
crops were not new but their production on a
large cheap scale was new and had a special significance because they catered to the demands of
the masses of men and thus made possible an
interchange of goods such as the luxury trade of
the Middle Ages catering to the rich could not
build. Black labor, therefore, beneath these crops
became an important part of the Industrial Revolution of the eighteenth and nineteenth centuries.

Moreover the black slave brought into common labor certain new spiritual values not yet
fully realized. As a tropical product with a sensuous receptivity to the beauty of the world he
was not as easily reduced to be the mechanical
draft-horse which the northern European laborer

became. He was not easily brought to recognize any ethical sanctions in work as such but tended to work as the results pleased him and refused to work or sought to refuse when he did not find the spiritual returns adequate; thus he was easily accused of laziness and driven as a slave when in truth he brought to modern manual labor a renewed valuation of life.

The Negro worked as farm hand and peasant proprietor, as laborer, artisan and inventor and as servant in the house, and without him, America as we know it, would have been impossible.

The numerical growth of the Negro population in America indicates his economic importance. The exact number of slaves exported to America will never be known. Probably 25,000 Negroes a year arrived in America between 1698 and 1707. After 1713 this rose to 30,000 and by 1775 to over 40,000 a year. The American Revolution stopped the trade, but it was revived afterward and reached enormous proportions. One estimate is that a million Negroes came in the sixteenth century, three million in the seventeenth, seven million in the eighteenth and four million in the nineteenth or fifteen million in all. Certainly at least ten million came and this meant sixty million killed and stolen in Africa because of the methods of capture and the horror of the middle passage. This, with the Asiatic trade, cost black Africa a hundred million souls.[1] Bancroft places the total slave population of the continental colonies at 59,000 in 1714, 78,000 in 1727, and 293,000 in 1754.

In the West Indies the whole laboring population early became Negro or Negro with an infiltration of Indian and white blood. In the United States at the beginning of our independent national existence, Negroes formed a fifth of the population of the whole nation. The exact figures are :[2]

PERCENTAGE NEGRO IN THE POPULATION

	United States	South
1920	9.9	2.61
1910	10.7	29.8
1900	11.6	32.3
1890	11.9	33.8
1880	13.1	36.0
1870	12.7	36.0
1860	14.1	36.8
1850	15.7	37.3
1840	16.8	38.0
1830	18.1	37.9

[1] Cf. Du Bois, *Suppression of the Slave Trade;* Du Bois, *The Negro* (Home University Library).
[2] United States Census, *Negro Population 1790-1915;* Fourteenth Census, Vol. 3.

	United States	South
1820	18.4	37.2
1810	19.0	36.7
1800	18.9	35.0
1790	19.3	35.2

If we consider the number of Negroes for each 1,000 whites, we have:

	United States	South
1920	110	369
1910	120	426
1900	132	480
1890	136	512
1880	152	564
1870	145	562
1860	165	582
1850	186	595
1840	203	613
1830	221	610
1820	225	592
1810	235	579
1800	233	539
1790	239	543

The proportion of Negroes in the North was small, falling from 3.4% in 1790 to 1.8% in 1910. Nevertheless even here the indirect in-

fluence of the Negro worker was large. The
trading colonies, New England and New York,
built up a lucrative commerce based largely on
the results of his toil in the South and in the
West Indies, and this commerce supported local
agriculture and manufacture. I have said in my
Suppression of the Slave Trade: "Vessels from
Massachusetts, Rhode Island, Connecticut, and,
to a less extent from New Hampshire, were early
and largely engaged in the carrying slave-trade.
'We know,' said Thomas Pemberton in 1795,
'that a large trade to Guinea was carried on for
many years by the citizens of Massachusetts
Colony, who were the proprietors of the vessels
and their cargoes, out and home. Some of the
slaves purchased in Guinea, and I suppose the
greatest part of them, were sold in the West
Indies.' Dr. John Eliot asserted that 'it made
a considerable branch of our commerce. . . .
It declined very little until the Revolution.' Yet
the trade of this colony was said not to equal
that of Rhode Island. Newport was the mart
for slaves offered for sale in the North, and a
point of reshipment for all slaves. It was principally this trade that raised Newport to her
commercial importance in the eighteenth century.
Connecticut, too, was an important slave-trader,

sending large numbers of horses and other com-
modities to the West Indies in exchange for slaves,
and selling the slaves in other colonies.

"This trade formed a perfect circle. Owners
of slavers carried slaves to South Carolina, and
brought home naval stores for their ship-build-
ing; or to the West Indies and brought home
molasses; or to other colonies, and brought home
hogsheads. The molasses was made into the
highly prized New England rum, and shipped in
these hogsheads to Africa for more slaves. Thus
the rum-distilling industry indicated to some extent the activity of New England in the slave-
trade. In May, 1752, one Captain Freeman
found so many slavers fitting out that, in spite
of the large importations of molasses, he could
get no rum for his vessel. In Newport alone
twenty-two stills were at one time running continuously; and Massachusetts annually distilled
15,000 hogsheads of molasses into this 'chief
manufacture.' "[3]

In New York and New Jersey Negroes formed
between 7 and 8 % of the total population in 1790,
which meant that they were probably 25 % of the
labor force of those colonies, especially on the
farms.

The growth of the great slave crops shows the

[3] Du Bois, *Suppression of the Slave Trade,* Chapter 4.

increasing economic value of Negro labor. In 1619, 20,000 pounds of tobacco went from Virginia to England. Just before the Revolutionary War, 100 million pounds a year were being sent, and at the beginning of the twentieth century, 800 millions were raised in the United States alone. Sugar was a luxury for the rich and physicians until the eighteenth century, when it began to pour out of the West Indies. By the middle of the nineteenth century a million tons of cane sugar were raised each year and this had increased to nearly 3 millions in 1900. The cotton crop rose correspondingly. England, the chief customer at first, consumed 13,000 bales in 1781, 572,000 in 1820, 871,000 in 1830 and 3,366,000 in 1860. The United States raised 6 million bales in 1880, and at the beginning of the twentieth century raised 11 million bales annually.

This tremendous increase in crops which formed a large part of modern commerce was due primarily to black labor. At first most of this labor was brute toil of the lowest sort. Our estimate of the value of this work and what it has done for America depends largely upon our estimate of the value of such toil. It must be confessed that, measured in wages and in public esteem, such work stands low in America and in the civilized world. On the other hand the fact that it does stand so low constitutes one of the greatest problems of social advance. Hard manual labor, and much of it of a disagreeable sort, must for a long time lie at the basis of civilized life. We are continually transmitting some of it to machines, but the residuum remains large. In an ideal society it would be highly-paid work because of its unpleasantness and necessity; and even to-day, no matter what we may say of the individual worker or of the laboring class, we know that the foundation of America is built on the backs of the manual laborer.

This was particularly true in the earlier centuries. The problem of America in the fifteenth and sixteenth centuries was the problem of manual labor. It was settled by importing white bond servants from Europe, and black servants from Africa, and compelling the American Indians to work. Indian slavery failed to play any great part because the comparatively small number of Indians in the West Indies were rapidly killed off by the unaccustomed toil or mingled their blood and pooled their destinies with the Negroes. On the continent, on the other hand, the Indians were too powerful, both in numbers and organization, to be successfully enslaved. The white bond servants and the Negroes therefore became the main laboring force of the new world and with their toil the economic development of the continent began.

There arose a series of special laws to determine the status of laborers which became the basis of the great slave codes. As the free European white artisans poured in, these labor codes gradually came to distinguish between slavery based on race and free labor. The slave codes greatly weakened the family ties and largely destroyed the family as a center of government or of economic organization. They made the plantation the center of economic life and left more or less religious autonomy. They provided punishment by physical torture, death or sale, but they always left some minimum of incentive by which the slave could have the beginnings of private possession.

In this way the economic organization was provided by which the middle classes of the world were supplied with a cheap sweetening material derived from sugar cane; a cheap luxury, tobacco; larger quantities of rice; and finally, and above all, a cheap and universal material for clothing, cotton. These were things that all men wanted who had anything to offer in labor or materials for the satisfaction of their wants. The cost of raising them was a labor cost almost entirely because land in America was at that time endless in fertility and extent. The old world trade there-

fore which sought luxuries in clothing, precious
metal and stones, spices, etc., for the rich, transformed itself to a world-wide trade in necessities
incomparably richer and bigger than its medieval
predecessor because of its enormous basis of demand. Its first appearance was in the slave trade
where the demand for the new American crops
showed itself in a demand for the labor necessary
to raise them; thus the slave trade itself was at
the bottom of the rise of great commerce, and
the beginning of modern international commerce.
This trade stimulated invention and was stimulated by it. The wellbeing of European workers
increased and their minds were stimulated. Economic and political revolution followed, to which
America fell heir. New immigrants poured in.
New conceptions of religion, government and
work arose and at the bottom of it all and one of
its efficient causes was the toil of the increasing
millions of black slaves.

As the nation developed this slave labor became confined more and more to the raising of
cotton, although sugar continued to be the chief
crop in the West Indies and Louisiana, and rice
on the southeast coast and tobacco in Virginia.
This world importance of cotton brought an economic crisis: Rich land in America, adapted to
slave methods of culture, was becoming limited,

and must either be increased or slavery would die an economic death. On the other hand, beside the plantation hands, there had grown up a large class of Negro servants and laborers who were distributed both north and south. These laborers in particular came into competition with the white laborer and especially the new immigrants. This and other economic causes led to riots in Philadelphia, New York and Cincinnati and a growing conviction on the part of a newly enfranchised white workingmen that one great obstacle in America was slave labor, together with the necessarily low status of the freedmen. These economic reasons overthrew slavery.[4]

After the legal disappearance of slavery its natural results remained in the mass of freedmen who had been trained in the necessary ignorance and inefficiency of slave labor. On such a foundation it was easy to build and emphasize race prejudice. On the other hand, however, there was still plenty of work for even the ignorant and careless working man, so that the Negro continued to raise cotton and the other great crops and to do throughout the country the work of the unskilled laborer and the servant. He continued to be the main laboring force of the South in industrial lines and began to invade the North.

[4] Cf. Du Bois, *The Philadelphia Negro,* Chapter 4.

His full power as a labor reservoir was not seen until the transformation of the World War. In a few short months 500,000 black laborers came North to fill the void made by the stoppage of immigration and the rush of white working men into the munitions industry. This was simply a foretaste of what will continue to happen. The Negro still is the mightiest single group of labor force in the United States. As this labor grows more intelligent, self-conscious and efficient, it will turn to higher and higher grades of work and it will reinforce the workingman's point of view.[5]

It must not be assumed, however, that the labor of the Negro has been simply the muscle-straining unintelligent work of the lowest grade. On the contrary he has appeared both as personal servant, skilled laborer and inventor. That the Negroes of colonial times were not all ignorant savages is shown by the advertisements concerning them. Continually runaway slaves are described as speaking very good English; sometimes as speaking not only English but Dutch and French. Some could read and write and play musical instruments. Others were blacksmiths, limeburners, bricklayers and cobblers. Others

[5] Cf. Woodson, *A Century of Negro Migration;* E. J. Scott: *Negro Migration During the War.*

were noted as having considerable sums of money.[6] In the early days in the South the whole conduct of the house was in the hands of the Negro house servant; as butler, cook, nurse, valet and maid, the Negro conducted family life.

Thus by social contact and mingling of blood the Negro house servant became closely identified with the civilization of the South and contributed to it in many ways. For a long time before emancipation the house servant had been pushing steadily upward; in many cases he had learned to read and write despite the law. Sometimes he had entered the skilled trades and was enabled by hiring his time to earn money of his own and in rare cases to buy his own freedom. Sometimes he was freed and sent North and given money and land; but even when he was in the South and in the family and an ambitious menial, he influenced the language and the imagination of his masters; the children were nursed at the breast of black women, and in daily intercourse the master was thrown in the company of Negroes more often than in the company of white people.

From this servile work there went a natural development. The private cook became the public cook in boarding houses, and restaurant keeper. The butler became the caterer; the "Black Mam-

[6] *Journal of Negro History,* Vol. I, p. 163.

my" became the nurse, and the work of all these in their various lines was of great influence. The cooks and caterers led and developed the art of good-eating throughout the South and particularly in cities like New Orleans and Charleston; and in northern cities like Philadelphia and New York their methods of cooking chicken and terrapin, their invention of ice cream and their general good taste set a standard which has seldom been surpassed in the world. Moreover, it gave economic independence to numbers of Negroes. It enabled them to educate their children and it furnished to the abolition movement a class of educated colored people with some money who were able to help. After emancipation these descendants of the house servant became the leading class of American Negroes. Notwithstanding the social stigma connected with menial service and still lingering there, partially because slaves and freedmen were so closely connected with it, it is without doubt one of the most important of the Negro's gifts to America.

During the existence of slavery all credit for inventions was denied the Negro slave as a slave could not take out a patent. Nevertheless Negroes did most of the mechanical work in the South before the Civil War and more than one suggestion came from them for improving machinery. We are told that in Virginia: "The county records of the seventeenth century reveal the presence of many Negro mechanics in the colony during that period, this being especially the case with carpenters and coopers.[7]

As example of slave mechanics it is stated that among the slaves of the first Robert Beverly was a carpenter valued at £30, and that Ralph Wormeley, of Middlesex county, owned a cooper and a carpenter each valued at £35. Colonel William Byrd mentions the use of Negroes in iron mining in 1732. In New Jersey slaves were employed as miners, ironworkers, sawmill hands, house and ship carpenters, wheelwrights, coopers, tanners, shoemakers, millers and bakers, among other employments, before the Revolutionary War. As early as 1708 there were enough slave mechanics in Pennsylvania to make the freemen feel their competition severely. In Massachusetts and other states we hear of an occasional artisan.[8]

During the early part of the nineteenth century the Negro artisans increased. The Spanish Governor Salcedo, early in the nineteenth century, in trying to keep the province of Louisiana loyal to Spain, made the militia officers swear allegiance and among them were two companies of colored

---

[7] Bruce, *Economic History of Virginia,* Vol. 2, pp. 405-6.
[8] Atlanta University Publications: Cf. *The Negro Artisan,* 1902-1912, and *Economic Cooperation among Negro Americans,* 1907.

men from New Orleans "who composed all the mechanics which the city possessed."[9]

Later, black refugees from San Domingo saved Louisiana from economic ruin. Formerly, Louisiana had had prosperous sugar-makers; but these industries had been dead for nearly twenty-five years when the attempt to market sugar was revived. Two Spaniards erected near New Orleans, a distillery and a battery of sugar kettles and began to manufacture rum and syrup. They had little success until Etienne de Boré, a colored San Dominican, appeared. "Face to face with ruin because of the failure of the indigo crop, he staked his all on the granulation of sugar. He enlisted the services of these successful San Dominicans and went to work. In all American history there can be fewer scenes more dramatic than the one described by careful historians of Louisiana, the day when the final test was made and the electrical word was passed around, 'It granulates!' "

De Boré sold $12,000 worth of sugar that year. Agriculture in the Delta began to flourish and seven years later New Orleans was selling 2,000,-000 gallons of rum, 250,000 gallons of molasses and 5,000,000 pounds of sugar. It was the beginning of the commercial reign of one of the

[9] Alice Dunbar Nelson in *Journal of Negro History*, Vol. 2, p. 52.

great commercial cities of America and it started
with the black refugees from San Domingo.[10]

In the District of Columbia many "were superior mechanics." Olmsted, in his journeys
through the slave states just before the Civil War,
found slave artisans in all the states. In Virginia
they worked in tobacco factories, ran steamboats,
made barrels, etc. On a South Carolina plantation he was told by the master that the Negro
mechanic "exercised as much skill and ingenuity
as the ordinary mechanics that he was used to
employ in New England." In Charleston and
some other places they were employed in cotton
factories. In Alabama he saw a black carpenter
—careful and accurate calculator and excellent
workman; he was bought for $2,000. In Louisi-
ana he was told that master mechanics often
bought up slave mechanics and acted as contrac-
tors. In Kentucky the slaves worked in factories
for hemp-bagging, and in iron work on the Cum-
berland river, and also in tobacco factories. In
the newspapers advertisements for runaway mechanics were often seen, as, for instance a black-
smith in Texas, "very smart"; a mason in Virginia, etc. In Mobile an advertisement read

[10] Alice Dunbar Nelson, in the *Journal of Negro History*, Vol. **1**,
p. 375.

"good blacksmiths and horseshoers for sale on reasonable terms."[11]

Such men naturally showed inventive genius, here and there. There is a strong claim that the real credit for the invention of the cotton gin is due to a Negro on the plantation where Eli Whitney worked. Negroes early invented devices for handling sails, corn harvesters, and an evaporating pan for refining sugar. In the United States patent office there is a record of 1500 inventions made by Negroes and this is only a part of those that should be credited to Negroes as the race of the inventor is not usually recorded.

In 1846 Norbert Rillieux, a colored man of Louisiana, invented and patented a Vacuum pan which revolutionized the method of refining sugar. He was a machinist and engineer of fine reputation, and devised a system of sewerage for New Orleans which the city refused to accept because of his color.

Sydney W. Winslow, president of the United Shoe Machinery Company, laid the foundation of his great organization by the purchase of an invention by a native of Dutch Guiana named Jan E. Matzeliger. Matzeliger was the son of a Negro woman and her husband, a Dutch engineer. He

[11] Olmsted, *A Journey in the Seaboard Slave States, Journey through Texas*, and *Journey in the Back Country*.

came to America as a young man and worked as a cobbler in Philadelphia and Lynn. He died in 1889 before he had realized the value of his invention.

Matzeliger invented a machine for lasting shoes. It held the shoe on the last, gripped and pulled the leather down around the sole and heel, guided and drove the nails into place and released a completed shoe from the machine. This patent was bought by Mr. Winslow and on it was built the great United Shoe Machinery Company, which now has a capital stock of more than twenty million dollars, and employs over 5,000 operatives in factories covering 20 acres of ground. This business enterprise is one of the largest in our country's industrial development. Since the formation of this company in 1890, the product of American shoe factories has increased from $200,000,000 to $552,631,000, and the exportation of American shoes from $1,000,000 to $11,000,000. This development is due to the superiority of the shoes produced by machines founded on the original Matzeliger type.[12] The cost of shoes has been cut in half, the quality greatly improved, the wages of workers increased,

[12] Prior to the Matzeliger machine the McKay machine was patented, designed for making the heaviest and cheapest kind of men's shoes. The Matzeliger machine was designed for light work, women's shoes, etc., and was the most important invention necessary to the formation of the United Shoe Machinery Company.

the hours of labor diminished, and all these factors have made "the Americans the best shod
people in the world."

After Matzeliger's death his Negro blood was
naturally often denied, but in the shoe-making districts the Matzeliger type of machine is still referred to as the "Nigger machine"; or the
"Niggerhead" machine; and "A certified copy of
the death certificate of Matzeliger, which was
furnished the writer by William J. Connery,
Mayor of Lynn, on October 23rd, 1912, states
that Matzeliger was a mulatto."[13]

Elijah McCoy is the pioneer inventor of automatic lubricators for machinery. He completed
and patented his first lubricating cup in 1872 and
since then has made some fifty different inventions
relating principally to the automatic lubrication
of machinery. He is regarded as the pioneer in
the art of steadily supplying oil to machinery in
intermittent drops from a cup so as to avoid the
necessity for stopping the machine to oil it. His
lubricating cup was in use for years on stationary
and locomotive machinery in the West including
the great railway locomotives, the boiler engines
of the steamers on the Great Lakes, on trans-
atlantic steamships, and in many of our leading
factories. "McCoy's lubricating cups were fam-

[13] H. E. Baker, in *Journal of Negro History*, Vol. 2, pp. 21ff.

ous thirty years ago as a necessary equipment in all up-to-date machinery, and it would be rather interesting to know how many of the thousands of machinists who used them daily had any idea then that they were the invention of a colored man."[14]

Another great Negro inventor was Granville T. Woods who patented more than fifty devices relating to electricity. Many of his patents were assigned to the General Electric Company of New York, the Westinghouse Company of Pennsylvania, the American Bell Telephone Company of Boston and the American Engineering Company of New York. His work and that of his brother Liates Wood has been favorably mentioned in technical and scientific journals.

J. H. Dickinson and his son S. L. Dickinson of New Jersey have been granted more than 12 patents for devices connected with player pianos. W. B. Purvis of Philadelphia was an early inventor of machinery for making paper bags. Many of his patents were sold to the Union Paper Bag Company of New York.

Today the Negro is an economic factor in the United States to a degree realized by few. His occupations were thus grouped in 1920:[15]

[14] Baker: *The Colored Inventor*, p. 7.
[15] U. S. Census of 1920. Wilcox-Du Bois, *Negroes in the United States* (U. S. Census bulletin No. 8, 1904).

The men were employed as follows:

in agriculture 1,566,627
in extraction of minerals 72,892
in manufacturing and mechanical industries 781,827
in transportation 308,896
in trade 129,309
in public service 49,586
in professional service 41,056
in domestic and personal service 273,959
in clerical occupations 28,710

The women were employed as follows:

in agriculture 612,261
in manufacturing and mechanical industries 104,983
in trade 11,158
in professional service 39,127
in domestic and personal service 790,631
in clerical occupations 8,301

A list of occupations in which at least 10,000
Negroes were engaged in 1920 is impressive:

MALES

Farmers 845,299
Farm laborers 664,567
Garden laborers 15,246
Lumber men 25,400
Coal miners 54,432
Masons 10,606
Carpenters 34,217
Firemen (not locomotive) 23,152
Laborers 127,860
Laborers in chemical industries 17,201
Laborers in cigar and tobacco factories 12,951
Laborers in clay, glass and stone industries 18,130

Laborers in food industries 24,638
Laborers in iron and steel industries 104,518
Laborers in lumber and furniture industries 103,154
Laborers in cotton mills 10,182
Laborers in other industries 80,583
Machinists 10,286
Semi-skilled operatives in food industries 11,160
Semi-skilled operatives in iron and steel industries 22,916
Semi-skilled operatives in other industries 14,745
Longshoremen 27,206
Chauffeurs 38,460
Draymen 56,556
Street laborers 35,673
Railway laborers 99,967
Delivery men 24,352
Laborers in coal yards, warehouses, etc. 27,197
Laborers, etc., in stores 39,446
Retail dealers 20,390
Laborers in public service 29,591
Soldiers, sailors 12,511
Clergymen 19,343
Barbers, etc. 18,692
Janitors 38,662
Porters not in stores 59,197
Servants 80,209
Waiters 31,681
Clerks except in stores 14,014
Messengers 12,587

FEMALES

Farmers 79,893
Farm laborers 527,937
Dressmakers and seamstresses 26,961
Semi-skilled operatives in cigar and tobacco
    factories 13,446

Teachers	29,244
Hairdressers and manicurists	12,660
Housekeepers and stewards	13,250
Laundresses not in laundries	283,557
Laundry operatives	21,084
Midwives and nurses (not trained)	13,888
Servants	401,381
Waiters	14,155

This has been the gift of labor, one of the greatest that the Negro has made to American nationality. It was in part involuntary, but whether given willingly or not, it was given and America profited by the gift. This labor was always of the highest economic and even spiritual importance. During the World War for instance, the most important single thing that America could do for the Allies was to furnish them with materials. The actual fighting of American troops, while important, was not nearly as important as American food and munitions; but this material must not only be supplied, it must be transported, handled and delivered in America and in France; and it was here that the Negro stevedore troops behind the battle line — men who received no medals and little mention and were in fact despised as all manual workers have always been despised,— it was these men that made the victory of the Allies certain by their desperately difficult but splendid work. The first colored stevedores went over in June, 1917, and were followed by about 50,000 volunteers. To these were added later nearly 200,000 drafted men.

To all this we must add the peculiar spiritual contribution which the Negro made to Labor. Always physical fact has its spiritual complement, but in this case the gift is apt to be forgotten or slurred over. This gift is the thing that is usually known as "laziness". Again and again men speak of the laziness of Negro labor and some suppose that slavery of Negroes was necessary on that account; and that even in freedom Negroes must be "driven". On the other hand and in contradiction to this is the fact that Negroes do work and work efficiently. In South Africa and in Nigeria, in the Sudan and in Brazil, in the West Indies and all over the United States Negro labor has accomplished tremendous tasks. One of its latest and greatest tasks has been the building of the Panama Canal. These two sets of facts, therefore, would seem to be mutually contradictory, and many a northern manager has seen the contradiction when, facing the apparent laziness of Negro hands, he has attempted to drive them and found out that he could not and at the same time has afterward seen someone used to Negro

labor get a tremendous amount of work out of
the same gangs. The explanation of all this iş
clear and simple: The Negro laborer has not
been trained in modern organized industry but
rather in quite a different school.

The European workman works long hours and
every day in the week because it is only in this
way that he can support himself and family. With
the present organization of industry and methods
of distributing the results of industry any failure
of the European workingman to toil hard and
steadily would mean either starvation or social
disgrace through the lowering of his standard of
living. The Negro workingman on the other
hand came out of an organization of industry
which was communistic and did not call for unlimited toil on the part of the workers. There
was work and hard work to do, for even in the
fertile tropical lands the task of fighting weeds,
floods, animals, insects and germs was no easy
thing. But on the other hand the distribution of
products was much simpler and fairer and the
wants of the people were less developed. The
black tropical worker therefore looked upon work
as a necessary evil and maintained his right to
balance the relative allurements of leisure and
satisfaction at any particular day, hour or season.
Moreover in the simple work-organization of

tropical or semi-tropical life individual desires of this sort did not usually disarrange the whole economic process or machine.[16]

The white laborer therefore brought to America the habit of regular, continuous toil which he regarded as a great moral duty. The black laborer brought the idea of toil as a necessary evil ministering to the pleasure of life. While the gift of the white laborer made America rich, or at least made many Americans rich, it will take the psychology of the black man to make it happy. New and better organization of industry and a clearer conception of the value of effort and a wider knowledge of the process of production must come in, so as to increase the wage of the worker and decrease rent, interest, and profit; and then the black laborer's subconscious contribution to current economics will be recognized as of tremendous and increasing importance.

[16] Olivier, *White Capital and Coloured Labor*, Chapter 8, London, 1906.

CHAPTER III

BLACK SOLDIERS

How the Negro fought in every American war for a cause that was not his and to gain for others a freedom which was not his own.

1. COLONIAL WARS

The day is past when historians glory in war. Rather, with all thoughtful men, they deplore the barbarism of mankind which has made war so large a part of human history. As long, however, as there are powerful men who are determined to have their way by brute force, and as long as these men can compel or persuade enough of their group, nation or race to support them even to the limit of destruction, rape, theft and murder, just so long these men will and must be opposed by force — moral force if possible, physical force in the extreme. The world has undoubtedly come to the place where it defends reluctantly such defensive war, but has no words of excuse for offensive war, for the initiation of the program of physical force.

There is, however, one further consideration:

the man in the ranks has usually little chance to decide whether the war is defensive or offensive, righteous or wrong. He is called upon to put life and limb in jeopardy. He responds, sometimes willingly with uplifted soul and high resolve, persuaded that he is under Divine command; sometimes by compulsion and by the iron of discipline. In all cases he has by every nation been given credit; and certainly the man who voluntarily lays down his life for a cause which he has been led to believe is righteous deserves public esteem, although the world may weep at his ignorance and blindness.

From the beginning America was involved in war because it was born in a day of war. First, there were wars, mostly of aggression but partly of self-defense, against the Indians. Then there was a series of wars which were but colonial echoes of European brawls. Next the United States fought to make itself independent of the economic suzerainty of England. After that came the conquest of Mexico and the war for the Union which resolved itself in a war against slavery, and finally the Spanish War and the great World War.

In all these wars the Negro has taken part. He cannot be blamed for them so far as they were unrighteous wars (and some of them were un-

righteous), because he was not a leader: he was
for the most part a common soldier in the ranks
and did what he was told. Yet in the majority of
cases he was not compelled to fight. He used his
own judgment and he fought because he believed
that by fighting for America he would gain the
respect of the land and personal and spiritual
freedom. His problem as a soldier was always
peculiar: no matter for what America fought and
no matter for what her enemies fought, the
American Negro always fought for his own freedom and for the self-respect of his race. Whatever the cause of war, therefore, his cause was
peculiarly just. He appears, therefore, in American wars always with double motive,—the desire
to oppose the so-called enemy of his country along
with his fellow white citizens, and before that, the
motive of deserving well of those citizens and
securing justice for his folk. In this way he
appears in the earliest times fighting with the
whites against the Indians as well as with the
Indians against the whites, and throughout the
history of the West Indies and Central America
as well as the Southern United States we find here
and there groups of Negroes fighting with the
whites. For instance: in Louisiana early in the
eighteenth century when Governor Perier took
office, the colony was very much afraid of a com-

bination between the Choctaw Indians and the fierce Banbara Negroes who had begun to make common cause with them. To offset this, Perier armed a band of slaves in 1729 and sent them against the Indians. He says: "The Negroes executed their mission with as much promptitude as secrecy." Later, in 1730, the Governor sent twenty white men and six Negroes to carry ammunition to the Illinois settlement up the Mississippi River. Perier says fifteen Negroes "in whose hands we had put weapons performed prodigies of valor. If the blacks did not cost so much and if their labor was not so necessary to the colony it would be better to turn them into soldiers and to dismiss those we have who are so bad and so cowardly that they seem to have been manufactured purposely for this colony." But this policy of using the Negroes against the Indians led the Indians to retaliate and seek alliance with the blacks and in August 1730, the Natchez Indians and the Chickshaws conspired with the Negroes to revolt. The head of the revolt, Samba, with eight of his confederates was executed before the conspiracy came to a head. In 1733, when Governor Bienville returned to power, he had an army consisting of 544 white men and 45 Negroes, the latter with free black officers.[1]

[1] Alice Dunbar Nelson, *Journal of Negro History,* Vol. 1, pp. 369, 370, 371.

In the colonial wars which distracted America
during the seventeenth and early part of the eighteenth centuries the Negro took comparatively
small part because the institution of slavery was
becoming more settled and the masters were
afraid to let their slaves fight. Notwithstanding
this, there were black freedmen who voted and
were enrolled in the militia and went to war, while
some masters sent their slaves as laborers and
servants. As early as 1652 a law of Massachusetts as to the militia required "Negro, Scotchmen and Indians" to enroll in the militia. Afterward the policy was changed and Negroes and
Indians were excluded but Negroes often acted as
sentinels at meeting-house doors. At other times
slaves ran away and enlisted as soldiers or as
sailors, thus often gaining their liberty. The
New York *Gazette* in 1760 advertises for a slave
who is suspected of having enlisted "in the provincial service." In 1763 the Boston *Evening
Post* was looking for a Negro who "was a soldier
last summer." One mulatto in 1746 is advertised
for in the Pennsylvania *Gazette*. He had threatened to go to the French and Indians and fight
for them. And in the Maryland *Gazette,* 1755,
gentlemen are warned that their slaves may run
away to the French and Indians.[2]

[2] Cf. Livermore, *Opinion of the Founders of the Republic,* etc., part 2 ;
Journal of Negro History, Vol. 1, p. 198ff.

2. THE REVOLUTIONARY WAR

The estimates of the Negro soldiers who fought on the American side of the Revolutionary War vary from four to six thousand, or one out of every 50 or 60 of the colonial troops.

On August 24, 1778, the following report was made of Negroes in the Revolutionary Army:[3]

Brigades	Present	Sick Absent	On Command	Total
North Carolina .	42	10	6	58
Woodford	36	3	1	40
Muhlenburg	64	26	8	98
Smallwood	20	3	1	24
2nd Maryland ..	43	15	2	60
Wayne	2	..	..	2
2nd Pennsylvania .	33	1	1	35
Clinton	33	2	4	62
Parsons	117	12	19	148
Huntington	56	2	4	62
Nixon	26	..	1	27
Paterson	64	13	12	89
Late Learned ...	34	4	8	46
Poor	16	7	4	27
Total	586	98	71	755

Alex. Scammell, *Adj. Gen.*

[3] G. H. Moore, *Historical Notes*, etc., N. Y., 1862.

This report does not include Negro soldiers enlisted in Rhode Island, Connecticut, New York, New Hampshire and other States not mentioned nor does it include those who were in the army at both earlier and later dates. Other records prove that Negroes served in as many as 18 brigades.

It was a Negro who in a sense began the actual fighting. In 1750 William Brown of Framingham, Mass., advertised three times for "A Molatto Fellow about 27 Years of Age, named *Crispas,* 6 Feet 2 Inches high, short Curl'd Hair." This runaway slave was the same Crispus Attucks who in 1779 led a mob on the 5th of March against the British soldiers in the celebrated "Boston Massacre."

Much has been said about the importance and lack of importance of this so-called "Boston Massacre." Whatever the verdict of history may be, there is no doubt that the incident loomed large in the eyes of the colonists. Distinguished men were orators on the 5th of March for years after, until that date was succeeded by the 4th of July. Daniel Webster in his great Bunker Hill oration said: "From that moment we may date the severance of the British Empire."

Possibly these men exaggerated the actual importance of a street brawl between citizens and soldiers, led by a runaway slave; but there is no doubt that the colonists, who fought for independence from England, thought this occasion of tremendous importance and were nerved to great effort because of it.

Livermore says: "The presence of the British soldiers in King Street excited the patriotic indignation of the people. The whole community was stirred, and sage counsellors were deliberating and writing and talking about the public grievances. But it was not for the 'wise and prudent' to be first to act against the encroachments of arbitrary power. 'A motley rabble of saucy boys, Negroes and mulattoes, Irish Teagues and outlandish Jack tars,' (as John Adams described them in his plea in defense of the soldiers) could not restrain their emotion or stop to enquire if what they *must do* was according to the letter of the law. Led by Crispus Attucks, the mulatto slave, and shouting, 'The way to get rid of these soldiers is to attack the main guard; strike at the root; this is the nest'; with more valor than discretion they rushed to King Street and were fired upon by Captain Preston's company. Crispus Attucks was the first to fall; he and Samuel Gray and Jonas Caldwell were killed on the spot. Samuel Maverick and Patrick Carr were mortally wounded. The excitement which followed was intense. The bells of the town were rung.

An impromptu town meeting was held and an immense assembly gathered. Three days after, on the 8th, a public funeral of the Martyrs took place. The shops in Boston were closed and all the bells of Boston and the neighboring towns were rung. It is said that a greater number of persons assembled on this occasion than ever before gathered on this continent for a similar purpose. The body of Crispus Attucks, the mulatto, had been placed in Faneuil Hall with that of Caldwell, both being strangers in the city. Maverick was buried from his mother's house in Union Street, and Gray from his brother's in Royal Exchange Lane. The four hearses formed a junction in King Street and then the procession marched in columns six deep, with a long file of coaches belonging to the most distinguished citizens, to the Middle Burying Ground, where the four victims were deposited in one grave over which a stone was placed with the inscription:

'Long as in Freedom's cause the wise contend,
Dear to your country shall your fame extend;
While to the world the lettered stone shall tell
Where Caldwell, Attucks, Gray and Maverick fell.'

"The anniversary of this event was publicly commemorated in Boston by an oration and other exercises every year until our National Independence was achieved, when the Fourth of July was substituted for the Fifth of March as the more proper day for a general celebration. Not only was the event commemorated but the martyrs who then gave up their lives were remembered and honored."[4]

The relation of the Negro to the Revolutionary War was peculiar. If his services were used by the Colonists this would be an excuse for the English to use the Indians and to emancipate the slaves. If he were not used not only was this source of strength to the small loyal armies neglected but there still remained the danger that the English would bid for the services of Negroes. At first then the free Negro went quite naturally into the army as he had for the most part been recognized as liable to military service. Then Congress hesitated and ordered that no Negroes be enlisted. Immediately there appeared the determination of the Negroes, whether deliberately arrived at or by the more or less unconscious development of thought under the circumstances, to give their services to the side which promised them freedom and decent treatment. When therefore Governor Dunmore of Virginia and English generals like Cornwallis and Clinton made a bid for the services of Negroes, coupled with prom-

[4] Livermore, pp. 115-16.

ises of freedom, they got considerable numbers and in the case of Dunmore one Negro unit fought a pitched battle against the Colonists.

The Continental Congress took up the question of Negroes in the Army in September, 1775. A committee consisting of Lynch, Lee and Adams reported a letter which they had drafted to Washington. Rutledge of South Carolina moved that Washington be instructed to discharge all Negroes whether slave or free from the army, but this was defeated. October 8th Washington and other generals in council of war, agreed unanimously that slaves should be rejected and a large majority declared that they refuse free Negroes. October 18th, the question came up again before the committee consisting of Benjamin Franklin, General Washington, certain deputies, governors and others. This council agreed that Negroes should be rejected and Washington issued orders to this effect November 12th, 1775. Meantime, however, Dunmore's proclamation came and his later success in raising a black regiment which greatly disturbed Washington. In July, 1776, the British had 200 Negro soldiers on Long Island and later two regiments of Negroes were raised by the British in North Carolina. The South lost thousands of Negroes through the British. In Georgia a corps of fugitives calling themselves the "King of England Soldiers" kept attacking on both sides of the Savannah River even after the Revolution and many feared a general insurrection of slaves.

The colonists soon began to change their attitude. Late in 1775, Washington reversed his decision and ordered his recruiting officers to accept free Negroes who had already served in the army and laid the matter before the Continental Congress. The Committee recommended that these Negroes be reenlisted but no others. Various leaders advised that it would be better to enlist the slaves, among them Samuel Hopkins, Alexander Hamilton, General Greene, James Madison. Even John Laurens of South Carolina tried to make the South accept the proposition.[5]

Thus Negroes again were received into the American army and from that time on they played important rôles. They had already distinguished themselves in individual cases at Bunker Hill. For instance, fourteen white officers sent the following statement to the Massachusetts Legislature on December 5, 1775: "The subscribers beg leave to report to your Honorable House (which we do in justice to the character of so brave a man) that under our own observation we declare

[5] Cf. Livermore and Moore as above; also *Journal of Negro History,* Vol. 1, pp. 114-20.

that a Negro man named Salem Poor, of Colonel Frye's regiment, Captain Ames' company, in the late battle at Charlestown, behaved like an experienced officer as well as an excellent soldier. To set forth particulars of his conduct would be tedious. We only beg leave to say, in the person of this said Negro, centers a brave and gallant soldier. The reward due to so great and distinguished a character we submit to the Congress."[6]

They afterward fought desperately in Long Island and at the battle of Monmouth. Foreign travellers continually note the presence of Negroes in the American army.

Less known however is the help which the black republic of Haiti offered to the struggling Colonists. In December 1778 Savannah was captured by the British, and Americans were in despair until the French fleet appeared on the coast of Georgia in September 1779. The fleet offered to help recapture Savannah. It had on board 1900 French troops of whom 800 were black Haitian volunteers. Among these volunteers were Christophe, afterward king of Haiti, Rigaud, André, Lambert and others. They were a significant and faithful band which began by helping freedom in America, then turned and through the French rev-

[6] Livermore, p. 122. See also the account of Peter Salem, *do.*, pp. 118-21.

olution freed Haiti and finally helped in the emancipation of South America. The French troops
landed below the city with the Americans at their
right and together they made an attack. American and French flags were planted on the British
outposts but their bearers were killed and a general retreat was finally ordered. Seven hundred
and sixty Frenchmen and 312 Americans were
killed and wounded. As the army began to retreat
the British general attacked the rear, determined
to annihilate the Americans. It was then that the
black and mulatto freedmen from Haiti under the
command of Viscount de Fontages made the charge
on the English and saved the retreating Americans.
They returned to Haiti to prepare eventually to
make that country the second one in America
which threw off the domination of Europe.[7]

Some idea of the number of Negro soldiers can
be had by reference to documents mentioning the
action of the States. Rhode Island raised a regiment of slaves, and Governor Cooke said that it
was generally thought that at least 300 would
enlist. Four companies were finally formed there
at a cost of over £10,000. Most of the 629 slaves
in New Hampshire enlisted and many of the
15,000 slaves in New York. Connecticut had
Negroes in her regiments and also a regiment of

[7] T. G. Steward, in *Publications American Negro Academy*, No. 5,
p. 12.

colored soldiers. Maryland sought in 1781 to raise 750 Negro troops. Massachusetts had colored troops in her various units from 72 towns in that State. "In view of these numerous facts it is safe to conclude that there were at least 4,000 Negro soldiers scattered throughout the Continental Army."[8]

In a debate in Congress in 1820 two men, one from the North and one from the South, gave the verdict of that time on the value of the Negro in the Revolutionary War. William Eustis of Massachusetts said: "The war over and peace restored, these men returned to their respective States, and who could have said to them on their return to civil life after having shed their blood in common with the whites in the defense of the liberties of the country, 'You are not to participate in the rights secured by the struggle or in the liberty for which you have been fighting?' Certainly no white man in Massachusetts."

Charles Pinckney of South Carolina said: that the Negroes, "then were, as they still are, as valuable a part of our population to the Union as any other equal number of inhabitants. They were in numerous instances the pioneers and, in all, the laborers of your armies. To their hands were

---

[8] W. B. Hartgrove, *Journal of Negro History*, Vol. 1, pp. 125-9.

owing the erection of the greatest part of the
fortifications raised for the protection of our
country; some of which, particularly Fort
Moultrie, gave at that early period of the inexperience and untried valor of our citizens, im-
mortality to American arms: and, in the Northern
States numerous bodies of them were enrolled
into and fought by the sides of the whites, the
battles of the Revolution."[9]

In 1779 in the war between Spain and Great
Britain, the Spanish Governor of Louisiana,
Galvez, had in his army which he led against the
British, numbers of blacks and mulattoes who he
said "behaved on all occasions with as much valor
and generosity as the whites."[10]

3. THE WAR OF 1812

In the War of 1812 the Negro appeared not
only as soldier but particularly as sailor and in
the dispute concerning the impressment of American sailors which was one of the causes of the
war, Negro sailors repeatedly figured as seized
by England and claimed as American citizens by
America for whose rights the nation was apparently ready to go to war. For instance, on the

[9] Wilson, *Black Phalanx,* p. 71.
[10] *Journal of Negro History,* Vol. 1, pp. 373-4; Gayarre's *History of Louisiana,* Vol. 3, p. 108.

Chesapeake were three Negro sailors whom the British claimed but whom the Americans declared were American citizens, — Ware, Martin and Strachen.   As Bryant says: "The citizenship of Negroes was sought and defended by England and America at this time but a little later it was denied by the United States Supreme Court that Negroes could be citizens."   On demand two of these Negroes were returned to America by the British government; the other one died in England.

Negroes fought under Perry and Macdonough. On the high seas Negroes were fighting. Nathaniel Shaler, captain of a privateer, wrote to his agent in New York in 1813:

"Before I could get our light sails on and almost before I could turn around, I was under the guns, not of a transport but of a large frigate! And not more than a quarter of a mile from her. . . . . Her first broadside killed two men and wounded six others. . . . . My officers conducted themselves in a way that would have done honor to a more permanent service. . . . . The name of one of my poor fellows who was killed ought to be registered in the book of fame, and remembered with reverence as long as bravery is considered a virtue. He was a black man by the name of John Johnson. . . . . . When America

has such tars, she has little to fear from the ty-
rants of the ocean."[11]

A few Negroes were in the northern armies. A
Congressman said in 1828: "I myself saw a battalion of them — as fine martial looking men as I
ever saw attached to the northern army in the last
war (1812) on its march from Plattsburg to
Sacketts Harbor where they did service for the
country with credit to New York and honor to
themselves."[12]

But it was in the South that they furnished the
most spectacular instance of participation in this
war. Governor Claiborne appealed to General
Jackson to use colored soldiers. "These men, Sir,
for the most part, sustain good characters. Many
of them have extensive connections and much
property to defend, and all seem attached to arms.
The mode of acting toward them at the present
crisis, is an inquiry of importance. If we give
them not our confidence, the enemy will be encouraged to intrigue and corrupt them."[13]

September 21, 1814, Jackson issued a spirited
appeal to the free Negroes of Louisiana:
"Through a mistaken policy, you have heretofore
been deprived of a participation in the glorious

[11] Niles' *Register,* Feb. 26, 1814.
[12] Wilson, *Black Phalanx,* p. 88.
[13] Alice Dunbar-Nelson in *Journal of Negro History,* Vol. 2, p. 58.

struggle for national rights in which our country is engaged. This no longer shall exist.

"As sons of freedom, you are now called upon to defend our most inestimable blessing. As Americans, your country looks with confidence to her adopted children for a valorous support as a faithful return for the advantages enjoyed under her mild and equitable government. As fathers, husbands and brothers, you are summoned to rally around the standard of the Eagle, to defend all which is dear in existence. . . . In the sincerity of a soldier and the language of truth I address you."[14]

He promised them the same bounty as whites and they were to have colored non-commissioned officers. There was some attempt to have Jackson tone down this appeal and say less of "equality," but he refused to change his first draft.

The news of this proclamation created great surprise in the North but not much criticism. Indeed, things were going too badly for the Americans. The Capitol at Washington had been burned, the State of Maine was in British hands, enlistment had stopped and Northern States like New York were already arming Negroes. The Louisiana legislature, a month after Jackson's proclamation, passed an act authorizing two regiments of

[14] Niles' Register, Vol. 7, p. 205.

"men of color" by voluntary enlistment. Slaves were allowed to enlist and were publicly manumitted for their services. There were 3200 white and 430 colored soldiers in the battle of New Orleans. The first battalion of 280 Negroes was commanded by a white planter, La Coste; a second battalion of 150 was raised by Captain J. B. Savary, a colored man, from the San Dominican refugees, and commanded by Major Daquin who was probably a quadroon.

Besides these soldiers slaves were used in throwing up the famous cotton bale ramparts, which saved the city, and this was the idea of a black slave from Africa, who had seen the same thing done at home. Colored men were used to reconnoitre, and the slave trader Lafitte brought a mixed band of white and black fighters to help. Curiously enough there were also Negroes on the other side, Great Britain having imported a regiment from the West Indies which was at the head of the attacking column moving against Jackson's right, together with an Irish regiment. Conceive this astounding anomaly!

The American Negro soldiers were stationed very near Jackson and his staff. Jackson himself in an address to the soldiers after the battle, complimenting the "embodied militia," said:

"To the Men of Color. — Soldiers! From the

shores of Mobile I collected you to arms, — I invited you to share in the perils and to divide the glory of your white countrymen. I expected much from you; for I was not uninformed of those qualities which must render you so formidable to an invading foe. I knew that you could endure hunger and thirst and all the hardships of war. I knew that you loved the land of your nativity and that, like ourselves, you had to defend all that is most dear to man. But you surpass my hopes. I have found in you, united to these qualities, that noble enthusiasm which impels to great deeds."[15]

In the celebration of the victory which followed in the great public square, the Place d'Armes, now Jackson Square, the colored troops shared the glory and the wounded prisoners were met by colored nurses.[16]

4. THE CIVIL WAR

There were a few Negroes in the Mexican War but they went mostly as body servants to white officers and there were probably no soldiers and certainly no distinct Negro organizations. The Negro, therefore, shares little of the blood guilt of that unhallowed raid for slave soil.

[15] Niles' Register, Vol. 7, pp. 345-6.
[16] Dunbar-Nelson in *Journal of Negro History*, Vol. 2, pp. 59-60.

At the time of the Civil War when the call came for volunteers free Negroes everywhere offered their services to the Northern States and everywhere their services were declined. Indeed, it was almost looked upon as insolence that they should offer to fight in this "white man's war." Not only was the war to be fought by white men but desperate effort was made to cling to the technical fact that this was a war to save the Union and not a war against slavery. Federal officials and northern army officers made effort to reassure the South that they were not abolitionists and that they were not going to touch slavery.[17]

Meantime there began to crystallize the demand that the real object of the war be made the abolition of slavery and that the slaves and colored men in general be allowed to fight for freedom.

This met bitter opposition. The New York *Herald* voiced this August 5, 1862. "The efforts of those who love the Negro more than the Union to induce the President to swerve from his established policy are unavailing. He will neither be persuaded by promises nor intimidated by threats. Today he was called upon by two United States Senators and rather peremptorily requested to accept the services of two Negro regiments. They were flatly and unequivocally rejected. The

[17] Williams, *Negro Race in America*, Vol. 2, pp. 244ff.

President did not appreciate the necessity of employing the Negroes to fight the battles of the country and take the positions which the white men of the nation, the voters, and sons of patriotic sires, should be proud to occupy; there were employments in which the Negroes of rebel masters might well be engaged, but he was not willing to place them upon an equality with our volunteers who had left home and family and lucrative occupations to defend the Union and the Constitution while there were volunteers or militia enough in the loyal States to maintain the Government without resort to this expedient. If the loyal people were not satisfied with the policy he had adopted, he was willing to leave the administration to other hands. One of the Senators was impudent enough to tell the President he wished to God he would resign."

In the spring of 1862 General Hunter was sent into South Carolina with less than 11,000 men and charged with the duty of holding the whole seacoast of Georgia, South Carolina and Florida. He asked for re-enforcement but was told frankly from Washington, "Not a man from the North can be spared." The only way to guard the position was to keep long lines of entrenchment thrown up against the enemy. General Hunter calmly announced his intention of forming a

Negro regiment to help him. They were to be paid as laborers by the quartermaster but he expected eventually to have them recognized as soldiers by the government. At first he could find no officers. They were shocked at being asked to command "niggers." Even non-commissioned officers were difficult to find. But eventually the regiment was formed and became an object of great curiosity when on parade. Reports of the first South Carolina infantry were sent to Washington but there was no reply. Then suddenly the matter came up in Congress and Hunter was ordered to explain whether he had enlisted fugitive slaves and upon what authority. Hunter immediately sent a sharp reply:

"To the first question, therefore, I reply: That no regiment of 'fugitive slaves' has been, or is being, organized in this department. There is, however, a fine regiment of loyal persons whose late masters are fugitive rebels — men who everywhere fly before the appearance of the National flag, leaving their loyal and unhappy servants behind them, to shift as best they can for themselves. So far, indeed, are the loyal persons composing the regiment from seeking to evade the presence of their late owners, that they are now one and all endeavoring with commendable zeal to acquire the drill and discipline requisite to place them in a position to go in full and effective pursuit of their fugacious and traitorous proprietors.

"The experiment of arming the blacks, so far as I have made it, has been a complete and even marvellous success. They are sober, docile, attentive and enthusiastic, displaying great natural capacities in acquiring the duties of the soldier. They are now eager beyond all things to take the field and be led into action; and it is the unanimous opinion of the officers who have had charge of them, that in the peculiarities of this climate and country, they will prove invaluable auxiliaries, fully equal to the similar regiments so long and so successfully used by the British authorities in the West India Islands.

"In conclusion, I would say, it is my hope — there appearing no possibility of other re-inforcements, owing to the exigencies of the campaign in the peninsula — to have organized by the end of next fall and to be able to present to the government from 48,000 to 50,000 of these hardy and devoted soldiers."[18]

The reply was read in Congress amid laughter despite the indignation of the Kentucky Congressman who instituted the inquiry.

Protests now came from the South but no answer was forthcoming and despite all the agita-

[18] Williams, *Negro Race in America,* Vol. 2, pp. 280-82.

tion the regiment remained until at last Hunter was officially ordered to raise 50,000 black laborers of whom 5,000 might be armed and dressed as soldiers.

Horace Greeley stated the case clearly August 20, 1862 in his "Prayer of Twenty Million":[19]

"On the face of this wide earth, Mr. President, there is not one disinterested, determined, intelligent champion of the Union cause who does not feel that all attempts to put down the rebellion and at the same time uphold its inciting cause are preposterous and futile — that the rebellion if crushed out tomorrow would be renewed within a year if slavery were left in full vigor — that army officers who remain to this day devoted to slavery can at best be but half-way loyal to the Union — and that every hour of deference to slavery is an hour of added and deepened peril to the Union. . . .

"I close as I began, with the statement that what an immense majority of the loyal millions of your countrymen require of you is a frank, declared, unqualified, ungrudging execution of the laws of the land, more especially of the Confiscation Act. That Act gives freedom to the slaves of rebels coming within our lines or whom those lines may at any time enclose, — we ask you to

[19] New York *Tribune*, Aug. 19, 1862.

render it due obedience by publicly requiring all your subordinates to recognize and obey it. The rebels are everywhere using the late anti-Negro riots in the North — as they have long used your officers' treatment of Negroes in the South — to convince the slaves that they have nothing to hope from a Union success — that we mean in that case to sell them into bitter bondage to defray the cost of the war. Let them impress this as a truth on the great mass of their ignorant and credulous bondsmen, and the Union will never be restored — never. We cannot conquer ten millions of people united in solid phalanx against us, powerfully aided by northern sympathizers and European allies. We must have scouts, guides, spies, cooks, teamsters, diggers and choppers from the blacks of the South — whether we allow them to fight for us or not — or we shall be baffled and repelled."

A month later, September 22, Abraham Lincoln issued the preliminary Emancipation Proclamation. He had considered this step before and his final decision was caused, first, by a growing realization of the immense task that lay before the Union armies and, secondly, by the fear that Europe was going to recognize the Confederacy, since she saw as between North and South little difference in attitude toward slavery.

The effect of the step was undoubtedly decisive
for ultimate victory, although at first it spread
dismay. Six of the Northern States went Democratic in the fall elections and elsewhere the Republicans lost heavily. In the army some officers
resigned and others threatened to because "The
war for the Union was changed into a war for
the Negro."

In the South men like Beauregard urged the
raising of the "Black Flag", while Jefferson Davis
in his third annual message wrote: "We may well
leave it to the instincts of that common humanity
which a beneficent Creator has implanted in the
breasts of our fellowmen of all countries to pass
judgment on a measure by which several millions
of human beings of an inferior race, peaceful and
contented laborers in their sphere, are doomed to
extermination."[20]

With emancipation foreshadowed the full recognition of the Negro soldier was inevitable. In
September 1862 came a black Infantry Regiment
From Louisiana and later a regiment of heavy
artillery and by the end of 1862 four Negro regiments had enlisted. Immediately after the signing of the Emancipation Proclamation came the
Kansas Colored volunteers and the famous 54th
Massachusetts Regiment. A Bureau was estab-

[20] Williams, Vol. 2, p. 271.

lished in Washington to handle the colored en-
listments and before the end of the war 178,975
Negroes had enlisted.

"In the Department [of War] the actual number of Negroes enlisted was never known, from
the fact that a practice prevailed of putting a live
Negro in a dead one's place. For instance, if a
company on picket or scouting lost ten men, the
officer would immediately put ten new men in their
places and have them answer to the dead men's
names. I learn from very reliable sources that
this was done in Virginia, also in Missouri and
Tennessee. If the exact number of men could be
ascertained, instead of 180,000 it would doubtless
be in the neighborhood of 220,000 who entered
the ranks of the army."[21]

General orders covering the enlistment of Negro troops were sent out from the War Department October 13, 1863. The Union League in
New York city raised 2,000 black soldiers in 45
days, although no bounty was offered them and
no protection promised their families. The regiment had a triumphal march through the city and
a daily paper stated: "In the month of July last
the homes of these people were burned and pillaged by an infuriated political mob; they and
their families were hunted down and murdered

[21] Wilson, p. 123.

in the public streets of this city; and the force and majesty of the law were powerless to protect them. Seven brief months have passed and a thousand of these despised and persecuted men marched through the city in the garb of the United States soldiers, in vindication of their own manhood and with the approval of a countless multitude — in effect saving from inevitable and distasteful conscription the same number of those who hunted their persons and destroyed their homes during those days of humiliation and disgrace. This is noble vengeance — a vengeance taught by Him who commanded, 'Love them that hate you; do good to them that persecute you.' "

The enlistment of Negroes caused difficulty and friction among the white troops. In South Carolina General Gilmore had to forbid the white troops using Negro troops for menial service in cleaning up the camps. Black soldiers in uniform often had their uniforms stripped off by white soldiers.

"I attempted to pass Jackson Square in New Orleans one day in my uniform when I was met by two white soldiers of the 24th Conn. They halted me and then ordered me to undress. I refused, when they seized me and began to tear my coat off. I resisted, but to no good purpose; a half dozen others came up and began to assist.

I recognized a sergeant in the crowd, an old ship-
mate on board of a New Bedford, Mass., whaler;
he came to my rescue, my clothing was restored
and I was let go. It was nothing strange to see a
black soldier *à la* Adam come into the barracks
out of the streets."[22]   This conduct led to the
killing of a portion of a boat's crew of the U. S.
Gunboat Jackson, at Ship Island, Miss., by members of a Negro regiment stationed there.

Then, too, there was contemptible discrimination in pay. While white soldiers received $13
a month and clothing, Negro soldiers, by act of
Congress, were given $10 a month with $3 de-
ducted for clothing, leaving only $7 a month as
actual pay. This was only remedied when the
54th Massachusetts Infantry refused all pay for
a year until it should be treated as other regiments. The State of Massachusetts made up the
difference between the $7 and $13 to disabled
soldiers until June 16, 1864, when the government finally made the Negroes' pay equal to that
of the whites.

On the Confederate side there was a movement to use Negro soldiers fostered by Judah
Benjamin, General Lee and others. In 1861 a
Negro company from Nashville offered its services to the Confederate states and free Negroes

22 Wilson, p. 132.

of Memphis were authorized by the Committee
of Safety to organize a volunteer company. Companies of free Negroes were raised in New Orleans,—"Very well drilled and comfortably uni-
formed." In Richmond colored troops were also
raised in the last days. Few if any of these saw
actual service. Plantation hands from Alabama
built the redoubts at Charleston, and Negroes
worked as teamsters and helpers throughout the
South. In February, 1864, the Confederate congress provided for the impressment of 20,000
slaves for menial service, and President Davis
suggested that the number be doubled and that
they be emancipated at the end of their service.
Before the war started local authorities had in
many cases enrolled free Negroes as soldiers and
some of these remained in the service of the Confederacy. The adjutant general of the Louisiana
militia issued an order which said "the Governor
and the Commander-in-Chief, relying implicitly
upon the loyalty of the free colored population
of the city and State, for the protection of their
homes, their property and for southern rights,
from the population of a ruthless invader, and
believing that the military organization which
existed prior to February 15, 1862, and elicited
praise and respect for the patriotic motives which
prompted it, should exist for and during the war,

calls upon them to maintain their organization
and hold themselves prepared for such orders as
may be transmitted to them." These native
guards did not leave the city when the Confederates did and explained to General Butler that
they dared not refuse to work with the Confederates and that they hoped by their service to
gain greater equality with the whites and that
they would be glad now to join the Union forces.
Two weeks after the fall of Sumter colored
volunteers passed through Georgia on their way
to Virginia. There were 16 or more companies. In November, 1861, a regiment of 1,400
free colored men were in the line of march at
New Orleans. The idea of calling the Negroes
grew as the power of the Confederacy waned and
the idea of emancipation as compensation spread.
President Davis said "Should the alternative ever
be presented of subjugation or of the employment
of slaves as soldiers there seems no reason to
doubt what should be our decision."

There was, of course, much difference of opinion. General Cobb said "If slaves make good
soldiers our whole theory of slavery is wrong,"
while a Georgian replied "Some say that Negroes
will not fight, I say they will fight. They fought
at Ocean Pond, Honey Hill and other places."
General Lee, in January '64, gave as his opinion

that they should employ them without delay. "I believe with proper regulations they may be made efficient soldiers." He continued, "Our chief aim should be to secure their fidelity. There have been formidable armies composed of men having no interest in the cause for which they fought beyond their pay or the hope of plunder. But it is certain that the surest foundation upon which the fidelity of an army can rest, especially in a service which imposes hardships and privations, is the personal interest of the soldier in the issue of the contest. Such an interest we can give our Negroes by giving immediate freedom to all who enlist, and freedom at the end of the war to the families of those who discharge their duties faithfully (whether they survive or not), together with the privilege of residing at the South. To this might be added a bounty for faithful service."

Finally, March 13, 1865, it was directed that slaves be enrolled in the Confederate army, each state to furnish its quota of 300,000. Recruiting officers were appointed, but before the plan could be carried out Lee and Johnson surrendered.[23]

The central fact which we forget in these days is that the real question in the minds of most

[23] Wesley, in *Journal of Negro History*, Vol. 4, pp. 239ff.

white people in the United States in 1863 was whether or not the Negro really would fight. The generation then living had never heard of the Negro in the Revolution and in the War of 1812, much less of his struggles and insurrections before. From 1820 down to the time of the war a determined and far-reaching propaganda had led most men to believe in the natural inferiority, cowardice and degradation of the Negro race. We have already seen Abraham Lincoln suggest that if arms were put into the hands of the Negro soldier it might be simply a method of arming the rebels. The New York *Times* discussed the matter soberly, defending the right to employ Negroes but suggesting four grounds which might make it inexpedient; that Negroes would not fight, that prejudice was so strong that whites would not fight with them, that no free Negroes would volunteer and that slaves could not be gotten hold of and that the use of Negroes would exasperate the South. "The very best thing that can be done under existing circumstances, in our judgment, is to possess our souls in patience while the experiment is being tried. The problem will probably speedily solve itself — much more speedily than heated discussion or harsh criminations can solve it."

This was in February 16, 1863. It was not

long before the results of using Negro troops
began to be reported and we find the *Times* saying editorially on the 31st of July: "Negro soldiers have now been in battle at Port Hudson
and at Milliken's Bend in Louisiana; at Helena
in Arkansas, at Morris Island in South Carolina, and at or near Fort Gibson in the Indian
Territory.   In two of these instances they
assaulted fortified positions and led the assault;
in two they fought on the defensive, and in one
they attacked rebel infantry.   In all of them they
acted in conjunction with white troops and under
command of white officers.   In some instances
they acted with distinguished bravery, and in all
they acted as well as could be expected of raw
troops."

On the 11th of February, 1863, the news columns of the *Times* were still more enthusiastic.
"It will not need many such reports as this —
and there have been several before it — to shake
our inveterate Saxon prejudice against the capacity and courage of Negro troops.   Everybody
knows that they were used in the Revolution, and
in the last war with Great Britain fought side by
side with white troops, and won equal praises
from Washington and Jackson.   It is shown also
that black sailors are on equal terms with their
white comrades.   If on the sea, why not on the

land? No officer who has commanded black
troops has yet reported against them. They are
tried in the most unfavorable and difficult circumstances, but never fail. When shall we learn
to use the full strength of the formidable ally
who is only waiting for a summons to rally under
the flag of the Union? Colonel Higginson says:
'No officer in this regiment now doubts that the
successful prosecution of this war lies in the unlimited employment of black troops.' The re-
mark is true in a military sense, and it has a still
deeper political significance.

"When General Hunter has scattered 50,000
muskets among the Negroes of the Carolinas,
and General Butler has organized the 100,000
or 200,000 blacks for whom he may perhaps
shortly carry arms to New Orleans, the possibility of restoring the Union as it was, with slavery again its dormant power, will be seen to have
finally passed away. The Negro is indeed the
key to success."

The Negroes began to fight and fight hard;
but their own and peculiar characteristics stood
out even in the blood of war. A Pennsylvania
Major wrote home: "I find that these colored
men learn everything that pertains to the duties
of a soldier much faster than any white soldiers

I have ever seen . . . They are willing, obe-
dient, and cheerful; move with agility, and are
full of music."[24]

Certain battles, carnivals of blood, stand out
and despite their horror must not be forgotten.
One of the earliest encounters was the terrible
massacre at Fort Pillow, April 18, 1863. The
fort was held with a garrison of 557 men, of
whom 262 were colored soldiers of the 6th United
States Heavy Artillery. The Union commander
refused to surrender.

"Upon receiving the refusal of Major Booth
to capitulate, Forrest gave a signal and his troops
made a frantic charge upon the fort. It was
received gallantly and resisted stubbornly, but
there was no use of fighting. In ten minutes the
enemy, assaulting the fort in the centre, and
striking it on the flanks, swept in. The Federal
troops surrendered; but an indiscriminate massacre followed. Men were shot down in their
tracks; pinioned to the ground with bayonet and
sabre. Some were clubbed to death while dying
of wounds; others were made to get down upon
their knees, in which condition they were shot to
death. Some were burned alive, having been
fastened into the buildings, while still others

[24] New York *Tribune*, Nov. 14, 1863; Williams, Vol. 2, p. 347.

were nailed against the houses, **tortured** and then burned to a crisp."[25]

May 27, 1863, came the battle of Port Hudson. "Hearing the firing apparently more fierce and continuous to the right than anywhere else, I turned in that direction, past the sugar house of Colonel Chambers, where I had slept, and advanced to near the pontoon bridge across the Big Sandy Bayou, which the Negro regiments had erected, and where they were fighting most desperately. I had seen these brave and hitherto despised fellows the day before as I rode along the lines, and I had seen General Banks acknowledge their respectful salute as he would have done that of any white troops; but still the question was — with too many — 'Will they fight?'

"General Dwight, at least, must have had the idea, not only that they were men, but something more than men, from the terrific test to which he put their valor. Before any impression had been made upon the earthworks of the enemy, and in full face of the batteries belching forth their 62-pounders, these devoted people rushed forward to encounter grape, canister, shell, and musketry, with no artillery but two small howitzers — that seemed mere popguns to their adversaries — and no reserve whatever.

[25] Williams, Vol. 2, p. 360.

"Their force consisted of the 1st Louisiana Native Guards (with colored field officers) under Lieutenant-Colonel Bassett, and the 3d Louisiana Native Guards, Colonel Nelson (with white field officers), the whole under command of the latter officer.

"On going into action they were 1,080 strong, and formed into four lines, Lieutenant-Colonel Bassett, Ist Louisiana, forming the first line, and Lieutenant-Colonel Henry Finnegas the second. When ordered to charge up the works, they did so with the skill and nerve of old veterans (black people, be it remembered who had never been in action before). Oh, but the fire from the rebel guns was so terrible upon the unprotected masses, that the first few shots mowed them down like grass and so continued.

"Colonel Bassett being driven back, Colonel Finnegas took his place, and his men being similarly cut to pieces, Lieutenant-Colonel Bassett reformed and recommenced; and thus these brave people went in from morning until 3:30 P. M., under the most hideous carnage that men ever had to withstand, and that very few white ones would have had nerve to encounter, even if ordered to.

"During this time, they rallied, and were ordered to make six distinct charges, losing 37

killed, and 155 wounded, and 116 missing,— the
majority, if not all, of these being, in all prob-
ability, now lying dead on the gory field, and
without the rites of sepulture; for when, by flag
of truce, our forces in other directions were permitted to reclaim their dead, the benefit, through
some neglect, was not extended to these black
regiments.

"The deeds of heroism performed by these
colored men were such as the proudest white men
might emulate. Their colors are torn to pieces
by shot and literally bespattered by blood and
brains. The color-sergeant of the 1st Louisiana,
on being mortally wounded, hugged the colors to
his breast, when a struggle ensued between the
two color-corporals on each side of him, as to
who should have the honor of bearing the sacred
standard, and during this generous contention one
was seriously wounded. One black lieutenant
actually mounted the enemy's works three or four
times, and in one charge the assaulting party came
within fifty paces of them. Indeed, if only ordi-
narily supported by artillery and reserve, no one
can convince us that they would not have opened
a passage through the enemy's works.

"Captain Callioux of the 1st Louisiana, a man
so black that he actually prided himself upon his

blackness, died the death of a hero, leading on
his men in the thickest of the fight."[26]

In July 13, 1863, came the draft riot in New
York when the daily papers told the people that
they were called upon to fight the battles of "niggers and abolitionists," when the governor did
nothing but "request" the rioters to await the
report of his demand that the President suspend
the draft.   Meantime the city was given over to
rapine and murder, property destroyed, Negroes
killed and the colored orphans' asylum burned to
the ground and property robbed and pillaged.

At that very time in South Carolina black
soldiers were preparing to take Fort Wagner,
their greatest battle.   It will be noted that continually Negroes were called upon to rescue lost
causes, many times as a sort of deliberate test of
their courage.   Fort Wagner was a case in point.
The story may be told from two points of view,
that of the white Unionist and that of the Confederate.   The Union account says:

"The signal given, our forces advanced rapidly
towards the fort, while our mortars in the rear
tossed their bombs over their heads.   The 54th
Massachusetts (a Negro Regiment) led the attack, supported by the 6th Connecticut, 48th New
York, 3rd New Hampshire, 76th Pennsylvania,

[26] New York *Times,* June 13, 1863.

and the 9th Maine Regiments . . . The silent
and shattered walls of Wagner all at once burst
forth into a blinding sheet of vivid light, as
though they had suddenly been transformed by
some magic power into the living, seething crater
of a volcano! Down came the whirlwind of destruction along the beach with the swiftness of
lightning! How fearfully the hissing shot, the
shrieking bombs, the whistling bars of iron, and
the whispering bullet struck and crushed through
the dense masses of our brave men! I never
shall forget the terrible sound of that awful blast
of death, which swept down, shattered or dead,
a thousand of our men. Not a shot had missed
its aim. Every bolt of steel, every globe of iron
and lead, tasted of human blood. . . .

"In a moment the column recovered itself, like
a gallant ship at sea when buried for an instant
under the immense wave.

"The ditch is reached; a thousand men leap
into it, clamber up the shattered ramparts, and
grapple with the foe, which yields and falls back
to the rear of the fort. Our men swarm over the
walls, bayoneting the desperate rebel cannoneers.
Hurrah! the fort is ours!

"But now came another blinding blast from
concealed guns in the rear of the fort, and our
men went down by scores. . . . The struggle

is terrific. Our supports hurry up to the aid of
their comrades, but as they reach the ramparts
they fire a volley which strikes down many of our
men. Fatal mistake! Our men rally once more;
but, in spite of an heroic resistance, they are
forced back again to the edge of the ditch. Here
the brave Shaw, with scores of his black warriors,
went down, fighting desperately."

When asking for the body of Colonel Shaw, a
confederate major said: "We have buried him
with his niggers."

The Confederate account is equally eloquent.

"The carnage was frightful. It is believed the
Federals lost more men on that eventful night
than twice the entire strength of the Confederate
garrison. . . . According to the statement of
Chaplain Dennison the assaulting columns, in two
brigades, commanded by General Strong and
Colonel Putnam (the division under General Seymour), consisted of the 54th Massachusetts, 3rd
and 7th New Hampshire, 6th Connecticut and
100th New York, with a reserve brigade commanded by General Stephenson. One of the
assaulting regiments was composed of Negroes
(the 54th Massachusetts) and to it was assigned
the honor of leading the white columns to the
charge. It was a dearly purchased compliment.
Their Colonel (Shaw) was killed upon the para-

pet and the regiment almost annihilated, although the Confederates in the darkness could not tell the color of their assailants."[27]

At last it was seen that Negro troops could do more than useless or helpless or impossible tasks, and in the siege of Petersburg they were put to important work. When the general attack was ordered on the 16th of June, 1864, a division of black troops was used. The Secretary of War, Stanton himself, saw them and said:

"The hardest fighting was done by the black troops. The forts they stormed were the worst of all. After the affair was over General Smith went to thank them, and tell them he was proud of their courage and dash. He says they cannot be exceeded as soldiers, and that hereafter he will send them in a difficult place as readily as the best white troops."[28]

It was planned to send the colored troops under Burnside against the enemy after the great mine was exploded. Inspecting officers reported to Burnside that the black division was fitted for this perilous work. The white division which was sent made a fiasco of it. Then, after all had been lost Burnside was ready to send in his black division and though they charged again and again

[27] Wilson, pp. 250-54.
[28] Williams, Vol. 2, p. 338.

they were repulsed and the Union lost over 4,000 men killed, wounded and captured.

All the officers of the colored troops in the Civil War were not white. From the first there were many colored non-commissioned officers, and the Louisiana regiments raised under Butler had 66 colored officers, including one Major and 27 Captains, besides the full quota of non-commissioned colored officers. In the Massachusetts colored troops there were 10 commissioned Negro officers and 3 among the Kansas troop. Among these officers was a Lieutenant-Colonel Reed of North Carolina, who was killed in battle. In Kansas there was Captain H. F. Douglas, and in other United States' volunteer regiments were Major M. H. Delaney and Captain O. S. B. Wall; Dr. A. T. Augusta, surgeon, was brevetted Lieutenant-Colonel. The losses of Negro troops in the Civil War, killed, wounded and missing has been placed at 68,178.

Such was the service of the Negro in the Civil War. Men say that the nation gave them freedom, but the verdict of history is written on the Shaw monument at the head of Boston Common:

THE WHITE OFFICERS

Taking Life and Honor in their Hands — Cast their lot with Men of a Despised Race Unproved in War —

and Risked Death as Inciters of a Servile Insurrection if Taken Prisoners, Besides Encountering all the Common Perils of Camp, March, and Battle.

THE BLACK RANK AND FILE

Volunteered when Disaster Clouded the Union Cause — Served without Pay for Eighteen Months till Given that of White Troops — Faced Threatened Enslavement if Captured — Were Brave in Action — Patient under Dangerous and Heavy Labors and Cheerful amid Hardships and Privations.

TOGETHER

They Gave to the Nation Undying Proof that Americans of African Descent Possess the Pride, Courage, and Devotion of the Patriot Soldier — One Hundred and Eighty Thousand Such Americans Enlisted Under the Union Flag in MDCCCLXIII-MDCCCLXV.

5. THE WAR IN CUBA

In the Spanish-American War four Negro regiments were among the first to be ordered to the front. They were the regular army regiments, 24th and 25th Infantry, and the 9th and 10th Cavalry. President McKinley recommended that new regiments of regular army troops be formed among Negroes but Congress took no action. Colored troops with colored officers were formed as follows: The 3rd North Carolina, the 8th Illinois, the 9th Battalion, Ohio and the 23rd

Kansas. Regiments known as the Immunes, being immune to Yellow fever, were formed with colored lieutenants and white captains and field officers, and called the 7th, 8th, 9th and 10th United States Volunteers. In addition to those there were the 6th Virginia with colored lieutenants and the 3rd Alabama with white officers. Indiana had two companies attached to the 8th Immunes. None of the Negro volunteer companies reached the front in time to take part in battle. The 8th Illinois formed a part of the Army of Occupation and was noted for its policing and cleaning up of Santiago. Colonel John R. Marshall, commanding the 8th Illinois, and Major Charles Young, a regular army commander, both colored, were in charge of the battalion.

The colored regular army regiments took a brilliant part in the war. The first regiment ordered to the front was the 24th Infantry. Negro soldiers were in the battles around Santiago. The Tenth Cavalry made an effective attack at Las Quasimas and at El Caney on July 1 they saved Roosevelt's Rough Riders from annihilation. The 24th Infantry volunteered in the Yellow fever epidemic and cleaned the camp in one day. *Review of Reviews* says: "One of the most gratifying incidents of the Spanish War has been the enthusiassm that the colored regiments of the regular army have aroused throughout the whole country. Their fighting at Santiago was magnificent. The Negro soldiers showed excellent discipline, the highest qualities of personal bravery, very superior physical endurance, unfailing good temper, and the most generous disposition toward all comrades-in-arms, whether white or black. Roosevelt's Rough Riders have come back singing the praises of the colored troops. There is not a dissenting voice in the chorus of praise. . . . Men who can fight for their country as did these colored troops ought to have their full share of gratitude and honor."

6. CARRIZAL

In 1916 the United States sent a punitive expedition under General Pershing into Mexico in pursuit of the Villa forces which had raided Columbus, New Mexico. Two Negro regiments, the 10th Cavalry and the 24th Infantry, were a part of his expedition. On June 21, Troop C and K of the 10th Cavalry were ambushed at Carrizal by some 700 Mexican soldiers. Although outnumbered almost ten to one, these black soldiers dismounted in the face of a withering machine-gun fire, deployed, charged the Mexicans and killed their commander.

This handful of men fought on until, of the
three officers commanding them, two were killed
and one was badly wounded. Seventeen of the
men were killed and twenty-three were made
prisoners. One of the many outstanding heroes
of this memorable engagement was Peter Bigstaff, who fought to the last beside his commander, Lieutenant Adair. A Southern white
man, with no love for blacks, wrote:

"The black trooper might have faltered and
fled a dozen times, saving his own life and leaving
Adair to fight alone. But it never seemed to
occur to him. He was a comrade to the last blow.
When Adair's broken revolver fell from his hand
the black trooper pressed another into it, and together, shouting in defiance, they thinned the
swooping circle of overwhelming odds before
them.

"The black man fought in the deadly shambles
side by side with the white man, following always,
fighting always as his lieutenant fought.

"And finally, when Adair, literally shot to
pieces, fell in his tracks, his last command to his
black trooper was to leave him and save his life.
Even then the heroic Negro paused in the midst
of that Hell of carnage for a final service to his
officer. Bearing a charmed life, he had fought
his way out. He saw that Adair had fallen with

his head in the water. With superb loyalty the black trooper turned and went back to the maelstrom of death, lifted the head of his superior, leaned him against a tree and left him there dead with dignity when it was impossible to serve any more.

"There is not a finer piece of soldierly devotion and heroic comradeship in the history of modern warfare than that of Henry Adair and the black trooper who fought by him at Carrizal."[29]

7. THE WORLD WAR

Finally we come to the World War the history of which is not yet written. At first and until the United States entered the war the Negro figured as a laborer and a great exodus took place from the South as we have already noted. Some effort was made to keep the Negro from the draft but finally he was called and although constituting less than a tenth of the population he furnished 13% of the soldiers called to the colors. The registry for the draft had insulting color discriminations and determined effort was made to confine Negroes to stevedore and labor regiments under white officers. Most of the Negro draftees were thus sent to the Service of Supplies where they

[29] John Temple Graves in *Review of Reviews.*

were largely under illiterate whites and suffered greatly. Finally a camp for training Negro officers was established and nearly 700 Negroes commissioned, none of them, however, above the rank of captain; Charles Young, the highest ranking Negro graduate of West Point and one of the best officers in the army was kept from the front, because being already a colonel with a distinguished record he would surely have become a general if sent to France.

Two Negro divisions were planned, the 92nd and the 93rd. The 93rd was to be composed of the Negro National Guard regiments all of whom had some and one all Negro officers. The latter division was never organized as a complete division but four of its regiments were sent to France and encountered bitter discrimination from the Americans on account of their Negro officers. They were eventually brigaded with the French and saw some of the hardest fighting of the war in the final drive toward Sedan. They were cited in General Orders as follows by General Goybet:[30]

"In transmitting to you with legitimate pride the thanks and congratulations of the General Garnier Duplessis, allow me, my dear friends of all ranks, Americans and

[30] MS. Copies of orders.

French, to thank you from the bottom of my heart as a chief and a soldier for the expression of gratitude for the glory which you have lent our good 157th Division. I had full confidence in you but you have surpassed my hopes.

"During these nine days of hard fighting you have progressed nine kilometers through powerful organized defenses, taken nearly 600 prisoners, 15 guns of different calibers, 20 minnewerfers, and nearly 150 machine guns, secured an enormous amount of engineering material, an important supply of artillery ammunition, brought down by your fire three enemy aeroplanes.

"Your troops have been admirable in their attack. You must be proud of the courage of your officers and men; and I consider it an honor to have them under my command.

"The bravery and dash of your regiment won the admiration of the 2nd Moroccan Division who are themselves versed in warfare. Thanks to you, during those hard days, the Division was at all times in advance of all other divisions of the Army Corps. I am sending you all my thanks and beg you to transmit them to your subordinates.

"I called on your wounded. Their morale is higher than any praise.

GOYBET."

The 92nd Division encountered difficulties in organization and was never assembled as a Division until it arrived in France. There it was finally gotten in shape and took a small part in the Argonne offensive and in the fight just preceding the armistice. Their Commanding General said:[31]

"Five months ago today the 92nd Division landed in France.

"After seven weeks of training, it took over a sector in the front line, and since that time some portion of the Division has been practically continuously under fire.

"It participated in the last battle of the war with creditable success, continuously pressing the attack against highly organized defensive works. It advanced successfully on the first day of the battle, attaining its objectives and capturing prisoners. This in the face of determined opposition by an alert enemy, and against rifle, machine-gun and artillery fire. The issue of the second day's battle was rendered indecisive by the order to cease firing at eleven A. M.—when the armistice became effective."

With the small chance thus afforded Negro troops nevertheless made a splendid record and especially those under Negro officers. If they had had larger opportunity and less organized prejudice they would have done much more. Perhaps their greatest credit is from the fact that they withstood so bravely and uncomplainingly the barrage of hatred and offensive prejudice aimed

[31] MS. Copies of orders.

against them.   The young Negro officers especially made a splendid record as to thinking, guid-
ing leaders of an oppressed group.

Thus has the black man defended America from
the beginning to the World War.   To him our independence from Europe and slavery is in no small
degree due.

CHAPTER IV

THE EMANCIPATION OF DEMOCRACY

How the black slave by his incessant struggle to
be free has broadened the basis of democracy
in America and in the world.

Help in exploration, labor unskilled and to
some extent skilled, and fighting, have been the
three gifts which so far we have considered as
having been contributed by black folk to America.
We now turn to a matter more indefinite and yet
perhaps of greater importance.

Without the active participation of the Negro
in the Civil War, the Union could not have been
saved nor slavery destroyed in the nineteenth century.[1] Without the help of black soldiers, the
independence of the United States could not have
been gained in the eighteenth century. But the
Negro's contribution to America was at once more
subtle and important than these things. Dramatically the Negro is the central thread of American
history. The whole story turns on him whether

[1] At least this was the opinion of Abraham Lincoln — cf. Wilson's
Black Phalanx, p. 108.

we think of the dark and flying slave ship in the
sixteenth century, the expanding plantations of the
seventeenth, the swelling commerce of the eighteenth, or the fight for freedom in the nineteenth.
It was the black man that raised a vision of democracy in America such as neither Americans nor
Europeans conceived in the eighteenth century and
such as they have not even accepted in the
twentieth century; and yet a conception which
every clear sighted man knows is true and inevitable.

1. DEMOCRACY

Democracy was not planted full grown in
America. It was a slow growth beginning in
Europe and developing further and more quickly
in America. It did not envisage at first the man
farthest down as a participant in democratic
privilege or even as a possible participant. This
was not simply because of the inability of the
ignorant and degraded to express themselves and
act intelligently and efficiently, but it was a failure
to recognize that the mass of men had any rights
which the better class were bound to respect. Thus
democracy to the world first meant simply the
transfer of privilege and opportunity from wan-
ing to waxing power, from the well-born to the
rich, from the nobility to the merchants. Divine

Right of birth yielded the Divine Right of wealth. Growing industry, business and commerce were putting economic and social power into the hands of what we call the middle class. Political opportunity to correspond with this power was the demand of the eighteenth century and this was what the eighteenth century called Democracy. On the other hand, both in Europe and in America, there were classes, and large classes, without power and without consideration whose place in democracy was inconceivable both to Europeans and Americans. Among these were the agricultural serfs and industrial laborers of Europe and the indentured servants and black slaves of America. The white serfs, as they were transplanted in America, began a slow, but in the end, effective agitation for recognition in American democracy. And through them has risen the modern American labor movement. But this movement almost from the first looked for its triumph along the ancient paths of aristocracy and sought to raise the white servant and laborer on the backs of the black servant and slave. If now the black man had been inert, unintelligent, submissive, democracy would have continued to mean in America what it means so widely still in Europe, the admission of the powerful to participation in government and privilege in so far and only in so far as their power becomes irresistible. It would not have meant a recognition of human beings as such and the giving of economic and social power to the powerless.

It is usually assumed in reading American history that whatever the Negro has done for America has been passive and unintelligent, that he accompanied the explorers as a beast of burden and accomplished whatever he did by sheer accident; that he labored because he was driven to labor and fought because he was made to fight. This is not true. On the contrary, it was the rise and growth among the slaves of a determination to be free and an active part of American democracy that forced American democracy continually to look into the depths; that held the faces of American thought to the inescapable fact that as long as there was a slave in America, America could not be a free republic; and more than that: as long as there were people in America, slave or nominally free, who could not participate in government and industry and society as free, intelligent human beings, our democracy had failed of its greatest mission.

This great vision of the black man was, of course, at first the vision of the few, as visions always are, but it was always there; it grew continuously and it developed quickly from wish to

active determination.   One cannot think then of
democracy in America or in the modern world
without reference to the American Negro.   The
democracy established in America in the eighteenth century was not, and was not designed to be,
a democracy of the masses of men and it was thus
singularly easy for people to fail to see the incongruity of democracy and slavery.   It was the
Negro himself who forced the consideration of
this incongruity, who made emancipation inevitable and made the modern world at least consider
if not wholly accept the idea of a democracy including men of all races and colors.

2. INFLUENCE ON WHITE THOUGHT

Naturally, at first, it was the passive presence
of the Negro with his pitiable suffering and
sporadic expression of unrest that bothered the
American colonists.   Massachusetts and Connecticut early in the seventeenth century tried to
compromise with their consciences by declaring
that there should be no slavery except of persons
"willingly selling themselves" or "sold to us."
And these were to have "All the liberties and
Christian usages which the law of God established
in Israel."   Massachusetts even took a strong
stand against proven "man stealing"; but it was
left to a little band of Germans in Pennsylvania,

in 1688, to make the first clear statement the moment they looked upon a black slave: "Now, though they are black, we cannot conceive there is more liberty to have them slaves than it is to have other white ones. There is a saying that we shall do to all men like as we will be done to ourselves, making no difference of what generation, descent or color they are. Here is liberty of conscience which is right and reasonable. Here ought also to be liberty of the body."[2]

In the eighteenth century, Sewall of Massachusetts attacked slavery. From that time down until 1863 man after man and prophet after prophet spoke against slavery and they spoke not so much as theorists but as people facing extremely uncomfortable facts. Oglethorpe would keep slavery out of Georgia because he saw how the strength of South Carolina went to defending themselves against possible slave insurrection rather than to defending the English colonies against the Spanish. The matter of baptizing the heathen whom slavery was supposed to convert brought tremendous heart searchings and argument and disputations and explanatory laws throughout the colonies. Contradictory benevolences were evident as when the Society for the Propagation of the Gospel sought to convert the

[2] Thomas, *Attitude of Friends toward Slavery*, p. 267 and Appendix.

Negroes and American legislatures sought to make the perpetual slavery of the converts sure.

The religious conscience, especially as it began to look upon America as a place of freedom and refuge, was torn by the presence of slavery. Late in the eighteenth and early in the nineteenth centuries pressure began to be felt from the more theoretical philanthropists of Europe and the position of American philanthropists was made correspondingly uncomfortable. Benjamin Franklin pointed out some of the evils of slavery; James Otis inveighing against England's economic tyranny acknowledged the rights of black men. Patrick Henry said that slavery was "repugnant to the first impression of right and wrong" and George Washington hoped slavery might be abolished. Thomas Jefferson made the celebrated statement: "Indeed I tremble for my country when I reflect that God is just; that His justice cannot sleep forever; that considering numbers, nature, and natural means only, a revolution of the wheel of fortune, an exchange of situation, is among possible events; that it may become probable by supernatural interference! The Almighty has no attribute which can take side with us in such a contest."[3]

Henry Laurens said to his son: "You know, my

[3] Jefferson's Writings, Vol. 8, pp. 403-4.

dear son, I abhor slavery. I was born in a country
where slavery had been established by British
kings and parliaments, as well as by the laws of
that country ages before my existence. I found
the Christian religion and slavery growing under
the same authority and cultivation. I nevertheless
disliked it. In former days there was no com-
bating the prejudices of men supported by interest; the day I hope is approaching when, from
principles of gratitude as well as justice, every man
will strive to be foremost in showing his readiness
to comply with the golden rule."[4]

The first draft of the Declaration of Independence harangued King George III of Britain for
the presence of slavery in the United States:

"He has waged cruel war against human nature
itself, violating its most sacred rights of life and
liberty in the persons of a distant people who
never offended him; captivating and carrying
them into slavery in another hemisphere, or to
incur miserable death in their transportation
thither. This piratical warfare, the opprobrium
of Infidel powers, is the warfare of the Christian
king of Great Britain. Determined to keep open
market where men should be bought and sold, he
has prostituted his negative for suppressing every

---

[4] George Livermore, *Opinions of the Founders of the Republic on
Negroes as Slaves, as Citizens, and as Soldiers*, Boston, 1862, p. 61.

legislative attempt to prohibit or to restrain this execrable commerce. And, that this assemblage of horrors might want no fact of distinguished die, he is now exciting those very people to rise in arms among us, and to purchase that liberty of which he has deprived them, by murdering the people on whom we also obtruded them; thus paying off former crimes committed against the liberties of one people with crimes which he urges them to commit against the lives of another."[5]

The final draft of the Declaration said: "We hold these truths to be self-evident:—that all men are created equal, that they are endowed by their Creator with certain inalienable rights; that among these are life, liberty, and the pursuit of happiness. That to secure these rights, governments are instituted among men, deriving their just powers from the consent of the governed."

It was afterward argued that Negroes were not included in this general statement and Judge Taney in his celebrated decision said in 1857:

"They had for more than a century before been regarded as beings of an inferior order, and altogether unfit to associate with the white race, either in social or political relations; and so far inferior that they had no rights which the white man was bound to respect; and that the Negro might justly

[5] Jefferson's Works, Vol. 1, pp. 23-4.

and lawfully be reduced to slavery for his benefit. . . ."[6]

This *obiter dictum* was disputed by equally
learned justices. Justice McLean said in his
opinion:

"Our independence was a great epoch in the
history of freedom; and while I admit the Government was not made especially for the colored
race, yet many of them were citizens of the New
England States, and exercised the rights of suffrage when the Constitution was adopted; and it
was not doubted by any intelligent person that its
tendencies would greatly ameliorate their condition."[7]

Justice Curtis also said:

"It has been often asserted, that the Constitution was made exclusively by and for the white
race. It has already been shown that in five of the
thirteen original States, colored persons then possessed the elective franchise and were among those
by whom the Constitution was ordained and established. If so, it is not true, in point of fact, that
the Constitution was made exclusively by the
white race. And that it was made exclusively for
the white race is, in my opinion, not only an
assumption not warranted by anything in the Con-

---

[6] Howard's Reports, Vol. 19.
[7] Howard's Reports, pp. 536-8.

stitution, but contradicted by its opening declaration, that it was ordained and established by the people of the United States, for themselves and their posterity. And, as free colored persons were then citizens of at least five States, they were among those for whom and whose posterity the Constitution was ordained and established."[8]

After the Revolution came the series of State acts abolishing slavery, beginning with Vermont in 1777; and then came the pause and retrogression followed by the slow but determined rise of the Cotton Kingdom. But even in that day the prophets protested. Hezekiah Niles said in 1819: "We are ashamed of the thing we practice; . . . there is no attribute of Heaven that takes part with us, and we know it. And in the contest that must come, and will come, there will be a heap of sorrows such as the world has rarely seen."[9] While the wild preacher, Lorenzo Dow, raised his cry from the wilderness even in Alabama and Mississippi, saying: "In the rest of the Southern States the influence of these Foreigners will be known and felt in its time, and the seeds from the HORY ALLIANCE and the DECAPIGANDI, who have a hand in those grades of Generals, from the Inquisitor to the Vicar General and

.[8] Howard's Reports, pp. 572-3, 582.
[9] Niles' Register, Vol. 16, May 22, 1819.

down. . . . The STRUGGLE will be DREAD-
FUL! The CUP will be BITTER! and when the
agony is over, those who survive may see better
days! FAREWELL!"[10]   Finally came William
Lloyd Garrison and John Brown.

3. INSURRECTION

It may be said, and it usually has been said, that
all this showed the natural conscience and humanity of white Americans protesting and eventually triumphing over political and economic temptations. But to this must be added the inescapable fact that the attitude, thought and action of
the Negro himself was in the largest measure back
of this heart searching, discomfort and warning;
and first of all was the physical force which the
Negro again and again and practically without
ceasing from the first days of the slave trade down
to the war of emancipation, used to effect his own
freedom.

We must remember that the slave trade itself
was war; that from surreptitious kidnapping of the
unsuspecting it was finally organized so as to set
African tribes warring against tribes, giving the
conquerors the actual aid of European or Arabian
soldiers and the tremendous incentive of high

[10] Benjamin Brawley, *A Social History of the American Negro*, New
York, 1921, p. 90.

prices for results of successful wars through the
selling of captives. The captives themselves
fought to the last ditch. It is estimated that every
single slave finally landed upon a slave ship meant
five corpses either left behind in Africa or lost
through rebellion, suicide, sickness, and murder on
the high seas. This which is so often looked upon
as passive calamity was one of the most terrible
and vindictive and unceasing struggles against mis-
fortune that a group of human beings ever put
forth. It cost Negro Africa perhaps sixty million
souls to land ten million slaves in America.

The first influence of the Negro on American
Democracy was naturally force to oppose force—
revolt, murder, assassination coupled with running
away. It was the primitive, ancient effort to
avenge blood with blood, to bring good out of
evil by opposing evil with evil. Whether right or
wrong, effective or abortive, it is the human answer to oppression which the world has tried for
thousands of years.

Two facts stand out in American history with
regard to slave insurrections: on the one hand,
there is no doubt of the continuous and abiding
fear of them. The slave legislation of the Southern States is filled with ferocious efforts to guard
against this. Masters were everywhere given per-
emptory and unquestioned power to kill a slave or

even a white servant who should "resist his master." The Virginia law of 1680 said: "If any Negro or other slave shall absent himself from his master's service and lie, hide and lurk in obscure places, committing injuries to the inhabitants, and shall resist any person or persons that shall by lawful authority be employed to apprehend and take the said Negro, that then, in case of such resistance, it shall be lawful for such person or persons to kill the said Negro or slave so lying out and resisting."[11]

In 1691 and in 1748, there were Virginia acts to punish conspiracies and insurrections of slaves. In 1708 and in 1712 New York had laws against conspiracies and insurrections of Negroes. North Carolina passed such a law in 1741, and South Carolina in 1743 was legislating "against the insurrection and other wicked attempts of Negroes and other slaves." The Mississippi code of 1839 provides for slave insurrections "with arms in the intent to regain their liberty by force." Virginia in 1797 decreed death for any one exciting slaves to insurrection. In 1830 North Carolina made it a felony to incite insurrection among slaves. The penal code of Texas, passed in 1857, had a severe section against insurrection.[12]

[11] Hening's Statutes.
[12] John C. Hurd, *The Law of Freedom and Bondage*, Boston, 1858-1862.

Such legislation, common in every slave state, could not have been based on mere idle fear, and when we follow newspaper comment, debates and arguments and the history of insurrections and attempted insurrections among slaves, we easily see the reason. No sooner had the Negroes landed in America than resistance to slavery began.

As early as 1503 the Governor of Hispaniola stopped the transportation of Negroes "because they fled to the Indians and taught them bad manners and they could never be apprehended." In 1518 in the sugar mills of Haiti the Negroes "quit working and fled whenever they could in squads and started rebellions and committed murders." In 1522 there was a rebellion on the sugar plantations. Twenty Negroes from Diego Columbus' mill fled and killed several Spaniards. They joined with other rebellious Negroes on neighboring plantations. In 1523 many Negro slaves "fled to the Zapoteca and walked rebelliously through the country." In 1527 there was an uprising of Indians and Negroes in Florida. In 1532 the Wolofs and other rebellious Negroes caused insurrection among the Carib Indians. These Wolofs were declared to be "haughty, disobedient, rebellious and incorrigible." In 1548 there was a rebellion in Honduras and the Viceroy Mendoza in Mexico writes of an uprising among the slaves and Indians in 1537.[13]   One of the most remarkable cases of resistance was the establishment and defense of Palmares in Brazil where 40 determined Negroes in 1560 established a city state which lived for nearly a half century growing to a population of 20,000 and only overthrown when 7,000 soldiers with artillery were sent against it. The Chiefs committed suicide rather than surrender.[14]

Early in the sixteenth century and from that time down until the nineteenth the black rebels whom the Spanish called "Cimarrones" and whom we know as "Maroons" were infesting the mountains and forests of the West Indies and South America.   Gage says between 1520 and 1530: "What the Spaniards fear most until they get out of these mountains are two or three hundred Negroes, Cimarrones, who for the bad treatment they received have fled from masters in order to resort to these woods; there they live with their wives and children and increase in numbers every year, so that the entire force of Guatemala (City) and its environments is not capable to subdue them."

[13] Wiener, *Africa and the Discovery of America*, Vol. 1, pp. 155-8.
[14] C. E. Chapman in *Journal of Negro History*, Vol. 3, p. 29.

Gage himself was captured by a mulatto corsair who was sweeping the seas in his own ship.[15]

The history of these Maroons reads like romance.[16] When England took Jamaica, in 1565, they found the mountains infested with Maroons whom they fought for ten years and finally, in 1663, acknowledged their freedom, gave them land and made their leader, Juan de Bolas, a colonel in the militia. He was killed, however, in the following year and from 1664 to 1778 some 3,000 black Maroons were in open rebellion against the British Empire. The English fought them with soldiers, Indians, and dogs and finally again, in 1738, made a formal treaty of peace with them, recognizing their freedom and granting them 25,000 acres of land. The war again broke out in 1795 and blood-hounds were again imported. The legislature wished to deport them but as they could not get their consent, peace was finally made on condition that the Maroons surrender their arms and settle down. No sooner, however, had they done this than the whites treacherously seized 600 of them and sent them to Nova Scotia. The Legislature voted a sword to the English general, who made the treaty; but he indignantly refused to accept it. Eventually these

[15] J. Kunst, *Negroes in Guatemala, Journal of Negro History*, Vol. I, pp. 392-8.
[16] Cf. Bryan Edward's *West Indies*, 4th Edition, Vol. I, pp. 337-98.

Maroons were removed to Sierra Leone where they saved that colony to the British by helping them put down an insurrection.

In the United States insurrection and attempts at insurrection among the slaves extended from Colonial times down to the Civil War. For the most part they were unsuccessful. In many cases the conspiracies were insignificant in themselves but exaggerated by fear of the owners. And yet a record of the attempts at revolt large and small is striking.

In Virginia there was a conspiracy in 1710 in Surrey County. In 1712 the City of New York was threatened with burning by slaves. In 1720 whites were attacked in the homes and on the streets in Charleston, S. C. In 1730 both in South Carolina and Virginia, slaves were armed to kill the white people and they planned to burn the City of Boston in 1723. In 1730 there was an insurrection in Williamsburg, Va., and five counties furnished armed men. In 1730 and 1731 homes were burned by slaves in Massachusetts and in Rhode Island and in 1731 and 1732 three ships crews were murdered by slaves. In 1729 the Governor of Louisiana reported that in an expedition sent against the Indians, fifteen Negroes had "performed prodigies of valor." But the very next year the Indians, led by a desperate Negro named

Samba, were trying to exterminate the whites.[17]
In 1741 an insurrection of slaves was planned in
New York City, for which thirteen slaves were
burned, eighteen hanged and eighty transported.
In 1754 and 1755 slaves burned and poisoned cer-
tain masters in Charleston, S. C.[18]

4. HAITI AND AFTER

On the night of August 23, 1791, the great
Haitian rebellion took place. It had been preceded by a small rebellion of the mulattoes who
were bitterly disappointed at the refusal of the
planters to assent to what the free Negroes
thought were the basic principles of the French
Revolution. When 450,000 slaves joined them,
they began a murderous civil war seldom paral-
leled in history. French, English and Spaniards
participated. Toussaint, the first great black
leader, was deceived, imprisoned and died perhaps
by poisoning. Twenty-five thousand French soldiers were sent over by Napoleon Bonaparte to
subdue the Negroes and begin the extension of his
American empire through the West Indies and up
the Mississippi valley. Despite all this, the
Negroes were triumphant, established an inde-

[17] Gayarre, *History of Louisiana*, Vol. I, pp. 435, 440.
[18] Du Bois' *Slave Trade*, pp. 6, 10, 22, 206; J. Coppin, *Slave Insur-rections*, 1860; Brawley, *Social History*, pp. 39, 86, 132.

pendent state, made Napoleon give up his dream
of American empire and sell Louisiana for a
song:[19] "Thus, all of Indian Territory, all of
Kansas and Nebraska and Iowa and Wyoming and
Montana and the Dakotas, and most of Colorado
and Minnesota, and all of Washington and Oregon states, came to us as the indirect work of a
despised Negro. Praise if you will, the work of
Robert Livingston or a Jefferson, but today let
us not forget our debt to Toussaint L'Ouverture
who was indirectly the means of America's expansion by the Louisiana Purchase of 1803."[20]

The Haitian revolution immediately had its
effect upon both North and South America. We
have read how Haitian volunteers helped in the
American revolution. They returned to fight for
their own freedom. Afterward when Bolivar, the
founder of five free republics in South America,
undertook his great rebellion in 1811 he at first
failed. He took refuge in Jamaica and implored
the help of England but was unsuccessful. Later
in despair he visited Haiti. The black republic
was itself at that time in a precarious position and
had to act with great caution. Neverthless President Pétion furnished Bolivar, soldiers, arms and

[19] Cf. T. G. Steward, *The Haitian Revolution.*
[20] DeWitt Talmadge in the *Christian Herald*, Nov. 28, 1906; Du
Bois' *Slave Trade*, Chapter 7.

money. Bolivar embarked secretly and again sought to free South America. Again he failed and a second time returned to Haiti. Money and reinforcements were a second time furnished him and with the help of these achieved the liberation of Mexico and Central America.

Thus black Haiti not only freed itself but helped to kindle liberty all through America. Refugees from Haiti and San Domingo poured into the United States both colored and white and had great influence in Maryland and Louisiana.[21] Moreover the news of the black revolt filtered through to the slaves in the United States. Here the chains of slavery were stronger and the number of whites much larger. As I have said in another place: "A long, awful process of selection chose out the listless, ignorant, sly and humble and sent to heaven the proud, the vengeful and the daring. The old African warrior spirit died away of violence and a broken heart."[22]

Nevertheless a series of attempted rebellions took place which can be traced to the influence of Haiti. In 1800 came the Prosser conspiracy in Virginia which planned a force of 11,000 Negroes to march in three columns in the city and seize the arsenal. A terrific storm thwarted these men and

[21] Cf. Dunbar-Nelson in the *Journal of Negro History*, Vol. i.
[22] Du Bois, *John Brown*, p. 81.

thirty-six were executed for the attempt. In 1791
Negroes of Louisiana sought to imitate Toussaint
leading to the execution of twenty-three slaves.
Other smaller attempts were made in South Carolina in 1816 and in Georgia in 1819. In 1822
came the celebrated attempt of Denmark Vesey,
an educated freedman who through his trade as
carpenter accumulated considerable wealth. He
spoke French and English and was familiar with
the Haitian revolution, the African Colonization
scheme and the agitation attending the Missouri
compromise. He openly discussed slavery and
ridiculed the slaves for their cowardice and submission; he worked through the church and
planned the total annihilation of the men, women
and children of Charleston. Thousands of slaves
were enrolled but one betrayed him and this led
to the arrest of 137 blacks of whom 35 were
hanged and 37 banished. A white South Caro-
linian writing after this plot said: "We regard our
Negroes as the Jacobins of the country, against
whom we should always be upon our guard and
who although we fear no permanent effects from
any insurrectionary movements on their part,
should be watched with an eye of steady and un-
remitted observation."[23]

[23] A. H. Grimke, *Right on the Scaffold in Occasional Papers*, No. 7,
American Negro Academy.

Less than ten years elapsed before another insurrection was planned and partially carried
through. Its leader was Nat Turner, a slave born
in Virginia in 1800. He was precocious and considered as "marked" by the Negroes. He had
experimented in making paper, gun powder and
pottery; never swore, never drank and never stole.
For the most part he was a sort of religious devotee, fasting and praying and reading the Bible.
Once he ran away but was commanded by spirit
voices to return. By 1825 he was conscious of a
great mission and on May 12, 1831, "a great
voice said unto him that the serpent was loosed,
that Christ had laid down the yoke." He believed
that he, Nat Turner, was to lead the movement
and that "the first should be last and the last first."
An eclipse of the sun in February, 1831 was a further sign to him. He worked quickly. Gathering
six friends together August 21, they made their
plans and then started the insurrection by killing
Nat's master and the family. About forty Negroes were gathered in all and they killed sixty-one
white men, women and children. They were
headed toward town when finally the whites began to arm in opposition. It was not, however,
until two months later, October 30, that Turner
himself was captured. He was tried November 5
and sentenced to be hanged. When asked if he

believed in the righteousness of his mission he
replied "Was not Christ crucified?" He made no
confession.[24]

T. R. Grey — Turner's attorney — said "As to
his ignorance, he certainly had not the advantages
of education, but he can read and write and for
natural intelligence and quickness of apprehension
is surpassed by few men I have ever seen. Further the calm, deliberate composure with which he
spoke of his late deeds and intentions, the expression of his fiend-like face when excited by enthusiasm; still bearing the stains of the blood of helpless innocence about him; clothed with rags and
covered with chains, yet daring to raise his man-
acled hands to heaven; with a spirit soaring above
the attributes of man, I looked on him and my
blood curdled in my veins."[25]

Panic seized the whole of Virginia and the
South. Military companies were mobilized, both
whites and Negroes fled to the swamps, slaves
were imprisoned and even as far down as Macon,
Ga., the white women and children were guarded
in a building against supposed insurrections. New
slave codes were adopted, new disabilities put
upon freedmen, the carrying of fire arms was especially forbidden. The Negro churches in the

[24] Brawley, p. 140; T. W. Higginson, *Atlantic Monthly*, Vol. 8,
p. 173.
[25] I. W. Cromwell, in *Journal of Negro History*, Vol. 5, pp. 208ff.

South were almost stopped from functioning and the Negro preachers from preaching. Traveling and meeting of slaves was stopped, learning to read and write was forbidden and incendiary pamphlets hunted down. Free Negroes were especially hounded, sold into slavery or driven out and a period of the worst oppression of the Negro in the land followed.

In 1839 and 1841 two cases of mutiny of slaves on the high seas caused much commotion in America. In 1839 a schooner, the Amistad, started from Havana for another West Indian port with 53 slaves. Led by a black man, Cinque, the slaves rose, killed the captain and some of the crew, allowed the rest of the crew to escape and put the two owners in irons. The Negroes then tried to escape to Africa, but after about two months they landed in Connecticut and a celebrated law case arose over the disposition of the black mutineers which went to the Supreme Court of the United States. John Quincy Adams defended them and won his case. Eventually money was raised and the Negroes returned to Africa. While this case was in the court the brig Creole in 1841 sailed from Richmond to New Orleans with 130 slaves. Nineteen of the slaves mutinied and led by Madison Washington took command of the vessel and sailed to the British West Indies.

Daniel Webster demanded the return of the slaves but the British authorities refused.

During these years, rebellion and agitation among Negroes, and agitation among white friends in Europe, was rapidly freeing the Negroes of the West Indies and beginning their incorporation into the body politic—a process not yet finished but which means possibly the eventual development of a free black and mulatto republic in the isles of the Caribbean.

It may be said that in most of these cases the attempts of the Negro to rebel were abortive, and this is true. Yet it must be remembered that in a few cases they had horrible success; in others nothing but accident or the actions of favorite slaves saved similar catastrophe, and more and more the white South had the feeling that it was sitting upon a volcano and that nothing but the sternest sort of repression would keep the Negro "in his place." The appeal of the Negro to force invited reaction and retaliation not only in the South, as we have noted, but also in the North. Here the common white workingman and particularly the new English, Scotch and Irish immigrants entirely misconceived the writhing of the black man. These white laborers, themselves so near slavery, did not recognize the struggle of the black slave as part of their own struggle; rather

they felt the sting of economic rivalry and under-
bidding for home and job; they easily absorbed
hatred and contempt for Negroes as their first
American lesson and were flattered by the white
capitalists, slave owners and sympathizers with
slavery into lynching and clubbing their dark fellow victims back into the pit whence they sought
to crawl. It was a scene for angels' tears.

In 1826 Negroes were attacked in Cincinnati
and also in 1836 and 1841. At Portsmouth, Ohio,
nearly one-half of the Negroes were driven
out of the city in 1830 while mobs drove
away free Negroes from Mercer County, Ohio.
In Philadelphia, Negroes were attacked in 1820,
1830 and 1834, having their churches and property burned and ruined. In 1838 there was
another anti-Negro riot and in 1842, when the
blacks attempted to celebrate abolition in the
West Indies. Pittsburg had a riot in 1839 and
New York in 1843 and 1863.[26]

Thus we can see that the fear and heart searchings and mental upheaval of those who saw the
anomaly of slavery in the United States was based
not only upon theoretical democracy but on force
and fear of force as used by the degraded blacks,
and on the reaction of that appeal on southern
legislatures and northern mobs.

[26] Cf. Du Bois' *Philadelphia Negro*, Chapter 4; Woodson's *Negro in
our History*, pp. 140-1.

5. THE APPEAL TO REASON

The appeal of the Negro to democracy, however, was not entirely or perhaps even principally an appeal of force. There was continually the appeal to reason and justice. Take the significant case of Paul Cuffee of Massachusetts, born in 1759, of a Negro father and Indian mother. When the selectmen of the town of Dartmouth refused to admit colored children to the public schools, or even to make separate provision for them, he refused to pay his school taxes. He was duly imprisoned, but when freed he built at his own expense a school house and opened it to all without race discrimination. His white neighbors were glad to avail themselves of this school as it was more convenient and just as good as the school in town. The result was that the colored children were soon admitted to all schools. Cuffee was a ship owner and trader, and afterward took a colony to Liberia at his own expense.[28] Again Prince Hall, the Negro founder of the African Lodge of Masons which the English set up in 1775, aroused by the revolution in Haiti and a race riot in Boston said in 1797:

"Patience, I say, for were we not possessed of a great measure of it you could not bear up under

[27] Brawley, pp. 123-4; *Journal of Negro History,* Vol. 2, pp. 209-28.

the daily insults you meet with in the streets of
Boston; much more on public days of recreation,
how are you shamefully abused, and that at such a
degree that you may truly be said to carry your
lives in your own hands. . . .

"My brethren, let us not be cast down under
these and many other abuses we at present labor
under; for the darkest hour is before the break of
day. My brethren, let us remember what a dark
day it was with our African brethren six years ago,
in the French West Indies. . . . But blessed be
to God, the scene is changed, they now confess
that God hath no respect of persons, and therefore receive them as their friends and treat them
as brothers. Thus doth Ethiopia begin to
stretch forth her hand from a sink of slavery to
freedom and equality."[28]

A more subtle appeal was made by seven
Massachusetts Negroes on taxation without representation. In a petition to the General Court of
Massachusetts in 1780 they said: "We being
chiefly of the African extract, and by reason of
long bondage and hard slavery, we have been
deprived of enjoying the profits of our labor or
the advantage of inheriting estates from our parents, as our neighbors the white people do, having

[28] Brawley, p. 71.

some of us not long enjoyed our own freedom; yet of late, contrary to the invariable custom and practice of the country, we have been, and now are, taxed both in our polls and that small pittance of estate which, through much hard labor and industry, we have got together to sustain ourselves and families withall. We apprehend it therefore, to be hard usage, and will doubtless (if continued) reduce us to a state of beggary, whereby we shall become a burden to others, if not timely prevented by the interposition of your justice and power.

"Your petitioners further show, that we apprehend ourselves to be aggrieved, in that, while we are not allowed the privilege of free men of the State, having no vote or influence in the election of those that tax us, yet many of our color (as is well known) have cheerfully entered the field of battle in the defence of the common cause, and that (as we conceive) against similar exertion of power (in regard to taxation) too well known to need a recital in this place."[29]

Perhaps though the most startling appeal and challenge came from David Walker, a free Negro, born of a free mother and slave father in North Carolina in 1785. He had some education, had traveled widely and conducted a second-hand

[29] Williams' *Negro Race*, Vol. 2, p. 126.

clothing store in Boston in 1827. He spoke to
various audiences of Negroes in 1828 and the
following year published the celebrated "Appeal
in four articles, together with a preamble to the
Colored Citizens of the World but in particular
and very expressly to those of the United States
of America." It was a thin volume of 76 octavol
pages, but it was frank and startlingly clear:

"Can our condition be any worse? Can it be
more mean and abject? If there are any changes,
will they not be for the better though they may
appear for the worst at first? Can they get us any
lower? Where can they get us? They cannot
treat us worse; for they well know the day they do
it they are gone. But against all accusations which
may or can be preferred against me, I appeal to
heaven for my motive in writing—who knows that
my object is if possible to awaken in the breasts
of my afflicted, degraded and slumbering brethren
a spirit of enquiry and investigation respecting our
miseries and wretchedness in this Republican land
of Liberty! ! ! !

"My beloved brethren:—The Indians of North
and South America—the Greeks—the Irish, subjected under the King of Great Britain—the Jews,
that ancient people of the Lord—the inhabitants
of the Islands of the Sea—in fine, all the inhabitants of the Earth, (except, however, the sons of

Africa) are called men and of course are and ought to be free.—But we, (colored people) and our children are brutes and of course are and ought to be slaves to the American people and their children forever—to dig their mines and work their farms; and thus go on enriching them from one generation to another with our blood and our tears! ! ! !

"I saw a paragraph, a few years since, in a South Carolina paper, which, speaking of the barbarity of the Turks, it said: 'The Turks are the most barbarous people in the world—they treat the Greeks more like brutes than human beings.' And in the same paper was an advertisement which said: 'Eight well built Virginia and Maryland Negro fellows and four wenches will positively be sold this day to the highest bidder!'

"Beloved brethren—here let me tell you, and believe it, that the Lord our God as true as He sits on His throne in heaven and as true as our Saviour died to redeem the world, will give you a Hannibal, and when the Lord shall have raised him up and given him to you for your possession, Oh! my suffering brethren, remember the divisions and consequent sufferings of Carthage and of Haiti. Read the history particularly of Haiti and see how they were butchered by the whites and do you take warning. The person whom God shall give you, give him your support and let him go his length and behold in him the salvation of your God. God will indeed deliver you through him from your deplorable and wretched condition under the Christians of America. I charge you this day before my God to lay no obstacle in his way, but let him go. . . . What the American preachers can think of us, I aver this day before my God I have never been able to define. They have newspapers and monthly periodicals which they receive in continual succession but on the pages of which you will scarcely ever find a paragraph respecting slavery which is ten thousand times more injurious to this country than all the other evils put together; and which will be the final overthrow of its government unless something is very speedily done; for their cup is nearly full.—Perhaps they will laugh at or make light of this; but I tell you, Americans! that unless you speedily alter your course, you and your Country are gone!

"Do you understand your own language? Hear your language proclaimed to the world, July 4, 1776—'We hold these truths to be self evident—that ALL men are created EQUAL!! That they are endowed by their Creator with certain unalienable rights; that among these are life, liberty and the pursuit of happiness!!! Compare your own language above, extracted from your Declaration of Independence, with your cruelties and murders inflicted by your cruel and unmerciful fathers and yourselves on our fathers and on us—men who have never given your fathers or you the least provocation!!!

"Now Americans! I ask you candidly, was your suffering under Great Britain one hundredth part as cruel and tryrannical as you have rendered ours under you? Some of you, no doubt, believe that we will never throw off your murderous government and provide new guards for our future 'security'. If Satan has made you believe it, will he not deceive you?"

The book had a remarkable career. It appeared in September, was in a third edition by the following March and aroused the South to fury. Special laws were passed and demands made that Walker be punished. He died in 1830, possibly by foul play.

6. THE FUGITIVE SLAVE

Beside force and the appeal to reason there was a third method which practically was more effective and decisive for eventual abolition, and that was the escape from slavery through running away. On the islands this meant escape to the mountains and existence as brigands. In South

America it meant escape to the almost impenetrable forest.

As I have said elsewhere:[30]

"One thing saved the South from the blood sacrifice of Haiti—not, to be sure, from so successful a revolt, for the disproportion of races was less, but from a desperate and bloody effort—and that was the escape of the fugitive.

"Along the Great Black Way stretched swamps and rivers and the forests and crests of the Alleghanies. A widening, hurrying stream of fugitives swept to the havens of refuge, taking the restless, the criminal and the unconquered—the natural leaders of the more timid mass. These men saved slavery and killed it. They saved it by leaving it to a false seductive dream of peace and the eternal subjugation of the laboring class. They destroyed it by presenting themselves before the eyes of the North and the world as living specimens of the real meaning of slavery."

"Three paths were opened to the slaves: to submit, to fight or to run away. Most of them submitted, as do most people everywhere, to force and fate. To fight singly meant death and to fight together meant plot and insurrection— a difficult thing, but one often tried. Easiest of all was to run away, for the land was wide and bare

[30] Du Bois' *John Brown,* pp. 82ff.

and the slaves were many. At first they ran to the swamps and mountains and starved and died. Then they ran to the Indians and in Florida founded a nation, to overthrow which cost the United States $20,000,000 and more in slave raids known as the Seminole 'wars.' Then gradually, after the War of 1812 had used so many black sailors to fight for free trade that the Negroes learned of the North and Canada as cities of refuge, they fled northward."

From the sixteenth century Florida Indians had Negro blood, but from early part of the nineteenth century the Seminoles gained a large new infiltration of Negro blood from the numbers of slaves who fled to them and with whom they intermarried. The first Seminole war, therefore, in 1818 was not simply a defense of the frontiers against the Indians and a successful raid to drive Spain from Florida, it was also a slave raid by Georgia owners determined to have back their property. By 1815 Negroes from Georgia among the Creeks and Seminoles numbered not less than 11,000 and were settled along the Appalachicola river, many of them with good farms and with a so-called Negro "fort" for protection. The war was disastrous to Negroes and Indians but not fatal and in 1822 some 800 Negroes were counted among the Indians who inhabited the new terri-

tory seized from Spain. Pressure to secure alleged
fugitives and Negroes from the Indians was kept
up for the next three years and the second Seminole war broke out because the whites treacherously seized the mulatto wife of the Indian chief
Osceola. The war broke out in 1837 and its real
nature, as a New Orleans paper said in 1839, was
to subdue the Seminoles and decrease the danger
of uprisings "among the serviles." Finally after
a total cost of twenty million dollars the Indians
were subdued and moved to the West and a part
of the Negroes driven back into slavery, but not
all.[31]

Through the organization which came to be
known as the Underground Railroad, thousands
of slaves escaped through Kentucky and into the
Middle West and thence into Canada and also by
way of the Appalachian Mountains into Pennsylvania and the East. Not only were they helped
by white abolitionists but they were guided by
black men and women like Joshua Henson and
Harriet Tubman.

Beside this there came the effort for emigration
to Africa which was very early suggested. Two
colored men sailed from New York for Africa in
1774 but the Revolutionary War stopped the
effort thus begun. The Virginia legislature in

[31] Cf. Joshua R. Giddings, *Exiles of Florida,* Columbus, Ohio, 1858.

secret session after Gabriel's insurrection in 1800, tried to suggest the buying of some land for the colonization of free Negroes, following the proposal of Thomas Jefferson made in 1781. Paul Cuffee, mentioned above, started the actual migration in 1815 carrying nine colored families, thirty-eight persons in all, to Sierra Leone at an expense of $4,000 which he paid himself. Finally came the American Colonization Society in 1817 but it was immediately turned from a real effort to abolish slavery gradually into an effort to get rid of free Negroes and obstreperous slaves. Even the South saw it and Robert Y. Hayne said in Congress: "While this process is going on, the colored classes are gradually diffusing themselves throughout the country and are making steady advances in intelligence and refinement and if half the zeal were displayed in bettering their condition that is now wasted in the vain and fruitless effort of sending them abroad, their intellectual and moral improvement would be steady and rapid."

7. BARGAINING

The Negro early learned a lesson which he may yet teach the modern world and which may prove his crowning gift to America and the world: Force begets force and you cannot in the end run away successfully from the world's problems. The

Negro early developed the shrewd foresight of recognizing the fact that as a minority of black folk in a growing white country, he could not win his battle by force. Moreover, for the mass of Negroes it was impracticable to run away and find refuge in some other land.

Even the appeal to reason had its limitations in an unreasoning land. It could not unfortunately base itself on justice and right in the midst of the selfish, breathless battle to earn a living. There was however a chance to prove that justice and self interest sometimes go hand in hand. Force and flight might sometimes help but there was still the important method of co-operating with the best forces of the nation in order to help them to win and in order to prove that the Negro was a valuable asset, not simply as a laborer but as a worker for social uplift, as an American. Sometimes this co-operation was in simple and humble ways and nevertheless striking. There was, for instance, the yellow fever epidemic in Philadelphia in 1793. The blacks were not suffering from it or at least not supposed to suffer from it as much as the whites. The papers appealed to them to come forward and help with the sick. Led by Jones, Gray and Allen, Negroes volunteered their services and worked with the sick and in burying the dead, even spending some of their own funds in the gruesome duty. The same thing happened much later in New Orleans, Memphis and Cuba.

In larger ways it must be remembered that the Abolition crusade itself could not have been successful without the co-operation of Negroes. Black folk like Remond, Frederick Douglass, and Sojourner Truth, were not simply advocates for freedom but were themselves living refutations of the whole doctrine of slavery. Their appeal was tremendous in its efficiency and besides, the free Negroes helped by work and money to spread the Abolition campaign.[32]

In addition to this there was much deliberate bargaining,—careful calculation on the part of the Negro that if the whites would aid them, they in turn would aid the whites at critical times and that otherwise they would not. Much of this went on at the time of the Revolution and was clearly recognized by the whites.

Alexander Hamilton (himself probably of Negro descent) said in 1779: "The contempt we have been taught to entertain for the blacks makes us fancy many things that are founded neither in reason nor experience; and an unwillingness to part with property of so valuable a kind will furnish a thousand arguments to show the impractic-

[32] Among the first subscribers to Garrison's *Liberator* were free Negroes and one report is that the very first paid subscriber was a colored Philadelphia caterer.

ability or pernicious tendency of a scheme which requires such a sacrifice. But it should be considered that if we do not make use of them in this way, the enemy probably will; and that the best way to counteract the temptations they will hold out will be to offer them ourselves. An essential part of the plan is to give them their freedom with their muskets. This will secure their fidelity, animate their courage, and, I believe, will have a good influence upon those who remain by opening a door to their emancipation. This circumstance, I confess, has no small weight in inducing me to wish the success of the project; for the dictates of humanity and true policy equally interest me in favor of this unfortunate class of men."[33]

Dr. Hopkins wrote in 1776: "God is so ordering it in His providence that it seems absolutely necessary something should speedily be done with respect to the slaves among us in order to our safety and to prevent their turning against us in our present struggle in order to get their liberty. Our oppressors have planned to gain the blacks and induce them to take up arms against us by promising them liberty on this condition; and this plan they are prosecuting to the utmost of their power. . . . The only way pointed out to prevent this threatening evil is to set the blacks at liberty our-

[33] Livermore, p. 170.

selves by some public acts and laws; and then give
them proper encouragement to labor or take arms
in the defense of the American cause, as they shall
choose. This would at once be doing them some
degree of justice and defeating our enemies in the
scheme they are prosecuting."[34]

When Dunmore appealed to the slaves of Virginia at the beginning of the Revolution, the
slave owners issued an almost plaintive counter
appeal:

"Can it, then, be supposed that the Negroes will
be better used by the English who have always
encouraged and upheld this slavery than by their
present masters who pity their condition; who
wish, in general, to make it easy and comfortable
as possible; and who would, were it in their power,
or were they permitted, not only prevent any
more Negroes from losing their freedom but restore it to such as have already unhappily lost
it?"[35]

In the South, where Negroes for the most part
were not received as soldiers, the losses of the
slaveholders by defection among the slaves was
tremendous. John Adams says that the Georgia
delegates gave him "a melancholy account of the
State of Georgia and South Carolina. They said

[34] Livermore, pp. 125-6.
[35] Force's Archives, 4th series, Vol. 3, p. 1387.

if one thousand regular troops should land in Georgia and their commander be provided with arms and clothes enough and proclaim freedom to all the Negroes who would join his camp, twenty thousand Negroes would join it from the two provinces in a fortnight. The Negroes have a wonderful art of communicating intelligence among themselves; it will run several hundreds of miles in a week or fortnight. They said their only security was this,—that all the King's friends and tools of Government have large plantations and property in Negroes, so that the slaves of the Tories would be lost as well as those of the Whigs."[36]

Great Britain, after Cornwallis surrendered, even dreamed of reconquering America with Negroes. A Tory wrote to Lord Dunmore in 1782:

"If, my Lord, this scheme is adopted, arranged and ready for being put in execution, the moment the troops penetrate into the country after the arrival of the promised re-enforcements, America is to be conquered with its own force (I mean the Provincial troops and the black troops to be raised), and the British and Hessian army could be spared to attack the French where they are most vulnerable. . . ."

[36] Works of John Adams, Vol. 2, p. 428.

" 'What! Arm the slaves? We shudder at the very idea, so repugnant to humanity, so barbarous and shocking to human nature,' etc. One very simple answer is, in my mind, to be given: Whether it is better to make this vast continent become an acquisition of power, strength and consequence to Great Britain again, or tamely give it up to France who will reap the fruits of American independence to the utter ruin of Britain? . . . experience will, I doubt not, justify the assertion that by embodying the most hardy, intrepid and determined blacks, they would not only keep the rest in good order but by being disciplined and under command be prevented from raising cabals, tumults, and even rebellion, what I think might be expected soon after a peace; but so far from making even our lukewarm friends and secret foes greater enemies by this measure, I will, by taking their slaves, engage to make them better friends."[37]

On the other hand, the Colonial General Greene wrote to the Governor of South Carolina the same year:

"The natural strength of the country in point of numbers appears to me to consist much more in the blacks than in the whites. Could they be incorporated and employed for its defence, it would

[37] Livermore, pp. 183, 184.

afford you double security. That they would make good soldiers, I have not the least doubt; and I am persuaded the State has it not in its power to give sufficient re-enforcements without incorporating them either to secure the country if the enemy mean to act vigorously upon an offensive plan or furnish a force sufficient to dispossess them of Charleston should it be defensive."

This spirit of bargaining, more or less carefully carried out, can be seen in every time of stress and war. During the Civil War certain groups of Negroes sought repeatedly to make terms with the Confederacy. Judah Benjamin said at a public meeting in Richmond in 1865:

"We have 680,000 blacks capable of bearing arms and who ought now to be in the field. Let us now say to every Negro who wishes to go into the ranks on condition of being free, go and fight —you are free. My own Negroes have been to me and said, 'Master, set us free and we'll fight for you.' You must make up your minds to try this or see your army withdrawn from before your town. I know not where white men can be found."[38]

Robert E. Lee said: "We should not expect slaves to fight for prospective freedom when they can secure it at once by going to the enemy in

[38] Wilson, pp. 491-92.

whose service they will incur no greater risk than
in ours. The reasons that induce me to recommend the employment of Negro troops at all render the effect of the measures I have suggested
upon slavery immaterial and in my opinion the
best means of securing the efficiency and fidelity of
the auxiliary force would be to accompany the
measure with a well-digested plan of gradual and
general emancipation. As that will be the result
of the continuance of the war and will certainly
occur if the enemy succeed, it seems to me most
advisable to adopt it at once and thereby obtain
all the benefits that will accrue to our cause.

"The employment of Negro troops under regulations similar to those indicated would, in my
opinion, greatly increase our military strength and
enable us to relieve our white population to some
extent. I think we could dispense with the reserve forces except in cases of emergency. It
would disappoint the hopes which our enemies
have upon our exhaustion, deprive them in a great
measure of the aid they now derive from black
troops and thus throw the burden of the war upon
their own people. In addition to the great political advantages that would result to our cause from
the adoption of a system of emancipation, it
would exercise a salutary influence upon our Negro
population by rendering more secure the fidelity

of those who become soldiers and diminishing inducements to the rest to abscond."[39]

At the time of the World War there was a distinct attitude on the part of the Negro population that unless they were recognized in the draft and had Negro officers and were not forced to become simply laborers, they would not fight and while expression of this determination was not always made openly it was recognized even by an administration dominated by Southerners. Especially were there widespread rumors of German intrigue among Negroes, which had some basis of fact.

Within the Negro group every effort for organization and uplift was naturally an effort toward the development of American democracy. The motive force of democracy has nearly always been the push from below rather than the aristocratic pull from above; the effort of the privileged classes to outstrip the surging forward of the bourgeoisie has made groups and nations rise; the determination of the "poor whites" in the South not to be outdone by the "nigger" has been caused by the black man's frantic efforts to rise rather than by any innate ambition on the part of the lower class of whites. It was a push from be-

[39] J. T. Wilson, *The History of the Black Phalanx*, Hartford, 1897, p. 490.

low and it made the necessity of recognizing the
white laborer even more apparent.   The great
democratic movement which took place during the
reign of Andrew Jackson from 1829-1837 was
caused in no small degree by the persistent striving
of the Negroes.   They began their meeting together in conventions in 1830, they organized migration to Canada.[40]   In the trouble with Canada
in 1837 and 1838 Negro refugees from America
helped to defend the frontiers.   Bishop Loguen
says: "The colored population of Canada at that
time was small compared to what it now is; nevertheless, it was sufficiently large to attract the
attention of the government.   They were almost
to a man fugitives from the States.   They could
not, therefore, be passive when the success of the
invaders would break the only arm interposed for
their security, and destroy the only asylum for
African freedom in North America.   The prompt-
ness with which several companies of blacks were
organized and equipped, and the desperate valor
they displayed in this brief conflict, are an earnest
of what may be expected from the welling thousands of colored fugitives collecting there, in the
event of a war between the two countries."[41]

In America during this time they sought to

[40] Cf. Cromwell, *Negro in American History,* Chapter 2.
[41] J. W. Loguen, *As a Slave and as a Freeman,* p. 344.

establish a manual training college, they established their first weekly newspaper and they made a desperate fight for admission to the schools. They helped thus immeasurably the movement for universal popular education, joined the anti-slavery societies and organized churches and beneficial societies; bought land and continued to appeal. Wealthy free Negroes began to appear even in the South, as in the case of Jehu Jones, proprietor of a popular hotel in Charleston, and later Thomé Lafon of New Orleans who accumulated nearly a half million dollars and eventually left it to Negro charities which still exist. In the North there were tailors and lumber merchants and the guild of the caterers; taxable property slowly but surely increased.

All this in a peculiar way forced a more all-embracing democracy upon America, and it blossomed to fuller efficiency after the Civil War.

CHAPTER V

THE RECONSTRUCTION OF FREEDOM

How the black fugitive, soldier and freedman
after the Civil War helped to restore the Union,
establish public schools, enfranchise the poor
white and initiate industrial democracy in
America.

There have been four great steps toward
democracy taken in America: The refusal to be
taxed by the English Parliament; the escape from
European imperialism; the discarding of New
England aristocracy; and the enfranchisement of
the Negro slave.

What did the Emancipation of the slave really
mean? It meant such property rights as would
give him a share in the income of southern
industry large enough to support him as a
modern free laborer; and such a legal status as
would enable him by education and experience to
bear his responsibility as a worker and citizen.
This was an enormous task and meant the transformation of a slave holding oligarchy into a
modern industrial democracy.

184

Who could do this?   Some thought it done
by the Emancipation Proclamation and the 13th
amendment and Garrison with naive faith in bare
law abruptly stopped the issue of the *Liberator*
when the slave was declared "free."   The Negro
was not freed by edict or sentiment but by the
Abolitionists backed by the persistent action of
the slave himself as fugitive, soldier and voter.

Slavery was the cause of the war.   There might
have been other questions large enough and important enough to have led to a disruption of the
Union but none have successfully done so except
slavery.   But the North fought for union and not
against slavery and for a long time it refused to
recognize that the Civil War was essentially a
war against Negro slavery.   Abraham Lincoln
said to Horace Greeley as late as August, 1862,
"If there be those who would not save the Union
unless they could at the same time destroy slavery,
I do not agree with them.   My paramount object
is to save the Union and not either to save or
destroy slavery."

Despite this attitude it was evident very soon
that the Nation was fighting against the symptom
of disease and not against the cause.   If we look
at the action of the North taken by itself, we find
these singular contradictions: They fought for the
Union; they suddenly emancipated the slave; they

enfranchised the Freedmen; they abandoned the Freedmen. If now this had been the deliberate action of the North it would have been a crazy program; but it was not. The action of the American Negro himself forced the nation into many of these various contradictions; and the motives of the Negro were primarily economic. He was trying to achieve economic emancipation. And it is this fact that makes Reconstruction one of the greatest attempts to spread democracy which the modern world has seen.

There were in the South in 1860, 3,838,765 Negro slaves and 258,346 free Negroes. The question of land and fugitive slaves had precipitated the war: that is, if slavery was to survive it had to have more slave territory, and this the North refused. Moreover if slavery was to survive the drain of fugitive slaves must stop or the slave trade be reopened. The North refused to consider the reopening of the slave trade and only half-heartedly enforced the fugitive slave laws.

No sooner then did the war open in April, 1861, than two contradictory things happened: Fugitive slaves began to come into the lines of the Union armies at the very time that Union Generals were assuring the South that slavery would not be interfered with. In Virginia, Colonel Tyler said "The relation of master and ser-

vant as recognized in your state shall be respected." At Port Royal, General T. W. Sherman declared that he would not interfere with
"Your social and local institution." Dix in Virginia refused to admit fugitive slaves within his
lines and Halleck in Missouri excluded them.
Later, both Buell at Nashville and Hooker on the
upper Potomac allowed their camps to be searched
by masters for fugitive slaves.[1]

Against this attitude, however, there appeared,
even in the first year of the War, some unanswer-
able considerations. For instance three slaves
escaped into General Butler's lines at Fortress
Monroe just as they were about to be sent to
North Carolina to work on Confederate fortifications. Butler immediately said "These men are
contraband of war, set them at work." Butler's
action was sustained.[2] But when Fremont, in
August freed the slaves of Missouri under martial
law, declaring it an act of war, Lincoln hastened
to repudiate his action;[3] and the same thing happened the next year when Hunter at Hilton
Head, S. C. declared "Slavery and martial law in
a free country . . . incompatible."[4] Neverthe-

[1] George W. Williams, *History of the Negro Race in America,* New York, 1882, Vol. 1, Chapter 15.
[2] Williams, Vol. 1, pp. 250-1.
[3] Williams, Vol. 2, pp. 255-7.
[4] Williams, Vol. 1, pp. 257-9.

less here loomed difficulty and the continued coming of the fugitive slaves increased the difficulty and forced action.

The year 1862 saw the fugitive slave recognized as a worker and helper within the Union lines and eventually as a soldier bearing arms. Thousands of black men during that year, of all ages and both sexes, clad in rags and with their bundles on their backs, gathered wherever the Union Army gained foothold — at Norfolk, Hampton, at Alexandria and Nashville and along the border towards the West. There was sickness and hunger and some crime but everywhere there was desire for employment. It was in vain that Burnside was insisting that slavery was not to be touched and that McClellan repeated this on his Peninsular Campaign.

A change of official attitude began to appear as indeed it had to. When for instance General Saxton, with headquarters at Beauford, S. C., took military control of that district, he began to establish market houses for the sale of produce from the plantations and to put the Negroes to work as wage laborers. When, in the West, Grant's army occupied Grand Junction, Mississippi and a swarm of fugitives appeared, naked and hungry, some were employed as teamsters, servants and cooks and finally Grant appointed a

"Chief of Negro affairs" for the entire district under his jurisdiction. Crops were harvested, wages paid, wood cutters swarmed in forests to furnish fuel for the Federal gun-boats, cabins were erected and a regular "Freedmen's Bureau" came gradually into operation. The Negroes thus employed as regular helpers and laborers in the army, swelled to more than 200,000 before the end of the war; and if we count transient workers and spies who helped with information, the number probably reached a half million.

If now the Negro could work for the Union Army why could he not also fight? We have seen in the last chapter how the nation hesitated and then yielded in 1862. The critical Battle of Antietam took place September 17th and the confederate avalanche was checked. Five days later, Abraham Lincoln proclaimed that he was going to recommend an appropriation by Congress for encouraging the gradual abolition of slavery through payment for the slaves; and that on the following January 1st, in all the territory which was still at war with the United States, he proposed to declare the slaves free as a military measure.[5] Thus the year 1862 saw the Negro as an active worker in the army and as a soldier.

[5] Preliminary Emancipation Proclamation, Sept. 22, 1862.

This fact together with the Emancipation Proclamation of January 1st, made the year 1863 a significant year. Not only were most of the slaves legally freed by military edict but by the very fact of their emancipation the stream of fugitives became a vast flood. The Army had to organize departments and appoint officials for the succor and guidance of these fugitives in their work; relief on a large scale began to appear from the North and the demand of the Negro for education began to be felt in the starting of schools here and there.

"The fugitives poured into the lines and gradually were used as laborers and helpers. Immediately teaching began and gradually schools sprang up. When at last the Emancipation Proclamation was issued and Negro soldiers called for, it was necessary to provide more systematically for Negroes. Various systems and experiments grew up here and there. The Freedmen were massed in large numbers at Fortress Monroe, Va., Washington, D. C., Beaufort and Port Royal, S. C., New Orleans, La., Vicksburg and Corinth, Miss., Columbus, Ky., Cairo, Ill., and elsewhere. In such places schools immediately sprang up under the army officers and chaplains. The most elaborate system, perhaps, was that under General Banks in Louisiana. It was established in 1863 and soon had a regular Board of Education, which laid and collected taxes and supported eventually nearly a hundred schools with ten thousand pupils, under 162 teachers. At Port Royal, S. C., were gathered Edward L. Pierce's 'Ten Thousand Clients'. . . . In the west, General Grant appointed Colonel John Eaton, afterwards United States Commissioner of Education to be Superintendent of Freedmen in 1862. He sought to consolidate and regulate the schools already established and succeeded in organizing a large system."[6]

The Treasury Department of the Government, solicitous for the cotton crop, took charge of certain plantations in order to encourage the workers and preserve the crop. Thus during the Spring of 1863, there were groups of Freedmen and refugeesin long broken lines between the two armies reaching from Maryland to the Kansas border and down the coast from Norfolk to New Orleans.

In 1864 a significant action took place: the petty and insulting discrimination in the pay of white and colored soldiers was stopped. The Negro began to be a free man and the center of the problem of Emancipation became land and organized industry. Eaton, the Superintendent of

[6] Atlanta University Publications, Atlanta, Ga., 1906, No. 8, p. 23.

Freedmen reports, July 15, for his particular district:

"These Freedmen are now disposed of as follows: In military service as soldiers' laundresses, cooks, officers' servants and laborers in the various staff departments, 41,150; in cities, on plantations and in freedmen's villages and cared for, 72,500. Of these 62,300 are entirely self-supporting—the same as any individual class anywhere else—as planters, mechanics, barbers, hackmen, draymen, etc., conducting on their own responsibility or working as hired laborers. The remaining 10,200 receive subsistence from the government. Three thousand of them are members of families whose heads are carrying on plantations and have under cultivation 4,000 acres of cotton. They are to pay the government for their subsistence from the first income of the crop. The other 7,200 include the paupers, that is to say, all Negroes over and under the self-supporting age, the crippled and sick in hospitals, of the 113,650, and those engaged in their care. Instead of being unproductive this class has now under cultivation 500 acres of corn, 970 acres of vegetables and 1,500 acres of cotton besides working at wood-chopping and other industries. There are reported in the aggregate over 100,000 acres of cotton under cultivation. Of these about 7,000 acres are leased and cultivated by blacks. Some Negroes are managing as high as 300 or 400 acres. . . ."[7]

The experiment at Davis Bend, Mississippi, was of especial interest: "Late in the season — in November and December, 1864,—the Freedmen's Department was restored to full control over the camps and plantations on President's Island and Palmyra or Davis Bend. Both these points had been originally occupied at the suggestion of General Grant and were among the most successful of our enterprises for the Negroes. With the expansion of the lessee system, private interests were allowed to displace the interest of the Negroes whom we had established there under the protection of the government, but orders issued by General N. J. T. Dana, upon whose sympathetic and intelligent co-operation my officers could always rely, restored to us the full control of these lands. The efforts of the freedmen on Davis Bend were particularly encouraging, and this property under Colonel Thomas' able direction, became in reality the "Negro Paradise" that General Grant had urged us to make of it."[8]

The United States Treasury went further in overseeing Freedmen and abandoned lands and appointed special agents over "Freedmen's home

[7] John Eaton, *Grant, Lincoln and the Freedmen,* New York, 1907, p. 134.
[8] Eaton, 165.

colonies." Down the Mississippi Valley, General
Thomas issued a lengthy series of instructions covering industry. He appointed three Commissioners to lease plantations and care for the employees; fixed the rate of wages and taxed cotton.
At Newbern, N. C., there were several thousand
refugees to whom land was assigned and about
800 houses rented. After Sherman's triumphant
March to the Sea, Secretary Stanton himself went
to Savannah to investigate the condition of the
Negroes.

It was significant that even this early Abraham
Lincoln himself was suggesting limited Negro
suffrage. Already he was thinking of the reconstruction of the states; Louisiana had been in
Union hands for two years and Lincoln wrote to
Governor Hahn, March 13th, 1864: "Now you
are about to have a convention, which, . . . will
probably define the elective franchise. I barely
suggest, for your private consideration, whether
some of the colored people may not be let in, as,
for instance, the very intelligent, and especially
those who have fought gallantly in our ranks.
They would probably help, in some trying time to
come, to keep the jewel of liberty within the family
of freedom. But this is only a suggestion, not to
the public, but to you alone."[9]

[9] Walter L. Fleming, *Documentary History of Reconstruction*, Cleveland, Ohio, 1907, Vol. 1, p. 112.

Here again the development had been logical.
The Negroes were voting in many Northern
states. At least one-half million of them were taking part in the war, nearly 200,000 as armed soldiers. They were beginning to be reorganized in
industry by the army officials as free laborers.
Naturally the question must come sooner or later:
Could they be expected to maintain their freedom, either political or economic, unless they had
a vote? And Lincoln with rare foresight saw
this several months before the end of the war.

The year 1865 brought fully to the front the
question of Negro suffrage and Negro free labor.
They were recognized January 16th, when Sherman settled large numbers of Negroes on the Sea
Islands. His order said:

"The Islands from Charleston, south, the
abandoned rice fields along the rivers for thirty
miles from the sea, and the country bordering the
St. John's river, Florida, are reserved and set
apart for the settlement of the Negroes now made
free by the acts of war and the proclamation of the
President of the United States.

"At Beaufort, Hilton Head, Savannah, Fernan-
dina, St. Augustine, and Jacksonville, the blacks
may remain in their chosen or accustomed voca-
tions but on the islands, and in the settlements hereafter to be established, no white person whatever,

unless military officers and soldiers detailed for
duty, will be permitted to reside; and the sole and
exclusive management of affairs will be left to the
freed people themselves, subject only to the
United States military authority and the acts
of Congress. By the laws of war and orders
of the President of the United States the
Negro is free, and must be dealt with as
such. He cannot be subjected to conscription
or forced military service, save by the written
orders of the highest military authority of the
department, under such regulations as the President or Congress may prescribe. Domestic
servants, blacksmiths, carpenters, and other
mechanics, will be free to select their own work
and residence, but the young and able-bodied
Negroes must be encouraged to enlist as soldiers
in the service of the United States, to contribute
their share towards maintaining their own freedom, and securing their rights as citizens of the
United States.

"Whenever three respectable Negroes, heads of
families shall desire to settle on lands, and shall
have selected for that purpose an island or a
locality clearly defined, within the limits above
designated, the Inspector of Settlements and
Plantations will himself, or by such subordinate
officer as he may appoint, give them a license to

settle such island or district, and afford them such
assistance as he can to enable them to establish a
peaceful agricultural settlement.   The three parties named will subdivide the land, under the
supervision of the Inspector, among themselves
and such others as may choose to settle near them,
so that each family shall have a plot of not more
than forty (40) acres of tillable ground, and when
it borders on some water channel, with not more
than 800 feet water front, in the possession of
which land the military authorities will afford
them protection until such time as they can protect themselves, or until Congress shall regulate
their title."[10]

On March 3, 1865 the Nation came to the part-
ing of the ways.   Two measures passed Congress on this momentous date.   First, a Freedmen's Bank was incorporated at Washington "to
receive on deposit therefore, by or on behalf of
persons heretofore held in slavery in the United
States or their descendants, and investing the same
in the stocks, bonds, Treasury notes, or other
securities of the United States."[11]   The first year
it had $300,000 of deposits and the deposits in-
creased regularly until in 1871 there were nearly
$20,000,000.   Also on March 3rd, the Freed-

[10] Fleming, Vol. 1, pp. 350-1.
[11] Fleming, Vol. 2, p. 382.

men's Bureau Act was passed. The war was over. Sometime the South must have restored home rule. When that came what would happen to the freedmen?

These paths were before the nation:

1. They might abandon the freedman to the mercy of his former masters.

2. They might for a generation or more make the freedmen the wards of the nation—protecting them, encouraging them, educating their children, giving them land and a minimum of capital and thus inducting them into real economic and political freedom.

3. They might force a grant of Negro suffrage, support the Negro voters for a brief period and then with hands off let them sink or swim.

The second path was the path of wisdom and statesmanship. But the country would not listen to such a comprehensive plan. If the form of this Bureau had been worked out by Charles Sumner today instead of sixty years ago, it would have been regarded as a proposal far less revolutionary than the modern labor legislation of America and Europe. A half-century ago, however, and in a country which gave the *laisser-faire* economics their extremest trial the Freedmen's Bureau struck the whole nation as unthinkable save as a very temporary expedient and to relieve the more

pointed forms of distress following war. Yet the
proposals of the Bureau as actually established
by the laws of 1865 and 1866 were both simple
and sensible:

1. To oversee the making and enforcement of
wage contracts.

2. To appear in the courts as the freedmen's
best friend.

3. To furnish the freedmen with a minimum of
land and of capital.

4. To establish schools.

5. To furnish such institutions of relief as hospitals, outdoor stations, etc.

How a sensible people could expect really to
conduct a slave into freedom with less than this is
hard to see. Of course even with such tutelage
extending over a period of two or three decades
the ultimate end had to be enfranchisement and
political and social freedom for those freedmen
who attained a certain set standard. Otherwise
the whole training had neither object nor guaran-
tee.

Naturally the Bureau was no sooner established
than it faced implacable enemies. The white
South naturally opposed to a man because it practically abolished private profit in the exploitation
of labor. To step from slave to free labor was
economic catastrophe in the opinion of the white

South: but to step further to free labor organized primarily for the laborers' benefit, this not only was unthinkable for the white South but it even touched the economic sensibilities of the white North. Already the nation owed a staggering debt. It would not face any large increase for such a purpose. Moreover, who could conduct such an enterprise? It would have taxed in ordinary times the ability and self sacrifice of the nation to have found men in sufficient quantity who could and would have conducted honestly and efficiently such a tremendous experiment in human uplift. And these were not ordinary times.

Nevertheless a bureau had to be established at least temporarily as a clearing house for the numberless departments of the armies dealing with freedmen and holding land and property in their name.

As General Howard, the head of the Bureau said, this Bureau was really a government and partially ruled the South from the close of the war until 1870. "It made laws, executed them and interpreted them. It laid and collected taxes, defined and punished crime, maintained and used military force and dictated such measures as it thought necessary and proper for the accomplishment of its varied ends." Its establishment was a herculean task both physically and socially, and it

accomplished a great work before it was repudiated. Carl Schurz in 1864 felt warranted in saying, "Not half of the labor that has been done in
the South this year, or will be done there next
year, would have been or would be done but for
the exertions of the Freedmen's Bureau. . . . No
other agency, except one placed there by the national government, could have wielded the moral
power whose interposition was so necessary to prevent the Southern society from falling at once into
the chaos of a general collision between its different elements."[12]

The nation knew, however, that the Freedmen's
Bureau was temporary. What should follow it?
The attitude of the South was not reassuring.
Carl Schurz reported that: "Some planters held
back their former slaves on their plantations
by brute force. Armed bands of white men pa-
trolled the country roads to drive back the Negroes wandering about. Dead bodies of murdered
Negroes were found on and near the highways
and by-paths. Gruesome reports came from the
hospitals—reports of colored men and women
whose ears had been cut off, whose skulls had
been broken by blows, whose bodies had been
slashed by knives or lacerated by scourges. A

[12] Report of Carl Schurz to President Johnson, in Senate Exec. Doc.
No. 2, 39th Cong., 1st Sess.

number of such cases I had occasion to examine myself. A veritable reign of terror prevailed in many parts of the South. The Negro found scant justice in the local courts against the white man. He could look for protection only to the military forces of the United States still garrisoning the 'states lately in rebellion' and to the Freedmen's Bureau."[14]

The determination to reconstruct the South without recognizing the Negro as a voter was manifest. The provisional governments set up by Lincoln and Johnson were based on white male suffrage. In Louisiana for instance, where free Negroes had wealth and prestige and had furnished thousands of soldiers under the proposed reconstruction and despite Lincoln's tactful suggestion—"Not one Negro was allowed to vote, though at that very time the wealthy, intelligent free colored people of the State paid taxes on property assessed at $15,000,000 and many of them were well known for their patriotic zeal and love for the Union. Thousands of colored men whose homes were in Louisiana served bravely in the national army and navy and many of the so-called Negroes in New Orleans could not be distinguished by the most intelligent strangers from the best class of white gentlemen either by color or manner, dress or language; still, as it was

known by tradition and common fame that they
were not of pure Caucasian descent, they could
not vote."[13]

Johnson feared this Southern program and like
Lincoln suggested limited Negro suffrage. August 15th, 1865, he wrote to Governor Sharkey of
Mississippi: "If you could extend the elective franchise to all persons of color who can read the
Constitution of the United States in English and
write their names, and to all persons of color
who own real estate valued at not less than two
hundred and fifty dollars, and pay taxes thereon,
you would completely disarm the adversary and
set an example the other states will follow. This
you can do with perfect safety and you thus place
the Southern States, in reference to free persons of
color, upon the same basis with the free States. I
hope and trust your convention will do this."[14]

The answer of the South to all such suggestions
was the celebrated "Black Codes": "Alabama
declared 'stubborn or refractory servants' or
'those who loiter away their time' to be 'vagrants'
who could be hired out at compulsory service by
law, while all Negro minors, far from being sent
to school, were to be 'apprenticed' preferably to
their father's former 'masters and mistresses.' In

[13] Brewster, *Sketches of Southern Mystery, Treason and Murder*,
p. 116.
[14] McPherson, *Reconstruction*, p. 19.

Florida it was decreed that no Negro could 'own, use or keep any bowie-knife, dirk, sword, fire-arms or ammunition of any kind' without a license from the Judge of Probate. In South Carolina the Legislature declared that 'no person of color shall pursue the practice of art, trade or business of an artisan, mechanic or shopkeeper or any other trade or employment besides that of husbandry or that of servant under contract for labor until he shall have obtained a license from the Judge of the District Court. Mississippi required that 'if a laborer shall quit the service of the employer be-fore the expiration of his term of service without just cause, he shall forfeit his wages for that year.' Louisiana said that 'every adult freed man or woman shall furnish themselves with a comfort-able home and visible means of support within twenty days after the passage of this act' and that any failing to do so should 'be immediately arrested', delivered to the court and 'hired out' by public advertisement, to some citizen, being the highest bidder, for the remainder year."[15]

These Codes were not reassuring to the friends of freedom. To be sure it was not a time to ex-pect calm, cool, thoughtful action on the part of the South. Its economic condition was pitiable. Property in slaves to the extent perhaps of two

[15] Atlanta University Publications, Atlanta, Ga., 1901, No. 6, p. 36.

thousand million dollars had suddenly disappeared.   One thousand five hundred more
millions representing the Confederate war debt,
had largely disappeared.   Large amounts of real
estate and other property had been destroyed, industry had been disorganized, 250,000 men had
been killed and many more maimed.   With this
went the moral effect of an unsuccessful war with
all its letting down of social standards and quick-
ening of hatred and discouragement—a situation
which would make it difficult under any circumstances to reconstruct a new government and a
new civilization.   Moreover any human being of
any color "doomed in his own person and his posterity to live without knowledge and without capacity to make anything his own and to toil that
another may reap the fruits," is bound on sudden
emancipation to loom like a great dread on the
horizon.

The fear of Negro freedom in the South was
increased by its own consciousness of guilt, yet it
was reasonable to expect from it something
more than mere repression and reaction toward
slavery.   To some small extent this expectation
was fulfilled: the abolition of slavery was recognized and the civil rights of owning property and
appearing as a witness in cases in which he was a
party were generally granted the Negro; yet with

these went such harsh regulations as largely neu-
tralized the concessions and gave ground for the
assumption that once free from Northern control
the South would virtually re-enslave the Negro.
The colored people themselves naturally feared
this and protested, as in Mississippi, "against the
reactionary policy prevailing and expressing the
fear that the Legislature will pass such proscrip-
tive laws as will drive the freedmen from the State
or practically re-enslave them."[16]

As Professor Burgess (whom no one accuses of
being Negrophile) says: "Almost every act, word
or gesture of the Negro not consonant with good
taste and good manners as well as good morals
was made a crime or misdemeanor, for which he
could first be fined by the magistrates and then be
consigned to a condition of almost slavery for an
indefinite time if he could not pay the bill."

All things considered, it seems probable that if
the South had been permitted to have its way in
1865 the harshness of Negro slavery would have
been mitigated so as to make slave trading difficult
and to make it possible for a Negro to hold property if he got any and to appear in some cases in
court; but that in most other respects the blacks
would have remained in slavery.   And no small

[16] October 7, 1865.

number of whites even in the North were quite willing to contemplate such a solution.

In October, the democratic platform of Louisiana said "This is a government of white people," and although Johnson reported in December that Reconstruction was complete in North and South Carolina, Georgia, Alabama, Mississippi, Louisiana, Arkansas and Tennessee, yet everyone knew that the real problems of Reconstruction had just begun. The war caused by slavery could be stopped only by a real abolition of slavery.

It was as though the Germans invading France had found flocking to their camps the laboring forces of the invaded land, poor and destitute, but willing to work and willing to fight. What would have been the attitude of the successful invader when the war was ended? Gratitude alone counseled help for the Freedmen; wisdom counseled a real abolition of slavery; so far slavery had not been abolished in spite of the fact that the 13th Amendment proposed in February had been proclaimed in December. Freedom and citizenship were primarily a matter of state legislation; and emancipation from slavery was an economic problem—a question of work and wages, of land and capital — all these things were matters of state legislation. Unless then something was done to insure a proper legal status and legal protection for the Freedmen, the so-called abolition of slavery would be but a name. Furthermore there were grave political difficulties: According to the celebrated compromise in the Constitution, three-fifths of the slaves were counted in the Southern states as a basis of representation and this gave the white South as compared with the North a large political advantage. This advantage was now to be increased because, as freemen, the whole Negro population was to be counted and still the voting was confined to whites. The North, therefore, found themselves faced by the fact that the very people whom they had overcome in a costly and bloody war were now coming back with increased political power, with determination to keep just as much of slavery as they could and with freedom to act toward the nation that they had nearly destroyed, in whatever way the deep hatreds of a hurt and conquered people tempted them to act. All this was sinister and dangerous. Assume as large minded and forgiving an attitude as one could, either the abolition of slavery must be made real or the war was fought in vain.

The Negroes themselves naturally began to insist that without political power it was impossible to accomplish their economic freedom. Frederick Douglass said to President Johnson: "Your noble and humane predecessor placed in our hands the sword to assist in saving the nation and we do hope that you, his able successor, will favorably regard the placing in our hands the ballot with which to save ourselves." And when Johnson demurred on account of the hostility between blacks and poor whites, a committee of prominent colored men replied:

"Even if it were true, as you allege, that the hostility of the blacks toward the poor whites must necessarily project itself into a state of freedom, and that this enmity between the two races is even more intense in a state of freedom than in a state of slavery, in the name of heaven, we reverently ask, how can you, in view of your professed desire to promote the welfare of the black man, deprive him of all means of defense and clothe him, whom you regard as his enemy, in the panoply of political power?"[17]

Again as the Negro fugitive slave was already in camp before the nation was ready to receive him and was even trying to drive him back to his master; just as the Negro was already bearing arms before he was legally recognized as a soldier; so too he was voting before Negro suffrage was contemplated; to cite one instance at Davis Bend, Mississippi. "Early in 1865 a system was

[17] McPherson, pp. 52, 56.

adopted for their government in which the freedmen took a considerable part. The Bend was divided into districts, each having a sheriff and
judge appointed from among the more reliable
and intelligent colored men. A general oversight
of the proceedings was maintained by our officers
in charge, who confirmed or modified the findings
of the court. The shrewdness of the colored
judges was very remarkable, though it was sometimes necessary to decrease the severity of the
punishment they proposed. Fines and penal service on the Home Farm were the usual sentences
they imposed. Petty theft and idleness were the
most frequent causes of trouble, but my officers
were able to report that exposed property was as
safe on Davis Bend as it would be anywhere. The
community distinctly demonstrated the capacity of
the Negro to take care of himself and exercised
under honest and competent direction the functions of self-government."[18]

Carl Schurz said in his celebrated report: "The
emancipation of the slaves is submitted to only in
so far as chattel slavery in the old form could not
be kept up. But although the freedman is no
longer considered the property of the individual
master, he is considered the slave of society and

[18] A. U. Publications, No. 12, p. 38; Cf. also Fleming, Vol. 1,
p. 355.

all independent State legislation will share the tendency to make him such.

"The solution of the problem would be very much facilitated by enabling all the loyal and free labor elements in the South to exercise a healthy influence upon legislation. It will hardly be possible to secure the freedman against oppressive class legislation and private persecution unless he be endowed with a certain measure of political power."

To the argument of ignorance Schurz replied: "The effect of the extension of the franchise to the colored people upon the development of free labor and upon the security of human rights in the South being the principal object in view, the objections raised on the ground of the ignorance of the freedmen become unimportant. Practical liberty is a good school. . . . It is idle to say that it will be time to speak of Negro suffrage when the whole colored race will be educated, for the ballot may be necessary to him to secure his education."[19]

Thus Negro suffrage was forced to the front, not as a method of humiliating the South; not as a theoretical and dangerous gift to the Freedmen; not according to any preconcerted plan but simply because of the grim necessities of the situation. The North must either give up the fruits of war,

[19] Schurz' Report.

keep a Freedmen's Bureau for a generation or use
the Negro vote to reconstruct the Southern states
and to insure such legislation as would at least
begin the economic emancipation of the slave.

*In other words the North being unable to free
the slave, let him try to free himself. And he did,
and this was his greatest gift to this nation.*

Let us return to the steps by which the Negro
accomplished this task.

In 1866, the joint committee of Congress on
Reconstruction said that in the South: "A large
proportion of the population had become, instead
of mere chattels, free men and citizens. Through
all the past struggle these had remained true and
loyal and had, in large numbers, fought on the
side of the Union. It was impossible to abandon
them without securing them their rights as free
men and citizens. The whole civilized world
would have cried out against such base ingratitude
and the bare idea is offensive to all right thinking
men. Hence it became important to inquire what
could be done to secure their rights, civil and
political."

The report then proceeded to emphasize the
increased political power of the South and recommended the Fourteenth Amendment, since: "It
appeared to your committee that the rights of
these persons by whom the basis of representation

had been thus increased should be recognized by the General Government. While slaves, they were not considered as having any rights, civil or political. It did not seem just or proper that all the political advantages derived from their becoming free should be confined to their former masters who had fought against the Union and withheld from themselves who had always been loyal."[20]

Nor did there seem to be any hope that the South would voluntarily change its attitude within any reasonable time. As Carl Schurz wrote: "I deem it proper, however, to offer a few remarks on the assertion frequently put forth, that the franchise is likely to be extended to the colored man by the voluntary action of the southern whites themselves. My observation leads me to a contrary opinion. Aside from a very few enlightened men, I found but one class of people in favor of the enfranchisement of the blacks: it was the class of Unionists who found themselves politically ostracised and looked upon the enfranchisement of the loyal Negroes as the salvation of the whole loyal element. . . . The masses are strongly opposed to colored suffrage; anybody that dares to advocate it is stigmatized as a dangerous fanatic.

"The only manner in which, in my opinion, the southern people can be induced to grant to the

[20] House Reports, No. 30, 39th Congress, 1st Session.

freedmen some measure of self-protecting power in the form of suffrage, is to make it a consideration precedent to 'readmission'."[21]

During 1866, the Freedmen's Bureau received over a million dollars mostly from the Freedmen's fund, sales of crop, rent of lands and buildings and school taxes. The chief expenditure was in wages, rent and schools. It was evident that the Negro was demanding education. Schools arose immediately among the refugees and Negro soldiers. They were helped by voluntary taxation of the Negroes and then by the activity of Northern religious bodies. Seldom in the history of the world has an almost totally illiterate population been given the means of self-education in so short a time. The movement started with the Negroes themselves and they continued to form the dynamic force behind it. "This great multitude arose up simultaneously and asked for intelligence." There can be no doubt that these schools were a great conservative steadying force to which the South owes much. It must not be forgotten that among the agents of the Freedmen's Bureau were not only soldiers and politicians but school teachers and educational leaders like Ware and Cravath.

[21] Schurz' Report.

In 1866, nearly 100,000 Negroes were in the schools under 1300 teachers and schools for Negroes had been opened in nearly all the southern states. A second Freedmen's Bureau act was passed extending the work of the Bureau, and the Freedmen's Bank which had been started in 1865 and had by 1866 twenty branches and $300,000 in savings.

Congress came to blows with President Johnson. His plan of reconstruction with white male suffrage was repudiated and the 14th Amendment was proposed by Congress which was designed to force the South to accept Negro suffrage on penalty of losing a proportionate amount of their representation in Congress. The 14th Amendment was long delayed and did not in fact become a law until July, 1868. Meantime, Congress adopted more drastic measures. By the Reconstruction Acts, the first of which passed March 2nd, the South was divided into five military districts, Negro suffrage was established for the constitutional conventions and the 14th Amendment made a prerequisite for readmission of states to the Union.

What was the result? No language has been spared to describe the results of Negro suffrage as the worst imaginable. Every effort of historical and social science and propaganda have supported this view; and its acceptance has been well nigh universal, because it was so clearly to the interests of the chief parties involved to forget their own shortcomings and put the blame on the Negro. As a colored man put it, they closed the "bloody chasm" but closed up the Negro inside. Yet, without Negro suffrage, slavery could not have been abolished in the United States and while there were bad results arising from the enfranchisement of the slaves as there necessarily had to be, the main results were not bad. Let us not forget that the white South believed it to be of vital interest to its welfare that the experiment of Negro suffrage should fail ignominiously and that almost to a man the whites were willing to insure this failure either by active force or passive resistance; that beside this there were, as might be expected in a day of social upheaval, men, white and black, Northern and Southern, only too eager to take advantage of such a situation for feathering their own nests. The results in such case had to be evil but to charge the evil to Negro suffrage is unfair. It may be charged to anger, poverty, venality and ignorance, but the anger and poverty were the almost inevitable aftermath of war; the venality was much more reprehensible as exhibited among whites than among Negroes, and while ignorance was the curse of the Negroes, the fault was not theirs and they took the initiative to correct it.

Negro suffrage was without doubt a tremendous experiment but with all its manifest failure it succeeded to an astounding degree; it made the immediate re-establishment of the old slavery impossible and it was probably the only quick method of doing this; it gave the Freedmen's sons a chance to begin their education. It diverted the energy of the white South from economic development to the recovery of political power and in this interval—small as it was—the Negro took his first steps toward economic freedom. It was the greatest and most important step toward world democracy of all men of all races ever taken in the modern world.

Let us see just what happened when the Negroes gained the right to vote, first in the conventions which reconstructed the form of government and afterward in the regular state governments. The continual charge is made that the South was put under Negro government—that ignorant ex-slaves ruled the land. This is untrue. Negroes did not dominate southern legislatures, and in only two states did they have a majority of the legislature at any time. In Alabama in the years of 1868-69 there were 106 whites and 27 Negroes in the legislature; in the year 1876 there were 104

whites and 29 Negroes. In Arkansas, 1868-69
there were 8 Negroes and 96 whites. In Georgia
there were 186 whites and 33 Negroes. In Mis-
sissippi, 1870-1, there were 106 whites and 34
Negroes and in 1876, 132 whites and 21 Negroes.
In North Carolina, 149 whites and 21 Negroes; in
South Carolina 1868-69, 72 whites and 85 Ne-
groes and in 1876, 70 whites and 54 Negroes. In
Texas, 1870-71 there were 110 whites and 10 Ne-
groes. In Virginia, 1868-69, 119 whites and 18
Negroes and in 1876, 112 whites and 13
Negroes.[22]

"Statistics show, however, that with the exception of South Carolina and Mississippi, no state
and not even any department of a state government was ever dominated altogether by Negroes.
The Negroes never wanted and never had complete control in the Southern states. The most
important offices were generally held by white
men. Only two Negroes ever served in the United
States Senate, Hiram R. Revells and B. K. Bruce;
and only twenty ever became representatives in the
House and all these did not serve at the same
time, although some of them were elected for
more than one term."[23]

The Negroes who held office, held for the most

[22] *Journal of Negro History*, Vol. 5, p. 238.
[23] *Journal of Negro History*, Vol. 7, pp. 127ff.

part minor offices and most of them were ignorant
men. Some of them were venal and vicious but
this was not true in all cases. Indeed the Freedmen were pathetic too in their attempt to choose
the best persons but they were singularly limited
in their choice. Their former white masters were
either disfranchised or bitterly hostile or ready to
deceive them. The "carpet-baggers" often cheated
them; their own ranks had few men of experience
and training. Yet some of the colored men who
served them well deserve special mention:

Samuel J. Lee, a member of the South Carolina
legislature, was considered by the whites as one
of the best criminal lawyers of the state. When
he died local courts were adjourned and the whole
city mourned. Bishop Isaac Clinton who served
as Treasurer of Orangeburg, S. C. for eight years
was held in highest esteem by his white neighbors
and upon the occasion of his death business was
suspended as a mark of respect. In certain com-
munities Negroes were retained in office for years
after the restoration of Democratic party control
as, for example Mr. George Harriot in George-
town, S. C. who was Superintendent of Education
for the county. Beaufort, South Carolina, retained Negroes as sheriffs and school officials.

J. T. White who was Commissioner of Public
Works and Internal Improvements in Arkansas;

M. W. Gibbs who was Municipal Judge in Little Rock, and J. C. Corbin, who was State Superintendent of Schools in Arkansas, had creditable records.[24]   John R. Lynch, when speaker of Mississippi House of Representatives, was given a public testimonial by Republicans and Democrats and the leading Democratic paper said: "His bearing in office had been so proper and his rulings in such marked contrast to the partisan conduct of the ignoble whites of his party who have aspired to be leaders of the blacks, that the conservatives cheerfully joined in the testimonial."[25]

Of the colored treasurer of South Carolina, Governor Chamberlain said: "I have never heard one word or seen one act of Mr. Cardoza's which did not confirm my confidence in his personal integrity and his political honor and zeal for the honest administration of the State Government. On every occasion and under all circumstances he has been against fraud and jobbery and in favor of good measures and good men."[26]

Jonathan C. Gibbs, a colored man and the first State Superintendent of Instructions in Florida, was a graduate of Dartmouth.   He established the system and brought it to success, dying in har-

---

[24] *Journal of Negro History*, Vol. 7, p. 424.
[25] Jackson, Miss., *Clarion*, April 24, 1873.
[26] Walter Allen, *Governor Chamberlain's Administration in South Carolina*, New York, 1888, p. 82.

ness in 1874. The first Negro graduate of Harvard College served in South Carolina, before he became chief executive officer of the association that erected the Grant's Tomb in New York.

In Louisiana we may mention Acting-Governor Pinchback, and Lieutenant-Governor Dunn, and Treasurer Dubuclet who was investigated by United States officials. E. P. White, afterward Chief Justice of the United States, reported that his funds had been honestly handled. Such men —and there were others—ought not to be forgotten or confounded with other types of colored and white Reconstruction leaders.

Between 1871 and 1901, twenty-two Negroes sat in Congress—two as senators and twenty as representatives; three or four others were undoubtedly elected but were not seated. Ten of these twenty-two Negroes were college bred: Cain of South Carolina was trained at Wilberforce and afterward became bishop of the African Methodist Church; Revels was educated at Knox College, Illinois, or at a Quaker Seminary, in Indiana; Cheatham was a graduate of Shaw; Murray was trained at the University of South Carolina; Langston was a graduate of Oberlin; five others were lawyers of whom the most brilliant was Robert Brown Elliott; he was a graduate of Eton College, England; Rapier was educated in Canada and O'Hara studied at Howard University; Miller graduated from Lincoln and White from Howard University. The other twelve men were self-taught: one was a thriving merchant tailor, one a barber, three were farmers, one a photographer, one a pilot and one a merchant.[27]

Of those who served in the Senate, one served an unexpired term and the other six years. In the House, one representative served one term from Virginia. From North Carolina one served one term and two, two terms. Georgia was represented by a Negro for one term and Mississippi for two terms. South Carolina had eight representatives, two of them served five terms, three two terms, and the rest one term. Beside these there were other Negro office holders who were fully the peers of white men; and those without formal training in the schools were in many cases men of unusual force and native ability.

James G. Blaine who served with nearly all these men approved of sending them to Congress: "If it is to be viewed simply as an experiment, it was triumphantly successful. The colored men who took seats in both Senate and House did not appear ignorant or helpless. They were as a rule studious, earnest, ambitious men whose public

[27] *Journal of Negro History,* Vol. 7, pp. 127ff.

conduct—as illustrated by Mr. Revels and Mr.
Bruce in the Senate and by Mr. Rapier, Mr. Lynch
and Mr. Rainey in the House would be honorable
to any race. Coals of fire were heaped on the
heads of all their enemies when the colored men
in Congress heartily joined in removing the disabilities of those who had before been their oppressors, and who, with deep regret be it said,
have continued to treat them with injustice and
ignominy."[28]

He cites the magnanimity of Senator Rainey:
"When the Amnesty Bill came before the House
for consideration, Mr. Rainey of South Carolina,
speaking for the colored race whom he represented said: 'It is not the disposition of my con-
stituents that these disabilities should longer be
retained. We are desirous of being magnanimous;
it may be that we are so to a fault. Nevertheless
we have open and frank hearts towards those who
were our oppressors and taskmasters. We foster
no enmity now, and we desire to foster none, for
their acts in the past to us or to the Government we
love so well. But while we are willing to accord
them their enfranchisement and here today give
our votes that they may be amnestied, while we declare our hearts open and free from any vindictive
feelings toward them, we would say to those gen-

[28] Blaine, *Twenty Years in Congress*, Vol. 2, p. 515.

tlemen on the other side that there is another
class of citizens in the country who have certain
rights and immunities which they would like you,
sirs, to remember and respect. . . . We invoke
you gentlemen, to show the same kindly feeling
towards us, a race long oppressed, and in demon-
stration of this humane and just feeling, I implore
you, give support to the Civil Rights Bill, which
we have been asking at your hands, lo! these many
days."[29]

The chief charge against Negro governments
has to do with property. These governments are
charged with attacking property and the charge is
true. This, although not perhaps sensed at the
time, was their real reason for being. The ex-
slaves must have land and capital or they would
fall back into slavery. The masters had both;
there must be a transfer. It was at first proposed
that land be confiscated in the South and given to
the Freedmen. "Forty Acres and a Mule" was the
widespread promise made several times with official sanction. This was perhaps the least that the
United States Government could have done to insure emancipation, but such a program would have
cost money. In the early anger of the war, it
seemed to many fair to confiscate land for this
purpose without payment and some land was thus

[29] Blaine, *Twenty Years in Congress,* pp. 513-14.

sequestered.   But manifestly with all the losses of war and with the loss of the slaves it was unfair to take the land of the South without some compensation.   The North was unwilling to add to its tremendous debt anything further to insure the economic independence of the Freedmen.   The Freedmen therefore themselves with their political power and with such economic advantage as the war gave them, tried to get hold of land.

The Negro party platform of 1876, in one state, advocated "division of lands of the state as far as practical into small farms in order that the masses of our people may be enabled to become landholders."   In the Constitutional Convention of South Carolina, a colored man said: "One of the greatest of slavery bulwarks was the infernal plantation system, one man owning his thousand, another his twenty, another fifty thousands acres of land.   This is the only way by which we will break up that system, and I maintain that our freedom will be of no effect if we allow it to continue.   What is the main cause of the prosperity of the North.   It is because every man has his own farm and is free and independent.   Let the lands of the South be similarly divided.   I would not say for one moment they should be confiscated but if sold to maintain the war, now that slavery is destroyed, let the plantation system go with it. We will never have true freedom until we abolish the system of agriculture which existed in the Southern States. It is useless to have any schools while we maintain the stronghold of slavery as the agricultural system of the country."[30] This question kept coming up in the South Carolina convention and elsewhere. Such arguments led in South Carolina to a scheme to buy land and distribute it and some $800,000 was appropriated for this purpose.

In the second place, property was attacked through the tax system. The South had been terribly impoverished and was saddled with new social burdens. Many of the things which had been done well or indifferently by the plantations —like the punishment of crime and the care of the sick and the insane, and such schooling as there was, with most other matters of social uplift were, after the war, transferred to the control of the state. Moreover the few and comparatively indifferent public buildings of slavery days had been ruined either by actual warfare or by neglect. Thus a new and tremendous burden of social taxation was put upon the reconstructed states.

As a southern writer says of the state of Mississippi: "The work of restoration which the government was obliged to undertake, made in-

[30] Fleming, Vol. I, pp. 450-1.

creased expenses necessary. During the period of
the war, and for several years thereafter, public
buildings and state institutions were permitted to
fall into decay. The state house and grounds, the
executive mansion, the penitentiary, the insane
asylum, and the buildings for the blind, deaf and
dumb, were in a dilapidated condition and had to
be extended and repaired. A new building for the
blind was purchased and fitted up. The recon-
structionists established a public school system and
spent money to maintain and support it, perhaps
too freely, in view of the impoverishment of the
people. When they took hold, warrants were
worth but sixty or seventy cents on the dollar, a
fact which made the price of building materials
used in the work of construction correspondingly
higher."[31]

In addition to all this there was fraud and
stealing. There were white men who cheated and
secured large sums. Most of $800,000 appro-
priated for land in South Carolina was wasted in
graft. Bills for wine and furniture in South
Carolina were enormous; the printing bill of
Mississippi was ridiculously extravagant. Colored men shared in this loot but they at least had
some excuse. We may not forget that among slaves

[31] J. W. Garner, *Reconstruction in Mississippi*, New York, 1901.
p. 322.

stealing is not the crime that it becomes in free
industry. The slave is victim of a theft so hateful that nothing he can steal can ever match it.
The freedmen of 1868 still shared the slave
psychology. The larger part of the stealing was
done by white men—Northerners and Southerners
—and we must remember that it was not the first
time that there had been stealing and corruption
in the South and that the whole moral tone of
the nation had been ruined by war. For instance:

In 1839 it was reported in Mississippi that
ninety per cent of the fines collected by sheriffs
and clerks were unaccounted for. In 1841 the
State Treasurer acknowledged himself "at a loss
to determine the precise liabilities of the state and
her means of paying the same." And in 1839 the
auditor's books had not been posted for eighteen
months, no entries made for a year, and no
vouchers examined for three years. Congress
gave Jefferson College, Natchez, more than
46,000 acres of land; before the war this whole
property had "disappeared" and the college was
closed. Congress gave to Mississippi among
other states, the "16th section" of the public lands
for schools. In thirty years the proceeds of this
land in Mississippi were embezzled to the amount
of at least one and a half millions of dollars. In
Columbus, Mississippi a receiver of public monies

stole $100,000 and resigned. His successor stole
$55,000 and a treasury agent wrote: "Another
receiver would probably follow in the footsteps of
the two. You will not be surprised if I recommend
him being retained in preference to another ap-
pointment." From 1830 to 1860 southern men
in federal offices alone embezzled more than a
million dollars—a far greater sum then than now.

There might have been less stealing in the
South during Reconstruction without Negro suffrage but it is certainly highly instructive to remember that the mark of the thief which dragged
its slime across nearly every great Northern State
and almost up to the presidential chair could not
certainly in those cases be charged against the
vote of black men. This was the day when a
national Secretary of War was caught stealing, a
vice president presumably took bribes, a private
secretary of the president, a chief clerk of the
Treasury, and eighty-six government officials stole
millions in the Whiskey frauds; while the "Credit
Mobilier" filched millions and bribed the government to an extent never fully revealed; not to
mention less distinguished thieves like Tweed.

Is it surprising that in such an atmosphere a
new race learning the a-b-c of government should
have become the tools of thieves? And when they
did, was the stealing their fault or was it justly

chargeable to their enfranchisement? Then too,
a careful examination of the alleged stealing in
the South reveals much: First, there is repeated
exaggeration. For instance, it is said that the
taxation in Mississippi was fourteen times as great
in 1874 as in 1869. This sounds staggering until
we learn that the State taxation in 1869 was only
ten cents on one hundred dollars and that the expenses of government in 1874 were only twice as
great as in 1860 and that too with a depreciated
currency. It could certainly be argued that the
State government in Mississippi was doing enough
additional work in 1874 to warrant greatly increased cost. The character of much of the stealing shows who were the thieves. The frauds
through the manipulation of State and railway
bonds and of bank notes must have inured chiefly
to the benefit of experienced white men and this
must have been largely the case in the furnishing
and printing frauds. It was chiefly in the extravagance for "sundries and incidentals" and direct
money payments for votes that the Negroes received their share. The character of the real
thieving shows that white men must have been the
chief beneficiaries and that as a former South
Carolina slaveholder said:

"The legislature, ignorant as it is, could not
have been bribed without money; that must have

been furnished from some source that it is our duty
to discover. A legislature composed chiefly of our
former slaves has been bribed. One prominent
feature of this transaction is the part which native
Carolinians have played in it, some of our own
household men whom the State, in the past, has
delighted to honor, appealing to their cupidity and
avarice make them the instruments to effect the
robbery of their impoverished white brethren.
Our former slaves have been bribed by these men
to give them the privilege by law of plundering
the property holders of the state."[32]

Even those who mocked and sneered at Negro
legislators brought now and then words of praise:
"But beneath all this shocking burlesque upon
Legislative proceedings we must not forget that
there is something very real to this uncouth and
untutored multitude. It is not all shame, not all
burlesque. They have a genuine interest and a
genuine earnestness in the business of the assembly
which we are bound to recognize and respect. . . .
They have an earnest purpose, born of conviction
that their conditions are not fully assured, which
lends a sort of dignity to their proceedings. The
barbarous, animated jargon in which they so often
indulge is on occasion seen to be so transparently
sincere and weighty in their own minds that sym-

[32] Warley in *Brewster's Sketches*, p. 150 .

pathy supplants disgust. The whole thing is a
wonderful novelty to them as well as to observers.
Seven years ago these men were raising corn and
cotton under the whip of the overseer. Today
they are raising points of order and questions of
privilege. They find they can raise one as well as
the other. They prefer the latter. It is easier
and better paid. Then, it is the evidence of an
accomplished result. It means escape and defence
from old oppressors. It means liberty. It means
the destruction of prison walls only too real to
them. It is the sunshine of their lives. It is their
day of jubilee. It is their long promised vision of
the Lord God Almighty."[33]

But with the memory of the Freedmen's Bank
before it, America should utter no sound as to
Negro dishonesty during reconstruction. Here
from the entrenched philanthropy of America with
some of the greatest names of the day like Peter
Cooper, William Cullen Bryant, Simon P. Chase,
A. A. Low, Gerritt Smith, John Jay, A. S. Barnes,
S. G. Howe, George L. Stearns, Edward Atkinson, Levi Coffin and others, a splendid scheme was
launched to help the Freedmen save their pittance
and encourage thrift and hope. On the covers of
the pass books is said: "This is a benevolent insti-

[33] A Liberal Republican's description of the S. C. Legislature in 1871,
Fleming, Vol. 2, pp. 53-4.

tution and profits go to the depositors or to educational purposes for the Freedmen and their descendants. The whole institution is under the
charter of Congress and receives the commenda-
tion of the President, Abraham Lincoln." With
blare of trumpet it was chartered March 3rd,
1865; it collapsed in hopeless bankruptcy in 1873.
It had received fifty-six millions of dollars in de-
posits and failed owing over three millions most
of which was never repaid. A committee of Congress composed of both Democrats and Republicans said in 1876:

"The law lent no efficacy to the moral obligations assumed by the trustees, officers, and agents
and the whole concern inevitably became as a
'whited sepulchre'. . . . The inspectors . . .
were of little or no value, either through the connivance and ignorance of the inspectors or the in-
difference of the trustees to their reports. . . .
The committe of examination . . . were still
more careless and inefficient, while the board of
trustees, as a supervising and administrative body,
intrusted with the fullest power of general control
over the management, proved utterly faithless to
the trust reposed in them. . . .

"The depositors were of small account now
compared with the personal interest of the political jobbers, real estate pools, and fancy-stock

speculators, who were organizing a raid upon the Freedmen's money and resorted to . . . amendment of the charter to facilitate their operations. . . . This mass of putridity, the District government, now abhorred of all men, and abandoned and repudiated even by the political authors of its being, was represented in the bank by no less than five of its high officers . . . all of whom were in one way or other concerned in speculations involving a free use of the funds of the Freedmen's Bank. They were high in power, too, with the dominant influence in Congress, as the legislation they asked or sanctioned and obtained, fully demonstrated. Thus it was that without consulting the wishes or regarding the interests of those most concerned — the depositors — the vaults of the bank were literally thrown open to unscrupulous greed and rapacity. The toilsome savings of the poor Negroes hoarded and laid by for a rainy day, through the carelessness and dishonest connivance of their self-constituted guardians, melted away. . . ."[34]

Even in bankruptcy the institution was not allowed to come under the operation of the ordinary laws but was liquidated and protected by a special law, the liquidators picking its corpse and

[34] Fleming, Vol. I, pp. 382ff.

the helpless victims being finally robbed not only of their money but of much of their faith in white folk.

Let us laugh hilariously if we must over the golden spittoons of South Carolina but let us also remember that at most the freedmen filched bits from those who had all and not all from those who had nothing; and that the black man had at least the saving grace to hide his petty theft by enshrining the nasty American habit of spitting in the sheen of sunshine.

With all these difficulties and failings, what did the Freedmen in politics during the critical years of their first investment with the suffrage accomplish? We may recognize three things which Negro rule gave to the South:

1. Democratic government.
2. Free public schools.
3. New social legislation.

Two states will illustrate conditions of government in the South before and after Negro rule. In South Carolina there was before the war a property qualification for office holders, and in part, for voters. The Constitution of 1868, on the other hand, was a modern democratic document starting (in marked contrast to the old constitution) with a declaration that "We, the

People,"[35] framed it and preceded by a broad
Declaration of Rights which did away with property qualifications and based representation directly on population instead of property. It especially took up new subjects of social legislation,
declaring navigable rivers free public highways,
instituting homestead exemptions, establishing
boards of county commissioners, providing for a
new penal code of laws, establishing universal
manhood suffrage "without distinction of race or
color," devoting six sections to charitable and
penal institutions and six to corporations, providing separate property for married women, etc.
Above all, eleven sections of the Tenth Article
were devoted to the establishment of a complete
public school system.

So satisfactory was the constitution thus
adopted by Negro suffrage and by a convention
composed of a majority of blacks that the States
lived twenty-seven years under it without essential
change and when the constitution was revised in
1895, the revision was practically nothing more
than an amplification of the Constitution of 1868.
No essential advance step of the former document
was changed except the suffrage article to disfranchise Negroes.

[35] Some of the Reconstruction Constitutions preceding Negro Suffrage
showed tendencies toward democratization among the whites.

In Mississippi the Constitution of 1868 was, as compared with that before the war, more democratic. It not only forbade distinctions on account of color but abolished all property qualifications for jury service and property and educational qualifications for suffrage; it required less rigorous qualifications for office; it prohibited the lending of the credit of the State for private corporations —an abuse dating back as far as 1830. It increased the powers of the governor, raised the ·low State salaries, and increased the number of state officials. New ideas like the public school system and the immigration bureau were introduced and in general the activity of the State greatly and necessarily enlarged. Finally that was the only constitution of the State ever submitted to popular approval at the polls. This constitution remained in force twenty-two years.

In general the words of Judge Albion W. Tourgee, "a carpet-bagger," are true when he says of the Negro governments: "They obeyed the Constitution of the United States and annulled the bonds of states, counties and cities which had been issued to carry on the war of rebellion and maintain armies in the field against the Union. They instituted a public school system in a realm where public schools had been unknown. They opened the ballot box and jury box to thousands of white

men who had been debarred from them by a lack
of earthly possessions. They introduced home
rule in the South. They abolished the whipping
post, the branding iron, the stocks and other barbarous forms of punishment which had up to that
time prevailed. They reduced capital felonies
from about twenty to two or three. In an age of
extravagance they were extravagant in the sums
appropriated for public works. In all of that
time no man's rights of person were invaded under
the forms of law. Every Democrat's life, home,
fireside and business were safe. No man ob-
structed any white man's way to the ballot box,
interfered with his freedom of speech or boycotted
him, on account of his political faith."[36]

A thorough study of the legislation accompanying these constitutions and its changes since would,
of course, be necessary before a full picture of the
situation could be given. This has not been done
but so far as my studies have gone I have been
surprised at the comparatively small amount of
change in law and government which the overthrow of Negro rule brought about. There were
sharp and often hurtful economies introduced,
marking the return of property to power, there
was a sweeping change in officials but the main
body of Reconstruction legislation stood.

[36] Chicago Weekly *Inter-Ocean*, Dec. 26, 1890.

There is no doubt but that the thirst of the black man for knowledge—a thirst which has been too persistent and durable to be mere curiosity or whim—gave birth to the public free school system of the South. It was the question upon which the black voters and legislators insisted more than anything else and while it is possible to find some vestiges of free schools in some of the Southern States before the war yet a universal, well established system dates from the day that the black man got political power. Common school instruction in the South, in the modern sense of the term, was begun for Negroes by the Freedmen's Bureau and missionary societies, and the State public school systems for all children were formed mainly by Negro Reconstruction governments.

The earlier state constitutions of Mississippi "from 1817 to 1864 contained a declaration that 'Religion, morality and knowledge being necessary to good government, the preservation of liberty and the happiness of mankind, schools and the means of education shall forever be encouraged.' It was not, however, until 1868 that encouragement was given to any general system of public schools meant to embrace the whole youthful population." The Constitution of 1868 makes it the duty of the legislature to establish "a uniform system of free public schools by taxation or other-

wise for all children between the ages of five and
twenty-one years." In Alabama the Reconstruction Constiution of 1868 provided that "It shall be
the duty of the Board of Education to establish
throughout the State in each township or other
school district which it may have created, one
or more schools at which all children of the state
between the ages of five and twenty-one years
may attend free of charge." Arkansas in 1868,
Florida in 1869, Virginia in 1870, established
school systems. The Constitution of 1868 in
Louisiana required the general assembly to establish "at least one free public school in every
parish," and that these schools should make no
"distinction of race, color or previous condition."
Georgia's system was not fully established until
1873.

We are apt to forget that in all human prob-
ability the granting of Negro manhood suffrage
was decisive in rendering permanent the foundation of the Negro common school. Even after
the overthrow of the Negro governments, if the
Negroes had been left a servile caste, personally
free but politically powerless, it is not reasonable
to think that a system of common schools would
have been provided for them by the Southern
states. Serfdom and education have ever proven
contradictory terms. But when Congress, backed

by the nation, determined to make the Negroes
full-fledged voting citizens, the South had a hard
dilemma before her; either to keep the Negroes
under as an ignorant proletariat and stand the
chance of being ruled eventually from the slums
and jails, or to join in helping to raise these wards
of the nation to a position of intelligence and
thrift by means of a public school system.[37]

The "carpet-bag" governments hastened the
decision of the South and although there was a
period of hesitation and retrogression after the
overthrow of Negro rule in the early seventies,
yet the South saw that to abolish Negro schools
in addition to nullifying the Negro vote would
invite Northern interference; and thus eventually
every Southern state confirmed the work of the
Negro legislators and maintained the Negro
public schools along with the white.

Finally, in legislation covering property the
wider functions of the State, the punishment of
crime and the like, it is sufficient to say that the
laws on these points established by Reconstruction
legislatures were not only different and even revolutionary to the laws of the older South, but they
were so wise and so well suited to the needs of the
new South that in spite of a retrogressive movement following the overthrow of the Negro

[37] Cf. Atlanta University Pub. No. 6 and No. 16.

governments, the mass of this legislation with elaboration and development still stands on the statute books of the South.

Reconstruction constitutions, practically un-altered, were kept in

Florida, 1868-1885	17 years
Virginia, 1870-1902	32 years
South Carolina, 1868-1895	27 years
Mississippi, 1868-1890	22 years

Even in the case of states like Alabama, Georgia, North Carolina and Louisiana, which adopted new constitutions to signify the over-throw of Negro rule, the new constitutions are nearer the model of the Reconstruction document than they are to the previous constitutions. They differ from the Negro constitutions in minor de-tails but very little in general conception.

Here then on the whole was a much more favorable result of a great experiment in democ-racy than the world had a right to await. But even on its more sinister side and in the matter of the ignorance of inexperience and venality of the colored voters there came signs of better things. The theory of democratic government is not that the will of the people is always right, but rather that normal human beings of average intelligence will, if given a chance, learn the right and best course by bitter experience. This is precisely

what the Negro voters showed indubitable signs
of doing. First, they strove for schools to abolish
their ignorance, and second, a large and growing
number of them revolted against the carnival of
extravagance and stealing that marred the beginning of Reconstruction and joined with the best
elements to institute reform; and the greatest
stigma on the white South is not that it opposed
Negro suffrage and resented theft and incompet-
ence, but that when it saw the reform movement
growing and even in some cases triumphing, and
a larger and larger number of black voters learning to vote for honesty and ability, it still preferred a Reign of Terror to a campaign of education and disfranchised Negroes instead of punishing rascals.

No one has expressed this more convincingly
than a Negro who was himself a member of the
Reconstruction legislature of South Carolina and
who spoke at the convention which disfranchised
him, against one of the onslaughts of Tillman:

"The gentleman from Edgefield (Mr. Tillman)
speaks of the piling up of the State debt; of
jobbery and speculation during the period between
1869 and 1873 in South Carolina, but he has not
found voice eloquent enough nor pen exact enough
to mention those imperishable gifts bestowed upon
South Carolina between 1873 and 1876 by Negro

legislators — the laws relative to finance, the
building of penal and charitable institutions and,
greatest of all, the establishment of the public
school system. Starting as infants in legislation
in 1869, many wise measures were not thought
of, many injudicious acts were passed. But in the
administration of affairs for the next four years,
having learned by experience the result of bad
acts, we immediately passed reformatory laws
touching every department of state, county, municipal and town governments. These enactments
are today upon the statute books of South Carolina. They stand as living witnesses of the
Negro's fitness to vote and legislate upon the
rights of mankind.

"When we came into power, town governments
could lend the credit of their respective towns to
secure funds at any rate of interest that the council saw fit to pay. Some of the towns paid as high
as twenty percent. We passed an act prohibiting
town governments from pledging the credit of
their hamlets for money bearing a greater rate of
interest than five percent.

"Up to 1874, inclusive, the State Treasurer
had the power to pay out State funds as he
pleased. He could elect whether he would pay
out the funds on appropriations that would place
the money in the hands of the speculators, or

would apply them to appropriations that were
honest and necessary. We saw the evil of this
and passed an act making specific levies and col-
lections of taxes for specific appropriations.

"Another source of profligacy in the expenditure of funds was the law that provided for and
empowered the levying and collecting of special
taxes by school districts, in the name of the
schools. We saw its evil and by a Constitutional
amendment provided that there should only be
levied and collected annually a tax of two mills
for school purposes, and took away from the
school districts the power to levy and to collect
taxes of any kind. By this act we cured the evils
that had been inflicted upon us in the name of the
schools, settled the public school question for all
time to come and established the system upon an
honest financial basis.

"Next, we learned during the period from
1869 to 1874 inclusive, that what was denominated the floating indebtedness, covering the
printing schemes and other indefinite expenditures, amounted to nearly $2,000,000. A confer-
ence was called of the leading Negro representatives in the two Houses together with the State
Treasurer, also a Negro. After this conference
we passed an act for the purpose of ascertaining
the bona fide floating debt and found that it did

not amount to more than $250,000 for the four
years; we created a commission to sift that indebtedness and to scale it.   Hence when the Democratic party came into power they found the
floating debt covering the legislative and all other
expenditures, fixed at the certain sum of $250,000.
This same class of Negro legislators, led by the
State Treasurer, Mr. F. L. Cardoza, knowing
that there were millions of fraudulent bonds
charged against the credit of the State, passed
another act to ascertain the true bonded indebtedness and to provide for its settlement.   Under
this law, at one sweep, those entrusted with the
power to do so, through Negro legislators,
stamped six millions of bonds, denominated as
conversion bonds, 'fraudulent.'   The commission
did not finish its work before 1876.   In that year
when the Hampton government came into power,
there were still to be examined into and settled
under the terms of the act passed by us and providing for the legitimate bonded indebtedness of
the State, a little over two and a half million
dollars worth of bonds and coupons which had not
been passed upon.

"Governor Hampton, General Hagood, Judge
Simonton, Judge Wallace and in fact, all of the
conservative thinking Democrats aligned themselves under the provision enacted by us for the

certain and final settlement of the bonded indebtedness and appealed to their Democratic legislators to stand by the Republican legislation on the
subject and to confirm it.   A faction in the Democratic party obtained a majority of the Democrats
in the legislature against settling the question and
they endeavored to open up anew the whole subject of the State debt.   We had a little over thirty
members in the House and enough Republican
senators to sustain the Hampton conservative
faction and to stand up for honest finance, or by
our votes to place the debt question of the old
State into the hands of the plunderers and speculators.   We were appealed to by General Hagood,
through me, and my answer to him was in these
words: 'General, our people have learned the difference between profligate and honest legislation.
We have passed acts of financial reform, and with
the assistance of God, when the vote shall have
been taken, you will be able to record for the
thirty-odd Negroes, slandered though they have
been through the press, that they voted solidly
with you all for the honest legislation and the
preservation of the credit of the State.'   The
thirty-odd Negroes in the legislature and their
senators by their votes did settle the debt question
and saved the State $13,000,000.

"We were eight years in power.   We had built

school houses, established charitable institutions, built and maintained the penitentiary system, provided for the education of the deaf and dumb, rebuilt the jails and court houses, rebuilt the bridges and re-established the ferries. In short, we had reconstructed the State and placed it upon the road to prosperity and, at the same time, by our acts of financial reform, transmitted to the Hampton government an indebtedness not greater by more than $2,500,000 than was the bonded debt of the State in 1868, before the Republican Negroes and their white allies came into power."[38]

So too in Louisiana in 1872 and in Mississippi later the better element of the Republicans triumphed at the polls and joining with the Democrats instituted reforms, repudiated the worst extravagances and started toward better things. But unfortunately there was one thing that the white South feared more than Negro dishonesty, ignorance and incompetency, and that was Negro honesty, knowledge and efficiency.

Paint the "carpet-bag" governments and Negro rule as black as may be, the fact remains that the essence of the revolution which the overturning

[38] This speech was made in the South Carolina Constitutional Convention of 1890 which disfranchised the Negro, by the Hon. Thomas E. Miller, ex-congressman and one of the six Negro members of the Convention. The Convention did not have the courage to publish it in their proceedings but it may be found in the Occasional Papers of the American Negro Academy No. 6, pp. 11-13.

of the Negro governments made was to put these black men and their friends out of power. Outside the curtailing of expenses and stopping of extravagance, not only did their successors make few changes in the work which these legislatures and conventions had done, but they largely carried out their plans, followed their suggestions and strengthened their institutions. Practically the whole new growth of the South has been accomplished under laws which black men helped to frame thirty years ago. I know of no greater compliment to Negro suffrage, and no greater contribution to real American democracy.[39]

The counter revolution came but it was too late. The Negro had stepped so far into new economic freedom that he could never be put back into slavery; and he had widened democracy to include not only a goodly and increasing number of his own group but the mass of the poor white South. The economic results of Negro suffrage were so great during the years from 1865 to 1876 that they have never been overthrown. The Freedmen's Bureau came virtually to an end in 1869. General Howard's report of that year said: "In spite of all disorders that have pre-

[39] Cf. W. E. B. Du Bois, *Reconstruction* (American Historical Review, XV, No. 4, p. 871).
    W. E. B. Du Bois, *Economics of Negro Emancipation* (Sociological Review, Oct., 1911, p. 303).

vailed and the misfortunes that have fallen upon many parts of the South, a good degree of prosperity and success has already been attained. To the oft-repeated slander that the Negroes will not work and are incapable of taking care of themselves, it is a sufficient answer that their voluntary labor has produced nearly all the food that supported the whole people, besides a large amount of rice, sugar and tobacco for export, and two millions of bales of cotton each year, on which was paid into the United States Treasury during the years 1866 to 1867 a tax of more than forty millions of dollars ($40,000,000). It is not claimed that this result was wholly due to the care and oversight of this Bureau but it is safe to say as it has been said repeatedly by intelligent Southern white men, that without the Bureau or some similar agency, the material interests of the country would have greatly suffered and the government would have lost a far greater amount than has been expended in its maintenance. . . .

"Of the nearly eight hundred thousand (800,000) acres of farming land and about five thousand (5,000) pieces of town property transferred to this Bureau by military and treasury officers, or taken up by assistant commissioners, enough was leased to produce a revenue of nearly four hundred thousand dollars ($400,000).

Some farms were set apart in each state as homes for the destitute and helpless and a portion was cultivated by freedmen prior to its restoration. . . .
"Notice the appropriations by Congress:

For the year ending July 1st, 1867	$6,940,450.00
For the year ending July 1st, 1868	3,936,300.00
For the relief of the destitute citizens in District of Columbia	40,000.00
For relief of destitute freedmen in the same	15,000.00
For expenses of paying bounties in 1869	214,000.00
For expenses for famine in Southern states and transportation	1,865,645.00
For support of hospitals	50,000.00

Making a total received from all sources of . .$12,961,395.00

"Our expenditures from the beginning (including assumed accounts of the 'Department of Negro Affairs' from January 1st, 1865, to August 31, 1869) have been eleven million two hundred and forty-nine thousand and twenty-eight dollars and ten cents ($11,249,028.10). In addition to this cash expenditure the subsistence, medical supplies, quartermasters stores, issued to the refugees and freedmen prior to July 1st, 1866, were furnished by the commissary, medical and quartermasters department, and accounted for in the current expenses of those departments; they were not charged to nor paid for by my officers. They amounted to two million three hundred and thirty thousand seven hundred and eighty-eight dollars and seventy-two cents ($2,330,788.72) in original cost; but a large portion of these stores being damaged and condemned as unfit for issue to troops, their real value to the Government was probably less than one million dollars ($1,000,-000). Adding their original cost to the amount expended from appropriations and other sources, the total expenses of our Government for refugees and freedmen to August 31, 1869, have been thirteen million five hundred and seventy-nine thousand eight hundred and sixteen dollars and eighty-two cents ($13,579,816.82). And deducting fifty thousand dollars ($50,000) set apart as a special relief fund for all classes of destitute people in the Southern states, the real cost has been thirteen million twenty-nine thousand eight hundred and sixteen dollars and eighty-two cents ($13,029,816.82)."[40]

By 1875, Negroes owned not less than 2,000,-000 and perhaps as much as 4,000,000 acres of land and by 1880 this had increased to 6,000,000.

Notwithstanding the great step forward that the Negro had made this sinister fact faced him and his friends: he formed a minority of the population of the South. If that population was

[40] O. O. Howard, *Autobiography,* New York, 1907, Vol. 2, pp. 361-7, 371-2.

solidly arrayed against him his legal status was in danger and his economic progress was going to be difficult. It has been repeatedly charged that the action of the Negro solidified Southern opposition; and that the Negro refusing to listen to and make fair terms with his white neighbors, sought solely Northern alliance and the protection of Northern bayonets. This is not true and is turning facts hindside before. The ones who did the choosing were the Southern master class. When they got practically their full political rights in 1872 they had a chance to choose, if they would, the best of the Negroes as their allies and to work with them as against the most ruthless elements of the white South. Gradually there could have been built up a political party or even parties of the best of the black and white South. The Negroes would have been more than modest in their demands so long as they saw a chance to keep moving toward real freedom. But the master class did not choose this, although some like Wade Hampton of South Carolina, made steps toward it. On the whole, the masters settled definitely upon a purely racial line, recognizing as theirs everything that had a white skin and putting without the pale of sympathy and alliance, everything of Negro descent. By bitter and unyielding social pressure they pounded the whites into a solid phalanx, but in order to do this they had to give up much.

In the first place the leadership of the South passed from the hands of the old slave owners into the hands of the newer town capitalists who were largely merchants and the coming industrial leaders. Some of them represented the older dominant class and some of them the newer poor whites. They were welded, however, into a new economic mastership, less cultivated, more ruthless and more keen in recognizing the possibilities of Negro labor if "controlled" as they proposed to control it. This new leadership, however, did not simply solidify the South, it proceeded to make alliance in the North and to make alliance of the most effective kind, namely economic alliance. The sentimentalism of the war period had in the North changed to the recognition of the grim fact of destroyed capital, dead workers and high prices. The South was a field which could be exploited if peaceful conditions could be reached and the laboring class made sufficiently content and submissive. It was the business then of the "New" South to show to the northern capitalists that by uniting the economic interests of both, they could exploit the Negro laborer and the white laborer—pitting the two classes against each other, keeping out labor unions and building a new industrial South which would pay tremendous returns. This was the program which began with the withdrawal of Northern troops in 1876 and was carried on up to 1890 when it gained political sanction by open laws disfranchising the Negro.

But the experiment was carried on at a terrific cost. First, the Negro could not be cowed and beaten back from his new-found freedom without a mass of force, fraud and actual savagery such as strained the moral fibre of the white South to the utmost. It will be a century before the South recovers from this *débacle* and this explains why this great stretch of land has today so meager an output of science, literature and art and can discuss practically nothing but the "Negro" problem. It explains why the South is the one region in the civilized world where sometimes men are publicly burned alive at the stake.

On the other hand, even this display of force and hatred did not keep the Negro from advancing and the reason for this was that he was in competition with a white laboring class which, despite all efforts and advantages could not outstrip the Negroes and put them wholly under their feet. By judiciously using this rivalry, the Negro gained economic advantage after advantage, and foothold after foothold until today

while by no means free and still largely deprived
of political rights, we have a mass of 10,000,000
people whose economic condition may be thus
described: If we roughly conceive of something
like a tenth of the white population as below the
line of decent free economic existence, we may
guess that a third of the black American population of 12 millions is still in economic serfdom,
comparable to condition of the submerged tenth
in cities, and held in debt and crime peonage in
the sugar, rice and cotton belts. Six other millions
are emerging and fighting, in competition with
white laborers, a fairly successful battle for rising
wages and better conditions. In the last ten years
a million of these have been willing and able to
move physically from Southern serfdom to the
freer air of the North.

The other three millions are as free as the
better class of white laborers; and are pushing
and carrying the white laborer with them in their
grim determination to hold advantages gained
and gain others. The Negro's agitation for the
right to vote has made any step toward disfranchising the poor white unthinkable, for the white
vote is needed to help disfranchise the blacks; the
black man is pounding open the doors of exclusive
trade guilds; for how can unions exclude whites
when Negro competition can break a steel strike?

The Negro is making America and the world acknowledge democracy as feasible and desirable for all white folk, for only in this way do they see any possibility of defending their world wide fear of yellow, brown and black folk.

In a peculiar way, then, the Negro in the United States has emancipated democracy, reconstructed the threatened edifice of Freedom and been a sort of eternal test of the sincerity of our democratic ideals. As a Negro minister, J. W. C. Pennington, said in London and Glasgow before the Civil war: "The colored population of the United States has no destiny separate from that of the nation in which they form an integral part. Our destiny is bound up with that of America. Her ship is ours; her pilot is ours; her storms are ours; her calms are ours. If she breaks upon a rock, we break with her. If we, born in America, cannot live upon the same soil upon terms of equality with the descendants of Scotchmen, Englishmen, Irishmen, Frenchmen, Germans, Hungarians, Greeks and Poles, then the fundamental theory of American fails and falls to the ground."

This is still true and it puts the American Negro in a peculiar strategic position with regard to the race problems of the whole world. What do we mean by democracy? Do we mean democracy of the white races and the subjection of the colored

races? Or do we mean the gradual working forward to a time when all men will have a voice in
government and industry and will be intelligent
enough to express the voice?

It is this latter thesis for which the American
Negro stands and has stood, and more than any
other element in the modern world it has slowly
but continuously forced America toward that
point and is still forcing. It must be remembered
that it was the late Booker T. Washington who
planned the beginning of an industrial democracy
in the South, based on education, and that in our
day the National Association for the Advancement of Colored People, nine-tenths of whose
members are Negroes, is the one persistent agency
in the United States which is voicing a demand
for democracy unlimited by race, sex or religion.
American Negroes have even crossed the waters
and held three Pan-African Congresses to arouse
black men through the world to work for modern
democratic development. Thus the emancipation
of the Negro slave in America becomes through
his own determined effort simply one step toward
the emancipation of all men.

CHAPTER VI

THE FREEDOM OF WOMANHOOD

How the black woman from her low estate not
only united two great human races but helped
lift herself and all women to economic independence and self-expression.

The emancipation of woman is, of course, but
one phase of the growth of democracy. It deserves perhaps separate treatment because it is
an interesting example of the way in which the
Negro has helped American democracy.

In the United States in 1920 there were 5,253,-
695 women of Negro descent; over twelve hundred thousand of these were children, another
twelve hundred thousand were girls and young
women under twenty, and two and a half million
were adults. As a mass these women have but
the beginnings of education, — twelve percent of
those from sixteen to twenty years of age were
unable to write, and twenty-eight percent of those
twenty-one years of age and over. These women
are passing through, not only a moral, but an

economic revolution. Their grandmothers married at twelve and fifteen, but in 1910 twenty-seven percent of these women who had passed fifteen were still single.

Yet these black women toil and toil hard. There were in 1910 two and a half million Negro homes in the United States. Out of these homes walked daily to work two million women and girls over ten years of age, — one half of the colored female population as against a fifth in the case of white women. These, then, are a group of workers, fighting for their daily bread like men; independent and approaching economic freedom! They furnished a million farm laborers, 80,000 farmers, 22,000 teachers, 600,000 servants and washerwomen, and 50,000 in trades and merchandizing. In 1920, 38.9% of colored women were at work as contrasted with 17.2% of native white women. Of the colored women 39% were farming and 50% in service.

The family group, however, which is the ideal of the culture into which these folk have been born, is not based on the idea of an economically independent working mother. Rather its ideal harks back to the sheltered harem with the mother emerging at first as nurse and homemaker, while the man remains the sole breadwinner. Thus the

Negro woman more than the women of any other group in America is the protagonist in the fight for an economically independent womanhood in modern countries. Her fight has not been willing or for the most part conscious but it has, nevertheless, been curiously effective in its influence on the working world.

This matter of economic independence is, of course, the central fact in the struggle of women for equality. In the earlier days the slave woman was found to be economically as efficient as the man. Moreover, because of her production of children she became in many ways more valuable; but because she was a field hand the slave family differed from the free family. The children were brought up very largely in common on the plantation, there was comparatively small parental control or real family life and the chief function of the woman was working and not making a home. We can see here pre-figured a type of social development toward which the world is working again for similar and larger reasons. In our modern industrial organization the work of women is being found as valuable as that of men. They are consequently being taken from the home and put into industry and the rapidity by which this process is going on is only kept back by the problem of the child; and more and more the community is taking charge of the education of children for this reason.

In America the work of Negro women has not only pre-figured this development but it has had a direct influence upon it. The Negro woman as laborer, as seamstress, as servant and cook, has come into competition with the white male laborer and with the white woman worker. The fact that she could and did replace the white man as laborer, artisan and servant, showed the possibility of the white woman doing the same thing, and led to it. Moreover, the usual sentimental arguments against women at work were not brought forward in the case of Negro womanhood. Nothing illustrates this so well as the speech of Sojourner Truth before the second National Woman Suffrage Convention, in 1852.

Sojourner Truth came from the lowest of the low, a slave whose children had been sold away from her, a hard, ignorant worker without even a name, who came to this meeting of white women and crouched in a corner against the wall. "Don't let her speak," was repeatedly said to the presiding officer. "Don't get our cause mixed up with abolition and 'niggers'." The discussion became warm, resolutions were presented and argued. Much was said of the superiority of man's intellect, the general helplessness of women and their

need for courtesy, the sin of Eve, etc. Most of
the white women, being "perfect ladies," according to the ideals of the time, were not used to
speaking in public and finally to their dismay the
black woman arose from the corner. The audience
became silent.

Sojourner Truth was an Amazon nearly six
feet high, black, erect and with piercing eyes, and
her speech in reply was to the point:

"Dat man ober dar say dat women needs to be
helped into carriages, and lifted ober ditches, and
to have the best places every whar. Nobody eber
help me into carriages, or ober mud puddles, or
gives me any best place" (and raising herself to
her full height and her voice to a pitch like rolling
thunder, she asked), "and ai'n't I a woman?
Look at me! Look at my arm!" (And she bared
her right arm to the shoulder, showing her tremendous muscular power.) "I have plowed, and
planted, and gathered into barns, and no man
could head me — and ai'n't I a woman? I could
work as much and eat as much as a man (when I
could get it), and bear de lash as well — and
ai'n't I a woman? I have borne thirteen chilern
and seen 'em mos' all sold off into slavery, and
when I cried out with a mother's grief, none but
Jesus heard — and ai'n't I a woman? Den dey
talks 'bout dis ting in de head — what dis dey

call it?" ("Intellect," whispered some one near.)
"Dat's it honey. What's dat got to do with women's rights or niggers' rights? If my cup won't
hold but a pint and yourn holds a quart, wouldn't
ye be mean not to let me have my little half-
measure full?" . . . She ended by asserting that
"If de fust woman God ever made was strong
enough to turn the world upside down, all 'lone,
dese togedder" (and she glanced her eye over us,)
"ought to be able to turn it back and get it right
side up again, and now dey is asking to do it, de
men better let 'em. . . ."

"Amid roars of applause, she turned to her
corner, leaving more than one of us with streaming eyes and hearts beating with gratitude. She
had taken us up in her strong arms and carried us
safely over the slough of difficulty, turning the
whole tide in our favor. I have never in my life
seen anything like the magical influence that subdued the mobbish spirit of the day and turned the
jibes and sneers of an excited crowd into notes of
respect and admiration. Hundreds rushed up to
shake hands, and congratulate the glorious old
mother and bid her God speed on her mission of
'testifying again concerning the wickedness of this
'ere people'."[1]

[1] Testimony of the presiding officer, Mrs. Frances D. Gage, in *"Narrative of Sojourner Truth,"* 1884, pp. 134-5.

Again and in more concrete ways the Negro
woman has influenced America and that is by her
personal contact with the family — its men, women and children.   As housekeeper, maid and
nurse — as confidante, adviser and friend, she was
often an integral part of the white family life of
the South, and transmitted her dialect, her man-
nerisms, her quaint philosophy and her boundless
sympathy.

Beyond this she became the concubine.   It is a
subject scarcely to be mentioned today with our
conventional morals and with the bitter racial
memories swirling about this institution of slavery.   Yet the fact remains stark, ugly, painful,
beautiful.

Let us regard it dispassionately, remembering
that the concubine is as old as the world and that
birth is a biological fact.   It is usual to speak of
the Negro as being the great example of the
unassimiliated group in American life.   This, of
course, is flatly untrue; probably of the strains of
blood longest present in America since the discovery by Columbus, the Negro has been less
liable to absorption than other groups; but this
does not mean that he has not been absorbed and
that his blood has not been spread throughout the
length and breadth of the land.

"We southern ladies are complimented with the

names of wives; but we are only the mistresses of seraglios," said a sister of President Madison; and a Connecticut minister who lived 14 years in Carolina said: "As it relates to amalgamation, I can say, that I have been in respectable families (so-called), where I could distinguish the family resemblance in the slaves who waited upon the table. I once hired a slave who belonged to his own uncle. It is so common for the female slaves to have white children, that little is ever said about it. Very few inquiries are made as to who the father is."[2]

One has only to remember the early histories of cities like Charleston and New Orleans to see what the Negro concubine meant and how she transfigured America. Paul Alliot said in his reflections of Louisiana in 1803: "The population of that city counting the people of all colors is only twelve thousand souls. Mulattoes and Negroes are openly protected by the Government. He who strikes one of those persons, even though he had run away from him, would be severely punished. Also twenty whites could be counted in the prisons of New Orleans against one man of color. The wives and daughters of the latter are much sought after by the white men, and white

[2] Goodell, *Slave Code,* p. 111.

women at times esteem well-built men of color."[3]
The same writer tells us that few white men
marry, preferring to live with their slaves or with
women of color.

A generation later the situation was much the
same in spite of reaction. In 1818, a traveler says
of New Orleans: "Here may be seen in the same
crowds, Quadroons, Mulattoes, Samboes, Musti-
zos, Indians and Negroes; and there are other
commixtures which are not yet classified."[4]

"The minor distinctions of complexion and race
so fiercely adhered to by the Creoles of the old
regime were at their height at this time. The
glory and shame of the city were her quadroons
and octoroons, apparently constituting two aristocratic circles of society, the one as elegant as the
other, the complexions the same, the men the
same, the women different in race, but not in color,
nor in dress nor in jewels. Writers on fire with
the romance of this continental city love to speak
of the splendors of the French Opera House, the
first place in the country where grand opera was
heard, and tell of the tiers of beautiful women
with their jewels and airs and graces. Above the
orchestra circle were four tiers; the first filled with
the beautiful dames of the city; the second filled

<hr>

[3] Robertson, *Louisiana under the Rule of Spain,* Vol. 1, pp. 67, 103,
111; Dunbar-Nelson, in *Journal of Negro History,* Vol. 2, p. 56.
[4] Dunbar-Nelson, *loc. cit.*

with a second array of beautiful women, attired like those of the first, with no apparent difference; yet these were the octoroons and quadroons, whose beauty and wealth were all the passports needed. The third was for the *hoi polloi* of the white race, and the fourth for the people of color whose color was more evident. It was a veritable sandwich of races."[5]

Whatever judgment we may pass upon all this and however we may like or dislike it, the fact remains that the colored slave women became the medium through which two great races were united in America. Moreover it is the fashion to assume that all this was merely infiltration of white blood into the black; but we must remember it was just as surely infiltration of black blood into white America and not even an extraordinary drawing of the color line against all visible Negro blood has ever been able to trace its true limits.

There is scarcely an American, certainly none of the South and no Negro American, who does not know in his personal experience of Americans of Negro descent who either do not know or do not acknowledge their African ancestry. This is their right, if they do know, and a matter of but passing importance if they do not. But without

---

[5] Dunbar-Nelson, *op. cit.*, p. 62; Martineau, *Society in America,* p. 326ff.

doubt the spiritual legacy of Africa has been spread through this mingling of blood. First, of course, we may think of those more celebrated cases where the mixed blood is fairly well known but nevertheless the man has worked and passed as a white man. One of the earliest examples was that of Alexander Hamilton. Alexander Hamilton was a case in point of the much disputed "Creole" blood. Theoretically the Creole was a person of European descent on both sides born in the West Indies or America; but as there were naturally few such persons in earlier times because of the small number of European women who came to America, those descendants of European fathers and mulatto mothers were in practice called "Creole" and consequently it soon began to be *prima facie* evidence, in the West Indies, that an illegitimate child of a white father was of Negro descent. Alexander Hamilton was such an illegitimate child. He had colored relatives whose descendants still live in America and he was currently reported to be colored in the island of Nevis. Further than this, of course, proof is impossible. But to those who have given careful attention to the subject, little further proof is needed.

To this can be added a long list of American notables,—bishops, generals and members of Con-

gress.   Many writers and artists have found
hidden inspiration in their Negro blood and from
the first importation in the fifteenth century down
to today there has been a continual mingling of
white and Negro blood in the United States both
within and without the bonds of wedlock that
neither law nor slavery nor cruel insult and contempt has been able to stop.

Besides these influences in economics and the
home there has come the work of Negro women
in revolt which cannot be forgotten. We mention
two cases.

Harriet Tubman was a woman absolutely illiterate, who, from 1849 down to the Civil War,
spent her time journeying backward and forward
between the free and slave states and leading
hundreds of black fugitives into freedom. Thousands of dollars were put upon her head as rewards
for her capture; and she was continually sought
by northern abolitionists and was a confidant of
John Brown. During the War, she acted as a spy,
guide and nurse and in all these days, worked
without pay or reward. William H. Seward said:
"A nobler, higher spirit or truer, seldom dwells
in the human form," and Wendell Phillips added:
"In my opinion there are few captains, perhaps
few colonels who have done more for the loyal
cause since the War began and few men who did

before that time more for the colored race than our fearless and most sagacious friend, Harriet." Abraham Lincoln gave her ready audience.[6]

Quite a different kind of woman and yet strangely effective and influential was Mammy Pleasants of California. Here was a colored woman who became one of the shrewdest business minds of the State. She anticipated the development in oil; she was the trusted confidant of many of the California pioneers like Ralston, Mills and Booth and for years was a power in San Francisco affairs. Yet, she held her memories, her hatreds, her deep designs and throughout a life that was perhaps more than unconventional, she treasured a bitter hatred for slavery and a certain contempt for white people.

As a field hand in Georgia she had attracted the attention of a planter by her intelligence and was bought and sent to Boston for training. Here she was made a household drudge and eventually married Alexander Smith who was associated with Garrison and the abolitionists. With $50,000 from his estate, she came to California and made a fortune. The epitaph which she wanted on her tombstone was, "She was a friend of John Brown." When she first heard of the projects of Brown she determined to help him and April 5,

[6] Brownie's Book, March, 1921.

1858, when John Brown was captured at Harper's Ferry, they found upon him a letter reading: "The ax is laid at the foot of the tree; when the first blow is struck there will be more money to help." This was signed by three initials which the authorities thought were "W. E. P."—in fact they were "M. E. P." and stood for Mammy Pleasants. She had come East the spring before with a $30,000 United States draft which she changed into coin and meeting John Brown in Chatham or Windsor, Canada, had turned this money over to him. It was agreed, however, that he was not to strike his blow until she had helped to arouse the slaves. Disguised as a jockey, she went South and while there heard of Brown's raid and capture at Harper's ferry. She fled to New York and finally reached California on a ship that came around Cape Horn, sailing in the steerage under an assumed name.

Mammy Pleasants "always wore a poke bonnet and a plaid shawl," and she was "very black with thin lips" and "she handled more money during pioneers days in California than any other colored person."[7]

Here then, we have the types of colored women who rose out of the black mass of slaves not only to guide their own folk but to influence the nation.

[7] Beasley, *Negro Trail Blazers,* pp. 95-7.

We have noted then the Negro woman in America as a worker tending to emancipate all women workers; as a mother nursing the white race and uniting the black and white race; as a conspirator urging forward emancipation in various sorts of ways; and we have finally only to remember that to-day the women of America who are doing humble but on the whole the most effective work in the social uplift of the lowly, not so much by money as by personal contact, are the colored women. Little is said or known about it but in thousands of churches and social clubs, in missionary societies and fraternal organizations, in unions like the National Association of Colored Women, these workers are founding and sustaining orphanages and old folk homes; distributing personal charity and relief; visiting prisoners; helping hospitals; teaching children; and ministering to all sorts of needs. Their work, as it comes now and then in special cases to the attention of individuals of the white world, forms a splendid bond of encouragement and sympathy, and helps more than most realize in minimizing racial difficulties and encouraging human sympathy.[8]

[8] Cf. Annual Reports National Association of Colored Women; Atlanta University Publications, No. 14.

CHAPTER VII

THE AMERICAN FOLK SONG

How black folk sang their sorrow songs in the land of their bondage and made this music the only American folk music.

"Little of beauty has America given the world save the rude grandeur God himself stamped on her bosom; the human spirit in this new world has expressed itself in vigor and ingenuity rather than in beauty. And so by fateful chance the Negro folk-song — the rhythmic cry of the slave — stands today not simply as the sole American music, but as the most beautiful expression of human experience born this side the seas. It has been neglected, it has been persistently mistaken and misunderstood; but notwithstanding, it still remains as the singular spiritual heritage of the nation and the greatest gift of the Negro people."[1]

Around the Negro folk-song there has arisen much of controversy and of misunderstanding. For a long time they were utterly neglected; then every once in a while and here and there they

[1] Du Bois, *Souls of Black Folk,* Chapter No. 14.

forced themselves upon popular attention. In the thirties, they emerged and in tunes like "Near the lake where droop the willow" and passed into current song or were caricatured by the minstrels. Then came Stephen Foster who accompanied a mulatto maid often to the Negro church and heard the black folk sing; he struck a new note in songs like "Old Kentucky Home," "Old Folks at Home" and "Nellie was a Lady." But it was left to war and emancipation to discover the real primitive beauty of this music to the world.

When northern men and women who knew music, met the slaves at Port Royal after its capture by Federal troops, they set down these songs in their original form for the first time so that the world might hear and sing them. The sea islands of the Carolinas where these meetings took place "with no third witness" were filled with primitive black folk, uncouth in appearance, and queer in language, but their singing was marvellous. Thomas Wentworth Higginson and Miss McKim and others collected these songs in 1867, making the first serious study of Negro American music. The preface said:

"The musical capacity of the Negro race has been recognized for so many years that it is hard to explain why no systematic effort has hitherto been made to collect and preserve their melodies.

More than thirty years ago those plantation songs made their appearance which were so extraordinarily popular for a while; and if 'Coal-black Rose,' 'Zip Coon' and 'Ole Virginny nebber tire' have been succeeded by spurious imitations, manufactured to suit the somewhat sentimental taste of our community, the fact that these were called 'Negro melodies' was itself a tribute to the musical genius of the race.

"The public had well-nigh forgotten these genuine slave songs, and with them the creative power from which they sprung, when a fresh interest was excited through the educational mission to the Port Royal Islands in 1861."[2]

Still the world listened only half credulously until the Fisk Jubilee Singers sang the slave songs "so deeply into the world's heart that it can never wholly forget them again." The story of the Fisk Jubilee singers is romantic. In abandoned barracks at Nashville hundreds of colored children were being taught and the dream of a Negro University had risen in the minds of the white teachers. But even the lavish contribution for missionary work, which followed the war, had by 1870 begun to fall off. It happened that the treasurer of Fisk, George L. White, loved music.

W. F. Allen and others, *Slave Songs of the United States,* New York, 1867.

He began to instruct the Fisk students in singing
and he used the folk-songs. He met all sorts of
difficulties. The white people of the nation and
especially the conventional church folk who were
sending missionary money, were not interested in
"minstrel ditties." The colored people looked
upon these songs as hateful relics of slavery.
Nevertheless, Mr. White persisted, gathered a
pioneer band of singers and in 1871 started north.

"It was the sixth day of October in the year of
our Lord, one thousand eight hundred and sev-
enty-one, when George L. White started out from
Fisk School with his eleven students to raise
money, that Fisk might live. Professor Adam K.
Spence, who was principal of the school, gave Mr.
White all the money in his possession save one
dollar, which he held back, that the treasury might
not be empty. While friends and parents wept,
waved, and feared, the train puffed out of the
station. All sorts of difficulties, obstacles, opposi-
tions and failures faced them until through wonderful persistence, they arrived at Oberlin, Ohio.
Here the National Council of Congregational
Churches was in session. After repeated efforts,
Mr. White gained permission for his singers to
render one song. Many of the members of the
Council objected vigorously to having such singers. During the time of the session the weather

had been dark and cloudy. The sun had not shone one moment, it had not cast one ray upon the village. The singers went into the gallery of the church, unobserved by all save the moderator and a few who were on the rostrum. At a lull in the proceeding, there floated sweetly to the ears of the audience the measures of 'Steal Away to Jesus.' Suddenly the sun broke through the clouds, shone through the windows upon the singers, and verily they were a heavenly choir. For a time the Council forgot its business and called for more and more. It was at this point that Henry Ward Beecher almost demanded of Mr. White that he cancel all engagements and come straight to his church in Brooklyn. . . ."

The New York papers ridiculed and sneered at Beecher's "nigger minstrels." But Beecher stuck to his plan and it was only a matter of hearing them once when audiences went into ecstasies.

"When the Metropolitan newspapers called the company 'Nigger Minstrels,' Mr. White was face to face with a situation as serious as it was awkward. His company had no appropriate name, and the odium of the title attributed by the New York newspapers pained him intensely. If they were to be known as 'Nigger Minstrels,' they could never realize his vision; they were both handicapped and checkmated, and their career was dead. . . . The suggestiveness of the Hebrew Jubilee had been borne in upon his mind and with joy of a deep conviction he exclaimed, 'Children, you are the Jubilee Singers'."[3]

For seven years the career of this company of Jubilee Singers was a continual triumph. They crowded the concert halls of New England; they began to send money back to Fisk; they went to Great Britain and sang before Queen Victoria, Lord Shaftesbury and Mr. Gladstone. Gladstone cried: "It's wonderful!" Queen Victoria wept. Moody, the evangelist, brought them again and again to his London meetings, and the singers were loaded with gifts. Then they went to Germany, and again Kings and peasants listened to them. In seven years they were able to pay not only all of their own expenses but to send $150,000 in cash to Fisk University, and out of this money was built Jubilee Hall, on the spot that was once a slave market. "There it stands, lifting up its grateful head to God in His heaven."

For a long time after some people continued to sneer at Negro music. They declared it was a "mere imitation," that it had little intrinsic value, that it was not the music of Negroes at all. Gradually, however, this attitude has completely passed and today critics vie with each other in

[3] G. D. Pike, *The Jubilee Singers,* New York, 1873.

giving tribute to this wonderful gift of the black man to America.

Damrosch says: "The Negro's music isn't ours, it is the Negro's. It has become a popular form of musical expression and is interesting, but it is not ours. Nothing more characteristic of a race exists, but it is characteristic of the Negro, not the American race. Through it a primitive people poured out its emotions with wonderful expressiveness. It no more expresses our emotions than the Indian music does."

Recently, numbers of serious studies of the Negro folk-song have been made. James Weldon Johnson says: "In the 'spirituals,' or slave songs, the Negro has given America not only its only folk-songs, but a mass of noble music. I never think of this music but that I am struck by the wonder, the miracle of its production. How did the men who originated these songs manage to do it? The sentiments are easily accounted for; they are, for the most part, taken from the Bible. But the melodies, where did they come from? Some of them so weirdly sweet, and others so wonderfully strong. Take, for instance, 'Go Down, Moses'; I doubt that there is a stronger theme in the whole musical literature of the world.

"It is to be noted that whereas the chief characteristic of Ragtime is rhythm, the chief character-

istic of the 'spirituals' is melody.   The melodies
of 'Steal Away to Jesus,' 'Swing Low, Sweet
Chariot,' 'Nobody Knows de Trouble I See,' 'I
couldn't hear Nobody Pray,' 'Deep River,' 'O,
Freedom Over Me,' and many others of these
songs possess a beauty that is — what shall I say?
Poignant.   In the riotous rhythms of Ragtime
the Negro expressed his irrepressible buoyancy,
his keen response to the sheer joy of living; in the
'spirituals' he voiced his sense of beauty and his
deep religious feeling."[4]

H. E. Krehbiel says: "There was sunshine as
well as gloom in the life of the black slaves in the
Southern colonies and States, and so we have
songs which are gay as well as grave; but as a
rule the finest songs are the fruits of suffering
undergone and the hope of the deliverance from
bondage which was to come with translation to
heaven after death.   The oldest of them are the
most beautiful, and many of the most striking have
never yet been collected, partly because they contained elements, melodic as well as rhythmical,
which baffled the ingenuity of the early collectors.
Unfortunately, trained musicians have never entered upon the field, and it is to be feared that it
is now too late.   The peculiarities which the col-

---

[4] James Weldon Johnson, *Book of American Negro Poetry*, New York,
1922.

laborators on 'Slave Songs of the United States'
recognized, but could not imprison on the written
page, were elements which would have been of
especial interest to the student of art.

"Is it not the merest quibble to say that these
songs are not American? They were created in
America under American influences and by people
who are Americans in the same sense that any
other element of our population is American —
every element except the aboriginal. . . . Is it
only an African who can sojourn here without
becoming an American and producing American
things; is it a matter of length of stay in the
country? Scarcely that; or some Negroes would
have at least as good a claim on the title as the
descendants of the Puritans and Pilgrims. Negroes figure in the accounts of his voyages to
America made by Columbus. . . . A year before
the English colonists landed on Plymouth Rock
Negroes were sold into servitude in Virginia."[5]

The most gifted and sympathetic student of the
folk-song in Africa and America was Natalie
Curtis, and it is scarcely necessary to add to what
she has so carefully and sympathetically written.
She has traced the connection between African
and Afro-American music which has always been

[5] H. E. Krehbiel, *Afro-American Folksongs*, New York, 1914; cf.
also John W. Work, *Folksong of the American Negro*, Nashville, Tenn.,
1915.

assumed but never carefully proven. The African
rhythm, through the use of the drum as a leading
instrument, produced musical emphasis which we
call syncopation. Primitive music usually shows
rhythm and melody of the voice sung in unison.
But in Africa, part singing was developed long
before it appeared in Europe. The great difference between the music of Africa and the music of
Europe lies in rhythm; in Europe the music is
accented on the regular beats of the music while
in Africa the accents fall often on the unstressed
beats. It is this that coming down through the
Negro folk-song in America has produced what is
known as ragtime.

Mrs. Curtis Burlin shows that the folk-song of
the African in America can be traced direct to
Africa: "As a creator of beauty the black man is
capable of contributing to the great art of the
world.

"The Negro's pronounced gift for music is today widely recognized. That gift, brought to
America in slave-ships, was nurtured by that
mother of woe, human slavery, till out of suffering
and toil there sprang a music which speaks to the
heart of mankind — the prayer-song of the American Negro. In Africa is rooted the parent stem
of that out-flowering of Negro folk-song in other
lands.

"Through the Negro this country is vocal with a folk-music intimate, complete and beautiful. It is the Negro music with its by-product of 'ragtime' that today most widely influences the popular song-life of America, and Negro rhythms have indeed captivated the world at large. Nor may we foretell the impress that the voice of the slave will leave upon the art of the country — a poetic justice, this! For the Negro everywhere discriminated against, segregated and shunned, mobbed and murdered — he it is whose melodies are on all our lips, and whose rhythms impel our marching feet in a 'war for democracy.' The irresistible music that wells up from this sunny and unresentful people is hummed and whistled, danced to and marched to, laughed over and wept over, by high and low and rich and poor throughout the land. The downtrodden black man whose patient religious faith has kept his heart still unembittered, is fast becoming the singing voice of all America. And in his song we hear a prophecy of the dignity and worth of Negro genius."[6]

The Negro folk-song entered the Church and became the prayer song and the sorrow song, still with its haunting melody but surrounded by the inhibitions of a cheap theology and a conventional

[6] Natalie Curtis-Burlin, *Negro Folksongs,* 4 books, 1918-19; *Songs and Tales from the Dark Continent,* 1920.

morality. But the musical soul of a race un-
leashed itself violently from these bonds and in
the saloons and brothels of the Mississippi bot-
toms and gulf coast flared to that crimson license
of expression known as "ragtime," "jazz" and
the more singular "blues" retaining with all their
impossible words the glamour of rhythm and wild
joy. White composers hastily followed with songs
like "A Hot Time in the Old Town Tonight,"
and numerous successors in popular favor.

Out of ragtime grew a further development
through both white and black composers. The
"blues," a curious and intriguing variety of love
song from the levees of the Mississippi, became
popular and was spread by the first colored man
who was able to set it down, W. C. Handy of
Memphis. Other men, white and colored, from
Stephen Foster to our day, have taken another
side of Negro music and developed its haunting
themes and rippling melody into popular songs
and into high and fine forms of modern music,
until today the influence of the Negro reaches
every part of American music, of many foreign
masters like Dvorak; and certainly no program of
concert music could be given in America without
voicing Negro composers and Negro themes.

We can best end this chapter with the word of
a colored man: "But there is something deeper

than the sensuousness of beauty that makes for
the possibilities of the Negro in the realm of the
arts, and that is the soul of the race. The wail
of the old melodies and the plaintive quality that
is ever present in the Negro voice are but the
reflection of a background of tragedy. No race
can rise to the greatest heights of art until it has
yearned and suffered. The Russians are a case in
point. Such has been their background in oppression and striving that their literature and art are
to-day marked by an unmistakable note of power.
The same future beckons to the American Negro.
There is something very elemental about the heart
of the race, something that finds its origin in the
African forest, in the sighing of the night wind,
and in the falling of the stars. There is something grim and stern about it all, too, something
that speaks of the lash, of the child torn from its
mother's bosom, of the dead body riddled with
bullets and swinging all night from a limb by the
roadside."[7]

[7] Benjamin Brawley, *Negro in Literature and Art.*

CHAPTER VIII

NEGRO ART AND LITERATURE

How the tragic story of the black slave has become a central theme of the story of America and has inspired literature and created art.

The Negro is primarily an artist. The usual way of putting this is to speak disdainfully of his "sensuous" nature. This means that the only race which has held at bay the life destroying forces of the tropics, has gained therefrom in some slight compensation a sense of beauty, particularly for sound and color, which characterizes the race. The Negro blood which flowed in the veins of many of the mightiest of the Pharaohs accounts for much of Egyptian art, and indeed Egyptian civilization owes much in its origin to the development of the large strain of Negro blood which manifested itself in every grade of Egyptian society.

Semitic civilization also had its Negroid influences, and these continually turn toward art as in the case of black Nosseyeb, one of the five great poets of Damascus under the Ommiades, and the

black Arabian hero, Antar. It was therefore not
to be wondered at that in modern days one of
the greatest of modern literatures, the Russian,
should have been founded by Pushkin, the grandson of a full blooded Negro, and that among the
painters of Spain was the mulatto slave, Gomez.
Back of all this development by way of contact,
come the artistic sense of the indigenous Negro as
shown in the stone figures of Sherbro, the bronzes
of Benin, the marvelous hand work in iron and other
metals which has characterized the Negro race so
long that archaeologists today, with less and less
hesitation, are ascribing the discovery of the
welding of iron to the Negro race.

Beyond the specific ways in which the Negro
has contributed to American art stands undoubtedly his spirit of gayety and the exotic charm which
his presence has loaned the parts of America
which were spiritually free enough to enjoy it. In
New Orleans, for instance, after the war of 1812
and among the free people of color there was a
beautiful blossoming of artistic life which the sordid background of slavery had to work hard to
kill. The "people of color" grew in number and
waxed wealthy. Famous streets even today bear
testimony of their old importance. Congo Square
in the old Creole quarter where Negroes danced
the weird "Bamboula" long before colored Cole-

ridge-Taylor made it immortal and Gottschalk wrote his Negro dance. Camp street and Julia street took their names from the old Negro field and from the woman who owned land along the Canal. Americans and Spanish both tried to get the support and sympathy of the free Negroes. The followers of Aaron Burr courted them.

"Writers describing the New Orleans of this period agree in presenting a picture of a continental city, most picturesque, most un-American, and as varied in color as a street of Cairo. There they saw French, Spaniards, English, Bohemians, Negroes, mulattoes, varied clothes, picturesque white dresses of the fairer women, brilliant cottons of the darker ones. The streets, banquettes, we should say, were bright with color, the nights filled with song and laughter. Through the scene, the people of color add the spice of color; in the life, they add the zest of romance."[1]

Music is always back of this gay Negro spirit and the folk song which the Negro brought to America was developed not simply by white men but by the Negro himself. Musicians and artists sprung from the Louisiana group. There was Eugene Warburg who distinguished himself as a sculptor in Italy. There was Victor Sejour who became a poet and composer in France, Dubuclet

[1] Alice Dunbar-Nelson in *Journal of Negro History,* Vol. 2, p. 55.

became a musician in Bordeaux and the seven
Lamberts taught and composed in America, France
and Brazil. One of the brothers Sydney was
decorated for his work by the King of Portugal.
Edmund Dèdè became a director of a leading
orchestra in France.[2]

Among other early colored composers of music
are J. Hemmenway who lived in Philadelphia
in the twenties; A. J. Conner of Philadelphia between 1846-57 published numbers of composi-
tions; in the seventies Justin Holland was well
known as a composer in Cleveland, Ohio; Samuel
Milady, known by his stage name as Sam Lucas,
was born in 1846 and died in 1916. He wrote
many popular ballads, among them "Grand-
father's Clock Was Too Tall For The Shelf."
George Melbourne, a Negro street minstrel, composed "Listen to the Mocking-Bird," although a
white man got the credit. James Bland wrote
"Carry me Back to Ole Virginny"; Gussie L. Davis
composed popular music at Cincinnati.[3]

Coming to our day we remember that the
Anglo-African Samuel Coleridge-Taylor received
much of his inspiration from his visits to the
American Negro group; then comes Harry T.

[2] Washington, *Story of the Negro,* Vol. 2, pp. 276-7.
[3] Cf. Benjamin Brawley, *The Negro in Literature and Art,* New
York, 1921.

Burleigh, perhaps the greatest living song writer in America. Among his works are "Five Songs" by Laurence Hope; "The Young Warrior," which became one of the greatest of the war songs; "The Grey Wolf" and "Ethiopia Saluting the Colors." His adaptations of Negro folk-songs are widely known and he assisted Dvorak in his "New World Symphony." R. Nathaniel Dett has written "Listen to the Lambs," a carol widely known, and "The Magnolia Suite." Rosamond Johnson wrote "Under the Bamboo Tree" and a dozen popular favorites beside choruses and marches. Clarence Cameron White has composed and adapted and Maud Cuney Hare has revived and explained Creole music. Edmund T. Jenkins has won medals at the Royal Academy in London. Among the colored performers on the piano are R. Augustus Lawson, who has often been soloist at the concerts of the Hartford Philharmonic Orchestra; Hazel Harrison, a pupil of Busoni; and Helen Hagen who took the Sanford scholarship at Yale. Carl Diton is a pianist who has transcribed many Negro melodies. Melville Charlton has done excellent work on the organ.

Then we must remember the Negro singers, the "Black Swan" of the early 19th century whose voice compared with Jenny Lind's; the Hyer sisters, Flora Batson, Florence Cole Talbert, and

Roland W. Hayes, the tenor whose fine voice has charmed London, Paris and Vienna and who is now one of the leading soloists of the Boston Symphony Orchestra.

The Negro has been one of the greatest originators of dancing in the United States and in the world. He created the "cake walk" and most of the steps in the "clog" dance which has so enthralled theatre audiences. The modern dances which have swept over the world like the "Tango" and "Turkey Trot" originated among the Negroes of the West Indies. The Vernon Castles always told their audiences that their dances were of Negro origin.[4]

We turn now to other forms of art and more particularly literature. Here the subjects naturally divides itself into three parts: *first,* the influence which the Negro has had on American literature,—and *secondly,* the development of a literature for and by Negroes. And lastly the number of Negroes who have gained a place in National American literature.

From the earliest times the presence of the black man in America has inspired American writers. Among the early Colonial writers the Negro was a subject as, for instance, in Samuel

[4] Cf. Preface to James Weldon Johnson's *The Book of American Negro Poetry*, New York, 1922.

Sewall's "Selling of Joseph," the first American
anti-slavery tract published in 1700. But we espe-
cially see in the influence of the Negro's condition
in the work of the masters of the 19th century,
like Ralph Waldo Emerson, John Greenleaf
Whittier, James Russell Lowell, Walt Whitman,
Julia Ward Howe, Harriet Beecher Stowe and
Lydia Maria Child. With these must be named
the orators Wendell Phillips, Charles Sumner,
John C. Calhoun, Henry Ward Beecher. In our
own day, we have had the writers of fiction,
George U. Cable, Thomas Nelson Page, Thomas
Dixson, Ruth McEnery Stewart, William Dean
Howells, Thomas Wentworth Higginson.

It may be said that the influence of the Negro
here is a passive influence and yet one must remember that it would be inconceivable to have an
American literature, even that written by white
men, and not have the Negro as a subject. He
has been the lay figure, but after all, the figure
has been alive, it has moved, it has talked, felt
and influenced.

In the minds of these and other writers how
has the Negro been portrayed? It is a fascinating
subject which I can but barely touch: in the days
of Shakespeare and Southerne the black man of
fiction was a man, a brave, fine, if withal over-
trustful and impulsive, hero. In science he was

different but equal, cunning in unusual but mighty
possibilities. Then with the slave trade he suddenly became a clown and dropped from sight.
He emerged slowly beginning about 1830 as a dull
stupid but contented slave, capable of doglike devotion, superstitious and incapable of education.
Then, in the abolition controversy he became a
victim, a man of sorrows, a fugitive chased by
bloodhounds, a beautiful raped octoroon, a crucified Uncle Tom, but a lay figure, objectively pitiable but seldom subjectively conceived. Suddenly
a change came after Reconstruction. The black
man was either a faithful old "Befoh de wah"
darky worshipping lordly white folk, or a
frolicking ape, or a villain, a sullen scoundrel, a
violator of womanhood, a low thief and mis-
birthed monster. He was sub-normal and con-
genitally incapable. He was represented as an unfit survival of Darwinian natural selection.
Philanthropy and religion stood powerless before
his pigmy brain and undeveloped morals. In a
"thousands years"? Perhaps. But at present, an
upper beast. Out of this today he is slowly but
tentatively, almost apologetically rising—a somewhat deserving, often poignant, but hopeless
figure; a man whose only proper end is dramatic
suicide physically or morally. His trouble is natural and inborn inferiority, slight by scientific

measurement but sufficient to make absolute limits
to his possibilities, save in exceptional cases.

And here we stand today. As a normal human
being reacting humanly to human problems the
Negro has never appeared in the fiction or the
science of white writers, with a bare half dozen
exceptions; while to the white southerner who
"knows him best" he is always an idiot or a
monster, and he sees him as such, no matter what
is before his very eyes. And yet, with all this, the
Negro has held the stage. In the South he is
everything. You cannot discuss religion, morals,
politics, social life, science, earth or sky, God or
devil without touching the Negro. It is a peren-
nial and continuous and continual subject of books,
editorials, sermons, lectures and smoking car con-
fabs. In the north and west while seldom in the
center, the Negro is always in the wings waiting
to appear or screaming shrill lines off stage. What
would intellectual America do if she woke some
fine morning to find no "Negro" Problem?

Coming now to the slowly swelling stream of a
distinct group literature, by and primarily for the
Negro, we enter a realm only partially known to
white Americans. First, there come the rich mass
of Negro folk lore transplanted from Africa and
developed in America. A white writer, Joel
Chandler Harris, first popularized "Uncle

Remus" and "Brer Rabbit" for white America; but he was simply the deft and singularly successful translator — the material was Negroid and appears repeatedly among the black peasants and various forms and versions. Take for instance the versions of the celebrated tar-baby story of Joel Chandler Harris. C. C. Jones took down a striking version apparently direct from Negro lips early in the 19th century:

" 'Do Buh Wolf, bun me: broke me neck, but don't trow me in de brier patch. Lemme dead one time. Don't tarrify me no mo.' Buh Wolf yet bin know wuh Buh Rabbit up teh. Eh tink eh bin guine tare Bur Rabbit hide off. So, wuh eh do? Eh loose Buh Rabbit from de spakleberry bush, an eh tek um by de hine leg, an eh swing um roun', en eh trow um way in de tick brier patch fuh tare eh hide and cratch eh yeye out. De minnit Buh Rabbit drap in de brier patch, eh cock up eh tail, eh jump, an holler back to Buh Wolf: 'Good bye, Budder! Dis de place me mammy fotch me up,— dis de place me mammy fotch me up.' An eh gone before Buh Wolf kin ketch um. Buh Rabbit too scheemy."

The Harris version shows the literary touch added by the white man. But the Negro version told by Jones has all the meat of the primitive tale.

Next we note the folk rhymes and poetry of Negroes, sometimes accompanying their music and sometimes not. A white instructor in English literature at the University of Virgina says:

"Of all the builders of the nation the Negro alone has created a species of lyric verse that all the world may recognize as a distinctly American production."

T. W. Talley, a Negro, has recently published an exhaustive collection of these rhymes. They form an interesting collection of poetry often crude and commonplace but with here and there touches of real poetry and quaint humor.[5]

The literary expression of Negroes themselves has had continuous development in America since the eighteenth century.[6] It may however be looked upon from two different points of view: We may think of the writing of Negroes as self-expression and as principally for themselves. Here we have a continuous line of writers. Only a few of these, however would we think of as contributing to American literature as such and yet this inner, smaller stream of Negro literature overflows faintly at first and now evidently more and more into the wider stream of American literature; on the other hand there have been figures in Ameri-

[5] T. W. Talley, *Negro Folk Rhymes.*
[6] Cf. W. E. B. Du Bois, *The Negro in Literature and Art* (Annals American Academy, Sept., 1913).

can literature who happen to be of Negro descent and who are but vaguely to be identified with the group stream as such. Both these points of view are interesting but let us first take up the succession of authors who form a group literature by and for Negroes.

As early as the eighteenth century, and even before the Revolutionary War the first voices of Negro authors were heard in the United States. Phyllis Wheatley, the black poetess, was easily the pioneer, her first poems appearing in 1773, and other editions in 1774 and 1793. Her earliest poem was in memory of George Whitefield. She was honored by Washington and leading Englishmen and was as a writer above the level of her American white contemporaries.

She was followed by Richard Allen, first Bishop of the African Methodist Church whose autobiography, published in 1793 was the beginning of that long series of personal appears and narratives of which Booker T. Washington's "Up From Slavery" was the latest. Benjamin Banneker's almanacs represented the first scientific work of American Negroes, and began to be issued in 1792.

Coming now to the first decades of the nineteenth century we find some essays on freedom by the African Society of Boston, and an apology for the new Negro church formed in Philadelphia. Paul Cuffe, disgusted with America, wrote an early account of Sierra Leone, while the celebrated Lemuel Haynes, ignoring the race question, dipped deeply into the New England theological controversy about 1815. In 1829 came the first full-voiced, almost hysterical, protest against slavery and the color line in David Walker's Appeal which aroused Southern legislatures to action. This was followed by the earliest Negro conventions which issued interesting minutes; two appeals against disfranchisement in Pennsylvania appeared in this decade, one written by Robert Purvis, who also wrote a biography of his father-in-law, Mr. James Forten, and the other appeal written by John Bowers and others. The life of Gustavus Vassa, also known by his African name of Olaudah Equiana, was published in America in 1837 continuing the interesting personal narratives.

In 1840 some strong writers began to appear. Henry Highland Garnet and J. W. C. Pennington preached powerful sermons and gave some attention to Negro history in their pamphlets: R. B. Lewis made a more elaborate attempt at Negro history. Whitfield's poems appeared in 1846, and William Wells Brown began a career of writing which lasted from 1847 until after the Civil War.

He began his literary career by the publication of his "Narrative of a Fugitive Slave" in 1847. This was followed by a novel in 1853, "Sketches" from abroad in 1855, a play in 1858, "The Black Man" in 1863, "The Negro in the American Rebellion" in 1867, and "The Rising Son" in 1874. The Colored Convention in Cincinnati and Cleveland published reports in this decade and Bishop Loguen wrote his life history. In 1845 Douglass' autobiography made its first appearance, destined to run through endless editions until the last in 1893. Moreover it was in 1841 that the first Negro magazine appeared in America, edited by George Hogarth and published by the A. M. E. Church.

In the fifties James Whitfield published further poems, and a new poet arose in the person of Frances E. W. Harper, a woman of no little ability who died lately; Martin R. Delaney and William Cooper Nell wrote further of Negro history, Nell especially making valuable contributions of the history of the Negro soldiers. Three interesting biographies were added in this decade to the growing number; Josiah Henson, Samuel C. Ward and Samuel Northrop; while Catto, leaving general history came down to the better known history of the Negro church.

In the sixties slave narratives multiplied, like

that of Linda Brent, while two studies of Africa
based on actual visits were made by Robert Campbell and Dr. Alexander Crummell; William Douglass and Bishop Daniel Payne continued the history of the Negro church, and William Wells
Brown carried forward his work in general Negro
history. In this decade, too, Bishop Tanner began
his work in Negro theology.

Most of the Negro talent in the seventies was
taken up in politics; the older men like Bishop
Wayman wrote of their experiences; Sojourner
Truth added her story to the slave narratives. A
new poet arose in the person of A. A. Whitman,
while James Monroe Trotter was the first to take
literary note of the musical ability of his race.
Robert Brown Elliott stirred the nation by his
eloquence in Congress. The Fisk edition of the
Songs of the Jubilee Singers appeared.

In the eighties there are signs of unrest and con-
flicting streams of thought. On the one hand the
rapid growth of the Negro church is shown by the
writers on church subjects like Moore and Wayman. The historical spirit was especially strong.
Still wrote of the Underground Railroad; Simmons issued his interesting biographical dictionary,
and the greatest historian of the race appeared
when George W. Williams issued his two-volume
history of the Negro Race in America. The

political turmoil was reflected in Langston's Freedom and Citizenship, Fortune's Black and White,
and Straker's New South, and found its bitterest
arraignment in Turner's pamphlets; but with all
this went other new thought: Scarborough published "First Greek Lessons"; Bishop Payne
issued his Treatise on Domestic Education, and
Stewart studied Liberia.

In the nineties came histories, essays, novels and
poems, together with biographies and social
studies. The history was represented by Payne's
History of the A. M. E. Church, Hood's "One
Hundred Years of the A. M. E. Zion Church,
Anderson's sketch of Negro Presbyterianism and
Hagood's Colored Man in the M. E. Church;
general history of the older type was represented
by R. L. Perry's Cushite and of the newer type in
E. A. Johnson's histories, while one of the secret
societies found their historian in Brooks; Crogman's essays appeared and Archibald Grimke's
biographies. The race question was discussed in
Frank Grimke's published sermons, social studies
were made by Penn, Wright, Mossell, Crummell,
Majors and others. Most notable, however, was
the rise of the Negro novelist and poet with national recognition: Frances Harper was still writing and Griggs began his racial novels, but both of
these spoke primarily to the Negro race; on the

other hand, Chesnutt's six novels and Dunbar's inimitable works spoke of the whole nation. J. T. Wilson's "Black Phalanx," the most complete study of the Negro soldier, came in these years.

Booker T. Washington's work began with his address at Atlanta in 1895, "Up From Slavery" in 1901, "Working with the Hands" in 1904, and "The Man Farthest Down" in 1912. The American Negro Academy, a small group, began the publication of occasional papers in 1897 and has published a dozen or more numbers including a "Symposium on the Negro and the Elective Franchise" in 1905, a "Comparative Study of the Negro Problem" in 1899, Love's "Disfranchisement of the Negro" in 1899, Grimke's Study of Denmark Vesey in 1901 and Steward's "Black St. Domingo Legion" in 1899. Since 1900 the stream of Negro writing has continued. Dunbar has found a successor in the critic and compiler of anthologies, W. S. Braithwaite; Booker T. Washington has given us his biography and Story of the Negro; Kelly Miller's trenchant essays have appeared in book form and he has issued numbers of critical monographs on the Negro problem with wide circulation. Scientific historians have appeared in Benjamin Brawley and Carter Woodson and George W. Mitchell. Sinclair's Aftermath of Slavery has attracted attention, as have the studies made by Atlanta University. The Negro in American Sculpture has been studied by H. F. M. Murray.

The development in poetry has been significant, beginning with Phyllis Wheatley.[7] Jupiter Hammon came in the 18th century, George M. Horton in the early part of the 19th century followed by Frances Harper who began publishing in 1854 and A. A. Whitman whose first attempts at epic poetry were published in the seventies. In 1890 came the first thin volume of Paul Lawrence Dunbar, the undoubted laureate of the race, who published poems and one or two novels up until the beginning of the 20th century. He was succeeded by William Stanley Braithwaite whose fame rests chiefly upon his poetic criticism and his anthologies, and finally by James Weldon Johnson, Claud McKay who came out of the West Indies with a new and sincere gift, Fenton Johnson, Georgia Johnson and Jessie Fauset. Joseph S. Cotter, Jr., Langston Hughes, Roscoe C. Jamison and Countée Cullen have done notable work in verse. Campbell, Davis and others have continued the poetic tradition of Negro dialect.

On the whole, the literary output of the American Negro has been both large and creditable, al-

---

[7] A. A. Schomberg, *A Bibliographical Checklist of American Negro Poetry*, New York, 1916.

though, of course, comparatively little known; few great names have appeared and only here and there work that could be called first class, but this is not a peculiarity of Negro literature.

The time has not yet come for the great development of American Negro literature. The economic stress is too great and the racial persecution too bitter to allow the leisure and the poise for which literature calls. "The Negro in the United States is consuming all his intellectual energy in this gruelling race-struggle. And the same statement may be made in a general way about the white South. Why does not the white South produce literature and art? The white South, too, is consuming all of its intellectual energy in this lamentable conflict. Nearly all of the mental efforts of the white South run through one narrow channel. The life of every southern white man and all of his activities are impassably limited by the ever present Negro problem. And that is why, as Mr. H. L. Mencken puts it, in all that vast region, with its thirty or forty million people and its territory as large as half a dozen Frances or Germanys, "there is not a single poet, not a serious historian, not a creditable composer, not a critic good or bad, not a dramatist dead or alive."

On the other hand, never in the world has a richer mass of material been accumulated by a people than that which the Negroes possess today and are becoming increasingly conscious of. Slowly but surely they are developing artists of technic who will be able to use this material. The nation does not notice this for everything touching the Negro has hitherto been banned by magazines and publishers unless it took the form of caricature or bitter attack, or was so thoroughly innocuous as to have no literary flavor. This attitude shows signs of change at last.

Most of the names in this considerable list except those toward the last would be unknown to the student of American literature. Nevertheless they form a fairly continuous tradition and a most valuable group expression. From them several have arisen, as I have said, to become figures in the main stream of American literature. Phyllis Wheatley was an American writer of Negro descent just as Dumas was a French writer of Negro descent. She was the peer of her best American contemporaries but she represented no conscious Negro group. Lemuel Haynes wrote for Americans rather than for Negroes.

Dunbar occupies a unique place in American literature. He raised a dialect and a theme from the minstrel stage to literature and became and remains a national figure. Charles W. Chesnutt followed him as a novelist, and many white people read in form of fiction a subject which they did not want to read or hearken to. He gained his way unaided and by sheer merit and is a recognized American novelist. Braithwaite is a critic whose Negro descent is not generally known and has but slightly influenced his work. His place in American literature is due more to his work as a critic and anthologist than to his work as a poet. "There is still another role he has played, that of friend of poetry and poets. It is a recognized fact that in the work which preceded the present revival of poetry in the United States, no one rendered more unremitting and valuable service than Mr. Braithwaite. And it can be said that no future study of American poetry of this age can be made without reference to Braithwaite."

Of McKay's poems, Max Eastman writes that it "should be illuminating to observe that while these poems are characteristic of that race as we most admire it—they are gentle, simple, candid, brave and friendly, quick of laughter and of tears —yet they are still more characteristic of what is deep and universal in mankind. There is no special or exotic kind of merit in them, no quality that demands a transmutation of our own natures to perceive. Just as the sculptures and wood and ivory carvings of the vast forgotten African Empires of Ife and Benin, although so wistful in their tranquility, are tranquil in the possession of the qualities of all classic and great art, so these poems, the purest of them, move with a sovereignty that is never new to the lovers of the high music of human utterance."[8]

The later writers like Jean Toomer, Claud McKay, Jessie Fauset and others have come on the stage when the stream of Negro literature has grown to be of such importance and gained so much of technique and merit that it tends to merge into the broad flood of American literature and any notable Negro writer became *ipso facto* a national writer.

One must not forget the Negro orator. While in the white world the human voice as a vehicle of information and persuasion has waned in importance until the average man is somewhat suspicious of "eloquence," in the Negro world the spoken word is still dominant and Negro orators have wielded great influence upon both white and black from the time of Frederick Douglass and Samuel Ward down to the day of J. C. Price and Booker T. Washington. There is here, undoubtedly, something of unusual gift and personal magnetism.

[8] Preface to Claud McKay's *Harlem Shadows*.

One must note in this connection the rise and
spread of a Negro press — magazines and week-
lies which are voicing to the world with increasing power the thought of American Negroes. The
influence of this new force in America is being
recognized and the circulation of these papers
aggregate more than a million copies.

On the stage the Negro has naturally had a
most difficult chance to be recognized. He has
been portrayed by white dramatists and actors,
and for a time it seemed but natural for a character like Othello to be drawn, or for Southerne's
Oroonoko to be presented in 1696 in England
with a black Angola prince as its hero. Beginning, however, with the latter part of the 18th
century the stage began to make fun of the Negro
and the drunken character Mungo was introduced
at Drury Lane.

In the United States this tradition was continued by the "Negro Minstrels" which began with
Thomas D. Rice's imitation of a Negro cripple,
Jim Crow. Rice began his work in Louisville in
1828 and had great success. Minstrel companies
imitating Negro songs and dances and blackening
their faces gained a great vogue until long after
the Civil War. Negroes themselves began to
appear as principals in minstrel companies after a
time and indeed as early as 1820 there was an

"African company" playing in New York. No sooner had the Negro become the principal in the minstrel shows than he began to develop and uplift the art. This took a long time but eventually there appeared Cole and Johnson, Ernest Hogan and Williams and Walker. Their development of a new light comedy marked an epoch and Bert Williams was at his recent death without doubt the leading comedian on the American stage.

In the legitimate drama there was at first no chance for the Negro in the United States. Ira Aldridge, born in Maryland, had to go to Europe for opportunity. There he became associated with leading actors like Edmund Keene and was regarded in the fifties as one of the two or three greatest actors in the world. He was honored and decorated by the King of Sweden, the King of Prussia, the Emperor of Austria and the Czar of Russia. He had practically no successor until Charles Gilpin triumphed in "The Emperor Jones" in New York during the season 1920-21.

Efforts to develop a new distinctly racial drama and portray the dramatic struggle of the Negro in America and elsewhere have rapidly been made. Mrs. Emily Hapgood made determined effort to initiate a Negro theatre. She chose the plays of Ridgeley Torrence, a white playwright, who wrote for the Negro players "Granny Maumee" and "The Rider of Dreams," pieces singularly true to Negro genius. The plays were given with unusual merit and gained the highest praise.

This movement, interrupted by the war, has been started again by the Ethiopian Players of Chicago and especially by the workers at Howard University where a Negro drama with Negro instructors, Negro themes and Negro players is being developed. One of the most interesting pageants given in America was written, staged and performed by Negroes in New York, Philadelphia and Washington.

Charles Gilpin had been trained with Williams and Walker and other colored companies. He got his first chance on the legitimate stage by playing the part of Curtis in Drinkwater's "Abraham Lincoln." Then he became the principal in O'Neill's wonderful play and was nominated by the Drama League in 1921 as one of the ten persons who had contributed most to the American theatre during the year. Paul Robeson and Evelyn Preer are following Gilpin's footsteps.

There is no doubt of the Negro's dramatic genius. Stephen Graham writes:

"I visited one evening a Negro theatre where a musical comedy was going on — words and music both by Negroes. It opened with the usual singing and dancing chorus of Negro girls. They were clad in yellow and crimson and mauve combinations with white tapes on one side from the lace edge of the knicker to their dusky arms. They danced from the thigh rather than from the knee, moving waist and bosom in unrestrained undulation, girls with large, startled seeming eyes and uncontrollable masses of dark hair.. A dance of physical joy and abandon, with no restraint in the toes or the knees, no veiling of the eyes, no half shutting of the lips, no holding in of the hair. Accustomed to the very aesthetic presentment of the Bacchanalia in the Russian ballet, it might be difficult to call one of those Negro dancers a Bacchante, and yet there was one whom I remarked again and again, a Queen of Sheba in her looks, a face like starry night, and she was clad slightly in mauve, and went into such ecstacies during the many encores that her hair fell down about her bare shoulders, and her cheeks and knees, glistening with perspiration, outshone her eyes. . . . I had seen nothing so pretty or so amusing, so bewilderingly full of life and color, since Sanine's production of the 'Fair of Sorochinsky' in Moscow."

Turning now to painting, we note a young African painter contemporary with Phyllis Wheatley who had gained some little renown.

Then a half century ago came E. M. Banister, the center of a group of artists forming the Rhode Island Art Club, and one of whose pictures took a medal at the Centennial Exposition in 1876.

William A. Harper died in 1910. His "Avenue of Poplars" took a prize of $100 at the Chicago Art Institute. William Edward Scott studied in Paris under Tanner. His picture "La Pauvre Voisine" was hung in the salon in 1910 and bought by the government of the Argentine Republic. Another picture was hung in Paris and took first prize at the Indiana State Fair, and a third picture was exhibited in the Royal Academy in London. Lately Mr. Scott has specialized in mural painting. His work is found in ten public schools in Chicago, in four in Indianapolis and in the latter city he decorated two units in the City Hospital with 300 life sized pictures. In many of these pictures he has especially emphasized the Negro type.

Richard Brown, Edwin Harleston, Albert A. Smith, Laura Wheeler and a number of rising young painters have shown the ability of the Negro in this line of art; but their dean is, of course, Henry Ossawa Tanner. Tanner is today one of the leading painters of the world and universally is so recognized. He was born an American Negro in Pittsburgh in 1859, the son of

an African Methodist minister; he studied at the
Academy of Fine Arts in Philadelphia and became a photographer in Atlanta. Afterward he
taught at Clark University in Atlanta. In all this
time he had sold less than $200 worth of pictures;
but finally he got to Paris and was encouraged by
Benjamin Constant. He soon turned toward his
greatest forte, religious pictures. His "Daniel in
the Lion's Den" was hung in the salon in 1896
and the next year the "Raising of Lazarus"
was bought by the French government and hung
in the Luxembourg. Since then he has won medals
in all the greatest expositions, and his works are
sought by connoisseurs. He has recently received
knighthood in the French Legion of Honor.

In sculpture we may again think of two points
of view, — first, there is the way in which the
Negro type has figured in American sculpture as,
for instance, the libyan Sybil of W. A. Story,
Bissell's Emancipation group in Scotland, the
Negro woman on the military monument in De-
troit, Ball's Negro in the various emancipation
groups, Ward's colored woman on the Beecher
monument, the panel on the Cleveland monument
of Scofield, Africa in D. C. French's group in
front of the Custom's House in New York City,
Calder's black boy in the Nations of the West
group in the Panama-Pacific exhibition and, of

course, the celebrated Shaw monument in Boston.[9]
On the other hand, there have been a few Negro
sculptors, three of whom merit mention: Edmonia
Lewis, who worked during the Civil War, Meta
Warrick Fuller, a pupil of Rodin, and May
Howard Jackson, who has done some wonderful
work in the portraying of the mulatto type.

To appraise rightly this body of art one must
remember that it represents mainly the work of
those artists whom accident set free; if the artist
had a white face his Negro blood did not militate
against him in the fight for recognition; if his
Negro blood was visible white relatives may have
helped him; in a few cases ability was united to
indomitable will. But the shrinking, modest,
black artist without special encouragement had
little or no chance in a world determined to make
him a menial. Today the situation is changing.
The Negro world is demanding expression in art
and beginning to pay for it. The white world is
able to see dimly beyond the color line. This sum
of accomplishment then is but a beginning and an
imperfect indication of what the Negro race is
capable of in America and in the world.

Science, worse luck, has in these drab days little
commerce with art and yet for lack of better place

[9] Cf. Freeman H. M. Murray, *Emancipation and the Freed in
American Sculpture*, Washington, D. C., 1916.

a word may drop here of the American Negro's contribution. Science today is a matter chiefly for endowed fellowships and college chairs. Negroes have small chance here because of race exclusion and yet no scientist in the world can today write of insects and ignore the work of C. H. Turner of St. Louis; or of insanity and forget Dr. S. C. Fuller of Massachusetts. Ernest Just's investigations of the origin of life make him stand among the highest two or three modern scientists in that line and the greatest American interpreter of Wasserman reactions is a colored man; Dr. Julien H. Lewis of the University of Chicago, is building a reputation in serology. There are also a number of deft Negro surgeons including Dr. Dan Williams who first sewed up a wounded human heart. The great precursors of all these colored men of science were Thomas Derham and Benjamin Banneker.

Derham was a curiosity more than a great scientist measuring by absolute standards, and yet in the 18th century and at the age of twenty-six he was regarded as one of the most eminent physicians in New Orleans. Dr. Rush of Philadelphia testified to his learning and ability.

Benjamin Banneker was a leading American scientist. He was the grandson of an English

woman and her black slave.   Their daughter married a Negro and Benjamin was their only son.
Born in 1731 in Maryland he was educated in a
private school with whites and spent his life on
his father's farm. He had taste for mathematics
and early constructed an ingenious clock.   He
became expert in the solution of difficult mathematical problems, corresponding with interested
persons of leisure.

Thomas Jefferson wrote to the Marquis de
Condorcet: "We now have in the United States a
Negro, the son of a black man born in Africa and
a black woman born in the United States, who is a
very respectable mathematician. I procured him
to be employed under one of our chief directors in
laying out the new Federal City on the Potomac
and in the intervals of his leisure, while on that
work, he made an almanac for the next year, which
he sent me in his own handwriting and which I
enclose to you. I have seen very elegant solutions
of geometrical problems by him. Add to this that
he is a very worthy and respectable member of
society. He is a free man. I shall be delighted to
see these instances of moral eminence so multiplied
as to prove that the want of talents observed in
them, is merely the effect of their degraded condition, and not proceeding from any difference in

the structure of the parts on which intellect depends."[10]

Banneker became greatly interested in astron-
omy. He made a number of calculations and
finally completed an almanac covering the year
1792. A member of John Adams' cabinet had
this almanac published in Baltimore. This patron,
James McHenry, said that the almanac was begun
and finished without outside assistance except the
loan of books "so that whatever merit is attached
to his present performance, is exclusively and
peculiarly his own." The publishers declared that
the almanac met the approbation of several of
the most distinguished astronomers of America.
The almanac was published yearly until 1802.
When the City of Washington was laid out in
1793 under Major Pierre Charles L'Enfant,
President Washington at the suggestion of
Thomas Jefferson appointed Banneker as one of
the six commissioners. He performed a most
important part of the mathematical calculations
of the survey and sat in conference with the other
commissioners. Later he wrote essays on bees and
studied methods to promote peace, suggesting a
Secretary of Peace in the president's cabinet. He
"was a brave looking pleasant man with some-

[10] *Journal of Negro History*, Vol. 3, p. 99ff. Later, Jefferson writing
to an American thought Banneker had "a mind of very common stature
indeed".

thing very noble in his appearance." His color was not jet black but decided Negroid. He died in 1806, with both an American and European reputation and was among the most learned men of his day in America.

CHAPTER IX

THE GIFT OF THE SPIRIT

How the fine sweet spirit of black folk, despite superstition and passion has breathed the soul of humility and forgiveness into the formalism and cant of American religion.

Above and beyond all that we have mentioned, perhaps least tangible but just as true, is the peculiar spiritual quality which the Negro has injected into American life and civilization. It is hard to define or characterize it — a certain spiritual joyousness; a sensuous, tropical love of life, in vivid contrast to the cool and cautious New England reason; a slow and dreamful conception of the universe, a drawling and slurring of speech, an intense sensitiveness to spiritual values — all these things and others like to them, tell of the imprint of Africa on Europe in America. There is no gainsaying or explaining away this tremendous influence of the contact of the north and south, of black and white, of Anglo Saxon and Negro.

One way this influence has been brought to bear

is through the actual mingling of blood. But this
is the smaller cause of Negro influence. Heredity
is always stronger through the influence of acts
and deeds and imitations than through actual
blood descent; and the presence of the Negro in
the United States quite apart from the mingling
of blood has always strongly influenced the land.
We have spoken of its influence in politics, literature and art, but we have yet to speak of that
potent influence in another sphere of the world's
spiritual activities: religion.

America early became a refuge for religion —
a place of mighty spaces and glorious physical and
mental freedom where silent men might sit and
think quietly of God and his world. Hither out
of the blood and dust of war-wrecked Europe
with its jealousies, blows, persecutions and fear of
words and thought, came Puritans, Anabaptists,
Catholics, Quakers, Moravians, Methodists —
all sorts of men and "isms" and sects searching
for God and Truth in the lonely bitter wilderness.

Hither too came the Negro. From the first he
was the concrete test of that search for Truth, of
the strife toward a God, of that body of belief
which is the essence of true religion. His presence rent and tore and tried the souls of men.
"Away with the slave!" some cried — but where
away and why? Was not his body there for work

and his soul — what of his soul? Bring hither
the slaves of all Africa and let us convert their
souls, this is God's good reason for slavery. But
convert them to what? to freedom? to emancipation? to being white men? Impossible. Convert
them, yes. But let them still be slaves for their
own good and ours. This was quibbling and good
men felt it, but at least here was a practical path,
follow it.

Thus arose the great mission movements to the
blacks. The Catholic Church began it and not
only were there Negro proselytes but black priests
and an order of black monks in Spanish America
early in the 16th century. In the middle of the
17th century a Negro freedman and charcoal
burner lived to see his son, Francisco Xavier de
Luna Victoria, raised to head the Bishopric of
Panama where he reigned eight years as the first
native Catholic Bishop in America.

In Spanish America and in French America the
history of Negro religion is bound up with the
history of the Catholic Church. On the other
hand in the present territory of the United States
with the exception of Maryland and Louisiana
organized religion was practically and almost exclusively Protestant and Catholics indeed were
often bracketed with Negroes for persecution.
They could not marry Protestants at one time in

colonial South Carolina; Catholics and Negroes could not appear in court as witnesses in Virginia by the law of 1705; Negroes and Catholics were held to be the cause of the "Negro plot" in New York in 1741.

The work then of the Catholic Church among Negroes began in the United States well into the 19th century and by Negroes themselves. In Baltimore, for instance, in 1829, colored refugees from the French West Indies established a sisterhood and academy and gave an initial endowment of furniture, real estate and some $50,000 in money. In 1842 in New Orleans, four free Negro women gave their wealth to form the Sisters of the Holy Family and this work expanded and grew especially after 1893 when a mulatto, Thomy Lafon, endowed the work with over three quarters of a million dollars, his life savings. Later, in 1896, a colored man, Colonel John McKee of Philadelphia, left a million dollars in real estate to the Catholic Church for colored and white orphans.

Outside of these colored sisterhoods and colored philanthropists, the church hesitated long before it began any systematic proselyting among Negroes. This was because of the comparative weakness of the church in early days and later when the Irish migration strengthened it the new

Catholics were thrown into violent economic competition with slaves and free Negroes, and their
fight to escape slave competition easily resolved
itself into a serious anti-Negro hatred which was
back of much of the rioting in Cincinnati, Philadelphia and New York. It was not then until the
20th century that the church began active work by
establishing a special mission for Negroes and
engaging in it nearly two hundred white priests.
This new impetus was caused by the benevolence
of Katherine Drexel and the Sisters of the Blessed
Sacrament. Notwithstanding all this and since
the beginning of the 18th century only six Negroes
have been ordained to the Catholic priesthood.

The main question of the conversion of the
Negro to Christianity in the United States was
therefore the task of the Protestant Church and
it was, if the truth must be told, a task which it
did not at all relish. The whole situation was
fraught with perplexing contradictions; Could
Christians be slaves? Could slaves be Christians?
Was the object of slavery the Christianizing of
the black man, and when the black man was
Christianized was the mission of slavery done and
ended? Was it possible to make modern Christians of these persons whom the new slavery began to paint as brutes? The English Episcopal
Church finally began the work in 1701 through

the Society for the Propagation of the Gospel. It
had notable officials, the Archbishop of Canter-
bury being its first president; it worked in America
82 years, accomplishing something but after all
not very much, on account of the persistent objection of the masters. The Moravians were more
eager and sent missionaries to the Negroes, con-
verting large numbers in the West Indies and
some in the United States in the 18th century.
Into the new Methodist Church which came to
America in 1766, large numbers of Negroes
poured from the first, and finally the Baptists in
the 18th century had at least one fourth of their
membership composed of Negroes, so that in 1800
there were 14,000 black Methodists and some
20,000 black Baptists.[1]

It must not be assumed that this missionary
work acted on raw material. Rather it reacted
and was itself influenced by a very definite and
important body of thought and belief on the part
of the Negroes. Religion in the United States
was not simply brought to the Negro by the missionaries. To treat it in that way is to miss the
essence of the Negro action and reaction upon
American religion. We must think of the transplanting of the Negro as transplanting to the

[1] Charles C. Jones, *Religious Instruction of the Negroes*, Savannah,
1842.

United States a certain spiritual entity, and an unbreakable set of world-old beliefs, manners, morals, superstitions and religious observances. The religion of Africa is the universal animism or fetishism of primitive peoples, rising to polytheism and approaching monotheism chiefly, but not wholly, as a result of Christian and Islamic missions. Of fetishism there is much misapprehension. It is not mere senseless degradation. It is a philosophy of life. Among primitive Negroes there can be, as Miss Kingsley reminds us, no such divorce of religion from practical life as is common in civilized lands. Religion is life, and fetish an expression of the practical recognition of dominant forces in which the Negro lives. To him all the world is spirit. Miss Kingsley says: "It is this power of being able logically to account for everything that is, I believe, at the back of the tremendous permanency of fetish in Africa, and the cause of many of the relapses into it by Africans converted to other religions; it is also the explanation of the fact that white men who live in the districts where death and danger are everyday affairs, under a grim pall of boredom, are liable to believe in fetish, though ashamed of so doing. For the African, whose mind has been soaked in fetish during his early and most impressionable years, the voice of fetish is almost irresistible when affliction comes to him."[2]

At first sight it would seem that slavery completely destroyed every vestige of spontaneous social movement among the Negroes; the home had deteriorated; political authority and economic initiative was in the hands of the masters; property, as a social institution, did not exist on the plantation; and, indeed, it is usually assumed by historians and sociologists that every vestige of internal development disappeared, leaving the slaves no means of expression for their common life, thought, and striving. This is not strictly true; the vast power of the priest in the African state still survived; his realm alone — the province of religion and medicine — remained largely unaffected by the plantation system in many important particulars. The Negro priest, therefore, early became an important figure on the plantation and found his function as the interpreter of the supernatural, the comforter of the sorrowing, and as the one who expressed, rudely, but picturesquely, the longing and disappointment and resentment of a stolen people. From such beginnings arose and spread with marvellous rapidity the Negro church, the first distinctively Negro American social institution. It was not at first by

[2] M. H. Kingsley, *West African Studies.*

any means a Christian Church, but a mere adapta-
tion of those heathen rites which we roughly
designate by the term Obe Worship or "Voo-
dooism."   Association and missionary effort soon
gave these rites a veneer of Christianity, and
gradually, after two centuries, the Church became
Christian, with a simple Calvinistic creed, but
with many of the old customs still clinging to the
services.   It is this historic fact that the Negro
Church today bases itself upon the sole surviving
social institution of the African fatherland, that
accounts for its extraordinary growth and vitality.
We easily forget that in the United States today
there is a Church organization for every sixty
Negro families.   This institution, therefore,
naturally assumed many functions which the other
harshly suppressed social organs had to surrender; the Church became the center of amusements,
of what little spontaneous economic activity remained, of education, and of all social intercourse, of music and art.[3]

For these reasons the tendency of the Negro
worshippers from the very first was to integrate
into their own organizations.   As early as 1775
distinct Negro congregations with Negro ministers began to appear here and there in the United·
States.   They multiplied, were swept away, effort

[3] Atlanta University Publications, *The Negro Church,* 1903.

was made to absorb them in the white church, but they kept on growing until they established national bodies with Episcopal control or democratic federation and these organizations today form the strongest, most inclusive and most vital of the Negro organizations. They count in the United States four million members and their churches seat these four million and six million other guests. They are houses in 40,000 centers, worth $60,-000,000 and have some 200,000 leaders.

On the part of the white church this tendency among the Negroes met with alternate encouragement and objection: encouragement because they did not want Negroes in their churches even when they occupied the back seats or in the gallery; objection when the church became, as it so often did, a center of intelligent Negro life and even of plotting against slavery. There arose out of the church the first leaders of the Negro group; and in the first rank among these stands Richard Allen.[4]

Richard Allen was born in 1760 as a slave in Philadelphia and was licensed to preach in 1782. He was ordained deacon by Bishop Asbury and he led the Negroes in their secession from St. George's Church in Philadelphia when they tried to stop black folk from praying on the main floor.

[4] Richard Allen, *Life, Experience and Gospel Labors*, Philadelphia, 1880.

He formed first the Free African Society and finally established Bethel Church.

As this church grew and multiplied it became the African Methodist Episcopal Church which now boasts three quarters of a million members. Allen was its first bishop. With Allen was associated Absalom Jones, born a slave in Delaware in 1746. He became the first Negro priest in the Episcopal Church. John Gloucester became the pioneer Negro minister among colored Presbyterians and gave that church his four sons as ministers. George Leile became a missionary of the American Negroes to the Negroes of Jamaica and began missionary work on that island while Lott Carey in a similar way became a missionary to Africa. Then came Nat Turner, the preacher revolutionist. James Varick, a free negro of New York who was the first bishop of the black Zion Methodist revolt, and afterward there followed the stream of Negro leaders who have built and led the organization of colored churches. But this is only part of the story.

It will be seen that the development of the Negro church was not separate from the white. Black preachers led white congregations, white preachers addressed blacks. In many other ways Negroes influenced white religion continuously and tremendously. There was the "Shout," com-

bining the trance and demoniac possession as old
as the world, and revivified and made wide-spread
by the Negro religious devotees in America.
Methodist and Baptist ways of worship, songs
and religious dances absorbed much from the
Negroes and whatever there is in American religion today of stirring and wild enthusiasm, of
loud conversions and every day belief in an an-
thropomorphic God owes its origin in a no small
measure to the black man.

Of course most of the influence of the Negro
preachers was thrown into their own churches and
to their own people and it was from the Negro
church as an organization that Negro religious influence spread most widely to white people. Many
would say that this influence had little that was
uplifting and was a detriment rather than an advantage in that it held back and holds back the
South particularly in its religious development.
There is no doubt that influences of a primitive
sort and customs that belong to the unlettered
childhood of the race rather than to the thinking
adult life of civilization crept in with the religious
influence of the slave. Much of superstition, even
going so far as witchcraft, conjury and blood
sacrifice for a long time marked Negro religion
here and there in the swamps and islands. But
on the other hand it is just as true that the cold

formalism of upper class England and New England needed the wilder spiritual emotionalism of
the black man to weld out of both a rational
human religion based on kindliness and social uplift; and whether the influence of Negro religion
was on the whole good or bad, the fact remains
that it was potent in the white South and still is.

Several black leaders of white churches are
worth remembering.[5]   Lemuel Hayes was born
in Connecticut in 1753 of a black father and white
mother.   He received his Master of Arts from
Middlebury College in 1804, was a soldier in the
Revolution and pastored various churches in New
England.   "He was the embodiment of piety and
honesty."   Harry Hosier, the black servant and
companion of Bishop Asbury, was called by Dr.
Benjamin Rush, the greatest orator in America.
He travelled north and south and preached to
white and black between 1784 and his death in
1810.

John Chavis was a full-blooded Negro, born in
Granville county, N. C., near Oxford, in 1753.
He was born free and was sent to Princeton, and
studied privately under Dr. Witherspoon, where
he did well.   He went to Virginia to preach to Negroes.   In 1802, in the county court, his freedom

<hr>

[5] Cf. Carter G. Woodson, *The History of the Negro Church,* Washington, D. C., 1921; Atlanta University Publications, *The Negro
Church;* and J. E. Bassett, *Slavery in North Carolina.*

and character were certified to and it was declared
that he had passed "through a regular course of
academic studies" at what is now Washington and
Lee University. In 1805 he returned to North
Carolina, where he, in 1809 was made a licentiate
in the Presbyterian Church and preached. His
English was remarkably pure, his manner impressive, his explanations clear and concise. For a
long time he taught school and had the best whites
as pupils — a United States senator, the sons of
a chief justice of North Carolina, a governor of
the state and many others. Some of his pupils
boarded in his family, and his school was regarded
as the best in the State. "All accounts agree that
John Chavis was a gentleman" and he was received socially among the best whites and asked to
table. In 1830 he was stopped from preaching
by the law. Afterward he taught school for free
Negroes in Raleigh.

Henry Evans was a full-blooded Virgina free
Negro, and was the pioneer of Methodism in Fay-
etteville, N. C. He found the Negroes there,
about 1800, without religious instruction. He began preaching and the town council ordered him
away; he continued and whites came to hear him.
Finally the white auditors outnumbered the black,
and sheds were erected for Negroes at the side of
the church. The gathering became a regular

Methodist Church, with a white and Negro membership, but Evans continued to preach. He exhibited "rare self-control before the most wretched of castes! Henry Evans did much good, but he would have done more good had his spirit been untrammelled by this sense of inferiority."[6]

His dying words uttered as he stood, aged and bent beside his pulpit, are of singular pathos:

"I have come to say my last word to you. It is this: None but Christ. Three times I have had my life in jeopardy for preaching the gospel to you. Three times I have broken ice on the edge of the water and swam across the Cape Fear to preach the gospel to you; and, if in my last hour I could trust to that, or anything but Christ crucified, for my salvation, all should be lost and my soul perish forever."

Early in the nineteenth century, Ralph Freeman was a slave in Anson county, N. C. He was a full-blooded Negro, and was ordained and became an able Baptist preacher. He baptised and administered communion, and was greatly respected. When the Baptists split on the question of missions he sided with the anti-mission side. Finally the law forbade him to preach.

The story of Jack of Virginia is best told in the words of a Southern writer:

[6] Bassett, pp. 58-9.

"Probably the most interesting case in the whole South is that of an African preacher of Nottoway county, popularly known as 'Uncle Jack,' whose services to white and black were so valuable that a distinguished minister of the Southern Presbyterian Church felt called upon to memorize his work in a biography.

"Kidnapped from his idolatrous parents in Africa, he was brought over in one of the last cargoes of slaves admitted to Virginia and sold to a remote and obscure planter in Nottoway county, a region at that time in the backwoods and destitute particularly as to religious life and instruction. He was converted under the occasional preaching of Rev. Dr. John Blair Smith, President of Hampden-Sidney College, and of Dr. William Hill and Dr. Archibald Alexander of Princeton, then young theologues, and by hearing the scriptures read. Taught by his master's children to read, he became so full of the spirit and knowledge of the Bible that he was recognized among the whites as a powerful expounder of Christian doctrine, was licensed to preach by the Baptist Church, and preached from plantation to plantation within a radius of thirty miles, as he was invited by overseers or masters. His freedom was purchased by a subscription of whites, and he was given a home and a tract of land for his support.

He organized a large and orderly Negro church, and exercised such a wonderful controlling influence over the private morals of his flock that masters, instead of punishing their slaves, often referred them to the discipline of their pastor, which they dreaded far more.

"He stopped a heresy among the Negro Christians of Southern Virginia, defeating in open argument a famous fanatical Negro preacher named Campbell, who advocated noise and 'the spirit' against the Bible, winning over Campbell's adherents in a body. For over forty years and until he was nearly a hundred years of age, he labored successfully in public and private among black and whites, voluntarily giving up his preaching in obedience to the law of 1832, the result of 'Old Nat's war.' . . .

"The most refined and aristocratic people paid tribute to him, and he was instrumental in the conversion of many whites. Says his biographer, Rev. Dr. William S. White: 'He was invited into their houses, sat with their families, took part in their social worship, sometimes leading the prayer at the family altar. Many of the most intelligent people attended upon his ministry and listened to his sermons with great delight. Indeed, previous to the year 1825, he was considered by the best judges to be the best preacher in that county. His

opinions were respected, his advice followed, and
yet he never betrayed the least symptoms of arro-
gance or self-conceit. His dwelling was a rude log
cabin, his apparel of the plainest and coarsest materials.' This was because he wished to be fully
identified with his class. He refused gifts of
better clothing saying 'These clothes are a great
deal better than are generally worn by people of
my color, and besides if I wear them I find shall
be obliged to think about them even at meeting'."

All this has to do with organized religion.

But back of all this and behind the half childish
theology of formal religion there has run in the
heart of black folk the greatest of human achievements, love and sympathy, even for their enemies,
for those who despised them and hurt them and
did them nameless ill. They have nursed the sick
and closed the staring eyes of the dead. They
have given friendship to the friendless, they have
shared the pittance of their poverty with the out-
cast and nameless; they have been good and true
and pitiful to the bad and false and pitiless and in
this lies the real grandeur of their simple religion,
the mightiest gift of black to white America.

Above all looms the figure of the Black
Mammy, one of the most pitiful of the world's
Christs. Whether drab and dirty drudge or dark
and gentle lady she played her part in the uplift

of the South. She was an embodied Sorrow, an
anomaly crucified on the cross of her own neglected children for the sake of the children of
masters who bought and sold her as they bought
and sold cattle. Whatever she had of slovenliness
or neatness, of degradation or of education she
surrendered it to those who lived to lynch her
sons and ravish her daughters. From her great
full breast walked forth governors and judges,
ladies of wealth and fashions, merchants and
scoundrels who lead the South. And the rest gave
her memory the reverence of silence. But a few
snobs have lately sought to advertise her sacrifice
and degradation and enhance their own cheap success by building on the blood of her riven heart a
load of stone miscalled a monument.

In religion as in democracy, the Negro has
been a peculiar test of white profession. The
American church, both Catholic and Protestant,
has been kept from any temptation to over-right-
eousness and empty formalism by the fact that
just as Democracy in America was tested by the
Negro, so American religion has always been
tested by slavery and color prejudice. It has kept
before America's truer souls the spirit of meekness and self abasement, it has compelled American religion again and again to search its heart
and cry "I have sinned;" and until the day comes

when color caste falls before reason and economic opportunity the black American will stand as the last and terrible test of the ethics of Jesus Christ.

Beyond this the black man has brought to America a sense of meekness and humility which America never has recognized and perhaps never will. If there is anybody in this land who thoroughly believes that the meek shall inherit the earth they have not often let their presence be known. On the other hand it has become almost characteristic of America to look upon position, self assertion, determination to go forward at all odds, as typifying the American spirit. This is natural. It is at once the rebound from European oppression and the encouragement which America offers physically, economically and socially to the human spirit. But on the other hand, it is in many of its aspects a dangerous and awful thing. It hardens and hurts our souls, it contradicts our philanthropy and religion; and here it is that the honesty of the black race, its hesitancy and heart searching, its submission to authority and its deep sympathy with the wishes of the other man comes forward as a tremendous, even though despised corrective. It is not always going to remain; even now we see signs of its disappearance before contempt, lawlessness and lynching. But it is still here, it still works and one of the most magnificent anomalies in modern human history is the labor and fighting of a half-million black men and two million whites for the freedom of four million slaves and these same slaves, dumbly but faithfully and not wholly unconsciously, protecting the mothers, wives and children of the very white men who fought to make their slavery perpetual.

This then is the Gift of Black Folk to the new world. Thus in singular and fine sense the slave became master, the bond servant became free and the meek not only inherited the earth but made that heritage a thing of questing for eternal youth, of fruitful labor, of joy and music, of the free spirit and of the ministering hand, of wide and poignant sympathy with men in their struggle to live and love which is, after all, the end of being.

POSTSCRIPT

Listen to the Winds, O God the Reader, that wail
across the whip-cords stretched taut on broken human
hearts; listen to the Bones, the bare bleached bones of
slaves, that line the lanes of Seven Seas and beat eternal
tom-toms in the forests of the laboring deep; listen to the
Blood, the cold thick blood that spills its filth across the
fields and flowers of the Free; listen to the Souls that
wing and thrill and weep and scream and sob and sing
above it all. What shall these things mean, O God the
Reader? You know. You know.

INDEX

Adair, Lieut., 129, 130
Adams, John, 87, 90, 159, 176, 177, 317
Adolphus, King Gustavus, 11
Aldridge, Ira, 310
Alexander, Dr. Archibald, 335
Allen, 173, 298, 329, 330
Allen, Walter, 220, 276
Alliot, Paul, 266
Almagro, 42
Alvarado, 42
Ames, Capt., 92
Anderson, 302
André, 92
Antar, 288
Atkinson, Edward, 232
Attucks, Crispus, 86, 87, 88
Augusta, Dr. A. T., 125

Baker, H. E., 72, 73
Balboa, 42
Ball, 314
Bancroft, H. H., 50, 55
Banister, E. M., 313
Banks, General, 118
Banneker, Benjamin, 298, 316, 317, 318
Bassett, Lieut.-Col., 119, 332, 334
Batson, Flora, 291
Beard, Charles A. & Mary R., 9, 12, 16
Beasley, 43, 49, 272
Beauregard, 137
Beecher, Henry Ward, 278, 293
Benjamin, Judah, 179
Beverly, Robert, 67
Bienville, Governor, 83
Bigstaff, Peter, 129
Bissell, 314
Blaine, James G., 222, 223, 224
Bland, James, 290

Bolas, Juan de, 151
Bolivar, 154, 155
Bonaparte, Napoleon, 153, 154
Booth, Major, 117, 271
Boré, Etienne de, 68
Bowers, John, 299
Braithwaite, W. S., 303, 304, 307
Brawley, Benjamin, 146, 153, 158, 162, 163, 285, 290, 303
Brent, Linda, 301
Brewster, 203
Bromwell, 17
Brooks, 302
Brown, John, 146, 270, 271, 272
Brown, Richard, 313
Brown, William, 86, 301, 299
Browne, 271
Bruce, B. K., 67, 218, 223
Bryant, William Cullen, 232
Buell, 187
Burgess, Prof., 206
Burleigh, Harry T., 290, 291
Burlin, Mrs. Curtis, 283, 284
Burnside, 124
Burr, Aaron, 289
Butler, General, 112, 116, 187
Byrd, Col. 67

Cable, George U., 293
Cain, 221
Calder, 314
Caldwell, Jonas, 87, 88
Calhoun, John C., 293
Callioux, Capt., 120
Campbell, Robert, 301, 304, 336
Carey, Lott, 330
Carr, Patrick, 87
Castaneda, Pedro de, 43
Castle, Vernon, 292
Catto, 300
Chamberlain, Governor, 220

343

Chambers, Colonel, 118
Chapman, C. E., 150
Charlton, Melville, 291
Chase, Simon P., 232
Chavis, John, 332, 333
Cheatham, 221
Chestnutt, Charles W., 303, 307
Child, Lydia Marcia, 293
Christophe, 92
Church, A. M. E., 300
Cinque, 159
Claiborne, Governor, 97
Clark, 49
Cleveland, 26
Clinton, Bishop Isaac, 89, 219
Cobb, General, 112
Cobb, Irvin S., 10
Coffin, Levi, 232
Cole, 310
Coleridge-Taylor, Samuel, 289, 290
Columbus, 35, 36, 37, 40, 265, 282
Commons, John R., 15
Conant, 36
Conner, A. J., 290
Connery, William J., 72
Constant, Benjamin, 314
Cooke, Governor, 93
Cooper, Peter, 232
Coppin, J., 153
Corbin, J. C., 220
Cordoza, F. L., 220-246
Cornwallis, 89, 177
Coronado, 44, 49
Cortes, 42, 45
Cotter, Joseph C. Jr., 304
Cravath, 214
Crogman, 302
Cromwell, J. W., 158, 182
Crummell, Dr. Alexander, 301, 302
Cuffee, Paul, 162, 172, 299
Cullen, Countée, 304
Curtis, Justice, 144
Curtis, Natalie, 282

Cushite, R. L. Perry, 302

Damrosch, 280
Dana, Gen. N. J. T., 193
Daquin, Major, 99
Davis, 304
Davis, Pres., 111, 112
Davis, Gussie L., 290
Davis, Jefferson, 107
De Charnay, 36
Dede, Edmund, 290
Delaney, Major M. H., 125
Delaney, Martin R., 300
Dennison, Chaplain, 123
Derham, Thomas, 316
De Soto, 43, 44
Dett, R. Nathaniel, 291
Dickinson, J. H., 73
Dickinson, S. L., 73
Diton, Carl, 291
Dix, 187
Dixon, Thomas, 293
Dodson, Jacob, 49
Dorantes, Stephen, 43, 44, 45
Douglas, Captain H. F., 125
Douglass, Frederick, 174, 208, 300, 301, 308
Dow, Lorenzo, 145
Drexel, Katherine, 324
Drinkwater, 311
DuBois, W. E. B., 13, 55, 58, 63, 153, 155, 161, 169, 249, 274, 297
DuBois, Wilcox, 73
Dubuclet, 221, 290
Dymas, 306
Dunbar, Paul Lawrence, 303, 304, 306
Dunmore, Governor, 89, 90, 176, 177
Dunn, Lieut.-Gov., 221
Duplessis, General Garnier, 131
Dvorak, 285, 291
Dwight, General, 118

Eaton, Col. John, 191, 193

Eastman, Max, 307
Edison, 28
Edward, Bryan, 151
Eliot, Dr. John, 57
Elliott, Robert Brown, 221, 301
Emerson, Ralph Waldo, 293
Equiana Olandah (See Gustavus Vassa)
Estevanico, 43, 44, 45, 46, 48, 49
Eustis, William, 94
Evans, Henry, 333, 334

Fairchild, Henry Pratt, 9
Fauset, Jessie, 304, 308
Finnegas, Lieut.-Col. Henry, 119
Fleming, Walter L., 194, 197, 226, 232, 234
Flipper, H. O., 43
Fontages, Viscount de, 93
Force, 176
Forrest, 117
Foster, Stephen, 275, 285
Forten, James, 299
Franklin, Benjamin, 90, 141
Freeman, Captain, 58
Freeman, Ralph, 334
Freemont, 49
French, D. C., 314
Frye, Colonel, 92
Fuller, Meta Warrick, 315

Gabriel, 172
Gage, Mrs. Frances D., 151, 264
Galvez, 95
Garner, J. W., 227
Garnet, Henry Highland, 299
Garrison, 174, 271
Garrison, William Lloyd, 146, 185
Gayarre, 95, 153
Geary, 25
Gibbs, Jonathan C., 220.
Gibbs, M. W., 220
Giddings, Joshua R., 171
Gilmore, General, 109

Gilpin, Charles, 310, 311
Gladstone, 279
Gloucester, John, 330
Gomez, 288
Gonino, 36
Goodell, 266
Gottschalk, 289
Goybet, General, 131, 132
Graham, Stephen, 311
Grant, General, 188, 191, 193
Graves, John Temple, 130
Gray, Samuel, 87, 88, 173
Greeley, Horace, 105, 185
Greene, General, 91, 178
Grey, T. R., 158
Griggs, 302
Grimke, A. H., 156, 302
Grimke, Frank, 302, 303

Hagen, Helen, 291
Hagood, General, 246, 247, 302
Hahn, Governor, 194
Hall, Prince, 162
Halleck, 187
Hamilton, Alexander, 91, 174, 269
Hammon, Jupiter, 304
Hampton, Governor, 246
Hampton, Wade, 283
Handy, W. C., 285
Hapgood, Mrs. Emily, 310
Hare, Maude-Cuney, 291
Harleston, Edwin, 313
Harper, Frances E. W., 300, 302, 304
Harper, William A., 313
Harriot, George, 29, 94
Harris, Joel Chandler, 295, 296
Harrison, Hazel, 291
Hartgrove, W. B., 94
Hayes, Roland W., 292
Hayne, Robert Y., 172
Haynes, Lemuel, 299, 306, 332
Helps, 42
Hemenway, J., 290
Hening, 148

Henry, Patrick, 141
Henson, Joshua, 171, 300
Henson, Matthew A., 50, 51
Higginson, Colonel, 116, 158, 275, 293
Hill, Dr. William, 335
Hogarth, George, 300
Hogan, Ernest, 310
Holland, Justin, 290
Hood, 302
Hooker, 187
Hope, Lawrence, 291
Hopkins, Samuel, 91, 175
Horton, George M., 304
Hosier, Harry, 332
Howard, General, 144, 145, 200, 249, 252
Howe, Julia Ward, 293
Howells, William Dean, 293
Hughes, Langston, 304
Hunter, General, 102, 103, 105, 116, 187
Hurd, John C., 148
Hyer, Sisters, 291

Jackson, General, 97, 99, 115, 182, 220
Jackson, M. Howard, 315
Jamison, J. F., 43
Jamison, Roscoe C., 304
Jay, John, 232
Jefferson, Thomas, 3, 141, 143, 154, 172, 317
Jenkins, Edmund T., 291
Johnson, E. A., 302
Johnson, Fenton, 304
Johnson, Georgia, 304
Johnson, James Weldon, 280, 292, 314
Johnson, John, 96, 113
Johnson, President, 201, 202, 203, 207, 208, 209, 214, 281
Johnson, Rosamond, 291
Jones, 173, 183, 330
Jones, C. C., 296, 325
Just, Ernest, 316

Kabell, 36
Keene, Edmund, 310
King George, 3rd of Britain, 142
Kingsley, Miss, 326, 327
Krehbiel, H. E., 281, 282
Kunst, J., 151

LaCoste, 99
Lafitte, 99
Lafon, Thomé, 183, 323
Lambert, 92, 291
Langston, 22, 302
Las Casas, 42
Laurens, Henry, 141
Laurens, John, 91
Lawrence, Joseph, 8
Lawson, A. Augustus, 291
Leader, 8
Lee, Samuel J., 219
Leile, George, 330
Leon, Ponce de, 38
L'Enfant, Major Pierre, 318
Lewis, 49
Lewis, Edmonia, 315
Lewis, Julien H., 316
Lewis, R. B., 299
Lind, Jenny, 291
Lincoln, Abraham, 28, 106, 114, 135, 185, 187, 189, 195, 202, 203, 233, 271
Livermore, 84, 87, 89, 91, 92, 142, 175, 176, 178, 194
Livingston, Robert, 154
Lodge, Henry Cabot, 12
Loguen, Bishop, 182, 300
Low, A. A., 232
Lowell, James Russell, 293
Lucas, Sam (See Samuel Milady)
Lynch, 90
Lynch, John R., 220, 223

Macdonough, 96
Madison, James, 91
Majors, 302
Maldonado, 44, 45
Marcos, Fray, 45, 46, 49

Marquis, de Cordocet, 317
Marshall, Colonel John R., 127
Martin, 96
Martineau, 268
Matzeliger, Jan E., 70, 71, 72
Maverick, Samuel, 87, 88
McCoy, Elijah, 72
McHenry, James, 318
McKay, 71, 304, 307
McKay, Claud, 308
McKee, Colonel John, 323
McKim, Miss, 275
McKinley, President, 126
McLean, Justice, 144
McLellan, 188
McPherson, 203, 209
McSweeney, Edw. F., Introduction to series
Melbourne, George, 290
Mencken, H. L., 305
Mendoza, 44, 45, 49, 150
Menendez, 43
Milady, Samuel, 290 (See Sam Lucas also)
Miller, Kelly, 303
Miller, Hon. Thomas E., 248
Mills, 271
Mitchell, George W., 303
Montalvo, Garcia de, 35
Moody, 279
Moore, G. H., 85, 91
Mossell, 302
Murray, 221
Murray, Freeman H. M., 304, 315

Narvaez, Panfilo de, 43
Nell, William Cooper, 300
Nelson, Alice Dunbar, 68, 69, 83, 97, 100, 145, 155, 267, 268, 289
Nelson, Colonel, 119
Niles, 97, 98, 100, 145
Northrop, Samuel, 300
Nosseyeb, 287

Oglethorpe, 140

O'Hara, 222
Olano, Nuflo de, 42
Olivier, 79
Olmstead, 69, 70
O'Neill, 311
Osceola, 171
Otis, James, 141
Ouverture, Toussaint, le, 154, 156
Ovando, 39
Oviedo, 38

Page, Thomas Nelson, 293
Payne, Bishop Daniel, 301, 302
Peary, Commodore, 50
Pemberton, Thomas, 57
Penn, 7, 302
Pennington, J. W. C., 257, 299
Perier, Governor, 82, 83
Perry, 96
Petien, President, 154
Phillips, Wendell, 270, 293
Pierce, Edward L., 191
Pike, G. D., 279
Pinchback, 221
Pinckney, Charles, 94
Pizarro, Marquis, 41
Plato, 2
Pleasants, Mammy, 271, 272
Poor, Salem, 92
Portugal, King of, 290
Preer, Evelyn, 311
Prendergast, J. P., 8
Preston, Captain, 87
Price, J. C., 308
Purvis, Robert, 299
Purvis, W. L., 73
Pushkin, 288
Putnam, Colonel, 123

Rainey, 223
Ralston, 271
Rapier, 221, 223
Redmond, 174
Reed, Lieut.-Col., 125
Revels, 221, 223
Revells, Hiram R., 218
Rice, Thomas D., 309

Rigaud, 92
Rillieux, Robert, 70
Rippy, J. F., 42, 43
Robertson, 267
Robeson, Paul, 311
Rodin, 315
Rush, Dr. Benjamin, 316, 332
Rutledge, 90

Salcedo, Governor, 67
Samba, 83
Sanine, 312
Savara, J. B. Capt., 99
Saxton, General, 188
Scammell, Alexander, 85
Scarborough, 302
Schomberg, A. A., 304
Schurz, Carl, 201, 210, 211, 213, 214
Scofield, 314
Scott, William Edward, 313
Sejour, Victor, 289
Selleck, 8
Sewall, 140
Seward, William H., 140
Seybert, Adam, 16
Seymour, General, 123
Shaftesbury, Lord, 279
Shakespeare, 293
Shaler, Governor, 203
Sharkey, Governor, 203
Sherman, General T. W., 187, 194
Shaw, Colonel, 123, 315
Simmons, 301
Simonton, Judge, 246
Sinclair, 303
Smith, Albert A., 313
Smith, Alexander, 271
Smith, Buckingham, 38
Smith, General, 124
Smith, Gerritt, 232
Smith, Rev. John Blair, 335
Southerne, 293, 309
Spence, Adam K., 277
Spencer, Rev. T. A., 9

Stanton, 124, 194
Stearns, George L., 232
Stephenson, General, 123
Steward, 93, 154, 303
Stewart, Ruth M., 293, 302
Story, W. A., 314
Stowe, Harriet Beecher, 293
Strachen, 96
Straker, 302
Strong, Gen., 123
Suarez, Illan, 41
Sumner, Charles, 198, 293

Talbert, Cole, 291
Talley, T. W., 297
Talmadge, DeWitt, 154
Taney, Judge, 143
Tanner, Bishop, 301, 313
Thacher, J. C., 36
Thebaud, A. J., 8
Thomas, General, 140, 193, 194
Thurston, 36
Tillman, 243
Toomer, Jean, 308
Tourgee, Judge Albion W., 237
Trotter, James Monroe, 301
Truth, Sojourner, 174
Tubman, Harriet, 171, 270, 271
Turner, C. H., 316
Turner, Nat., 157, 158, 302, 330
Tyler, Col., 186

Vaca de, 44, 45
Valdivia, 42
Vassa, Gustavus, 279 (See Olandah Equiana)
Varick, James, 330
Vela, Blasco Nunez, 41, 42
Vernon, Capt. John, 8
Vesey, Denmark, 156
Victoria, Francisco Xavier de, 322
Victoria, Queen, 279

Walker, David, 164, 168, 299, 310, 311
Wall, Capt. O. S. B., 125

Wallace, Judge, 246
Warburg, Eugene, 289
Ward, Samuel C., 300, 308, 314
Ware, 214
Wark, John W., 282
Warley, 231
Washington, 2, 38, 89, 102, 103, 115, 141, 298, 318
Washington, Booker T., 258, 298, 303, 308
Washington, Madison, 159
Wayman, Bishop, 301
Webster, Daniel, 86, 160
Weiner, 36, 37, 38, 40, 150
Wesley, 113
Wheatley, Phyllis, 298, 304, 306, 312
Wheeler, Laura, 313
White, Clarence Cameron, 291
White, E. P., 221
White, George L., 276, 277, 278
White, J. L., 219
White, Dr. William S., 336
Whitfield, James, 299, 300

Whitefield, George, 298
Whittier, John Greenleaf, 293
Whitman, A. A., 301, 304
Whitman, Walt, 293
Whitney, Eli, 70
Williams, 101, 104, 107, 117, 118, 124, 164, 187, 301, 310, 311,
Williams, Bert, 310
Williams, Dr. Dan, 316
Wilson, 26, 95, 97, 108, 110, 124, 135, 179, 181, 303
Winslow, Sydney W., 70, 71
Witherspoon, D., 332
Wood, Liates, 73
Woods, Granville T., 73
Woodson, Carter, 64, 161, 303, 332
Wormeley, Ralph, 67
Wright, 302

Yeomans, Robert, 8
Young, Major Charles, 17, 18, 127, 131

DATE DUE

NOV 9 '77			